11/09

# THE FREEZER COMPANION

MICHELLE BERRIEDALE-JOHNSON

Macdonald

A **Macdonald** BOOK

© Michelle Berriedale-Johnson 1986

First published in Great Britain in 1986
by Macdonald & Co (Publishers) Ltd
London & Sydney

A member of BPCC plc

**British Library Cataloguing in Publication Data**

Berriedale-Johnson, Michelle
   The freezer companion
   1. Home freezers – Amateurs' Manuals
   I. Title
   641.4'53     TX610,

ISBN 0–356–10763–9

Printed and bound in Great Britain
by Hazell Watson & Viney Limited,
Aylesbury, Bucks
A BPCC plc Company

*Editor:* Julie Dufour
*Designer:* Kate Poole
*Photographer:* Peter Chadwick
*Stylist:* Dawn Lane
*Home Economist:* Liza Collard
*Indexer:* Michèle Clarke
*Production:* Oscar Heini

Macdonald & Co (Publishers) Ltd
Greater London House
Hampstead Road
London NW1 7QX

**Acknowledgements**
The publishers would like to thank the
following firm for the loan of props:

Elizabeth David, London SW1

# CONTENTS

*Beef Tomatoes Stuffed with Bulgar Wheat and Chorizo* (see page 8), *Smoked Mackerel and Cockle Flan* (see page 32) *and Spinach and Mushroom Pâté* (see page 17)

# INTRODUCTION

Although frozen food is now a widely known and accepted part of twentieth-century life, most people think of deep-freezing as being a relatively modern invention or discovery. In fact, Eskimos, Russians and others who inhabit cold parts of the world have known about frozen 'convenience' food for many centuries. Even in England, as far back as the late sixteenth and early seventeenth centuries every large house had its icehouse and ice creams were all the rage. Scientists even tried stuffing chickens with snow to see whether they could preserve them. Indeed, it was said that the great Sir Francis Bacon actually caught his death of cold doing just that! Eighteenth-century travellers in Russia reported seeing frozen chunks of meat and fish on sale in the street markets and noted with interest that, when they were cooked, it was difficult to tell them from fresh. But it took the explorer Clarence Birdseye to observe that not only were the fish caught through holes in the Labrador ice instantly frozen in the Artic temperatures, but that they were protected from the intense dryness of the cold air (which would otherwise suck the moisture from the frozen fish) by a glaze of ice. When they were defrosted and cooked months later, they were indistinguishable from the original fresh fish. He made good use of his discovery!

## Principles of Freezing

Since all edible matter is composed of greater or lesser amounts of water held in suspension by fibres and solid matter, when subjected to sufficiently low temperature all edible matter will freeze. The speedier the freezing process is, the smaller will be the ice crystals in which it freezes. And the smaller the ice crystals that form, the less damage they will do to the surrounding fibres. It follows logically, therefore, that the faster the food is frozen, the less damage will be done to the texture of the food. Moreover, since freezing arrests all development, including the action of bacteria in the food, the faster the food is frozen, the better the condition in which it will be preserved.

However, because very cold air is very dry, over a prolonged period of storage the air surrounding a piece of frozen food (normally very moist in its unfrozen state) will gradually absorb moisture from it. Hence the importance of good, airtight packing. If air is packed in with the food, or allowed to penetrate to it through bad seals or holes in the packaging, it will gradually dehydrate the food. This is particularly relevant in relation to relatively dry foods, like baked goods, which will dry out and become stale and crumbly in no time unless very well packed. Contact with air (which also causes 'freezer burn' or marking of frozen food) is not harmful, it merely causes deterioration in texture and flavour.

Although there are many other ancient and successful ways of preserving food, all of them necessitate the application of some outside agent (salt, smoke, spices, sugar, pickling liquids, heat, etc.) to arrest the action of the bacteria in the food and prevent it going off. And all of these have flavours of their own – some of them desirable, some not. Freezing merely suspends the food in time; it does not apply any external agent to it and therefore does not change its flavour.

Having said this, it is true that frozen food does not always taste as good as fresh. However, the difference is normally due to a change in texture resulting from the formation and dispersal of the ice crystals – which affects the flavour, or to inefficient packaging, which has allowed cold air to penetrate. For example, food frozen very slowly or improperly packed may lose its texture, become dehydrated, be tainted by other flavours in the freezer, or get damaged by contact with the air – all of which will turn your delicious fillet steak or apple pie into a pale shadow of its original self. Moreover, the texture of some food stuffs is so delicate and the water content so high in relation to the solid matter that, no matter how small the ice crystals, their texture will be affected by freezing. Strawberries, for example, have a very high water content held together by very delicate fibres in a relatively large mass. No matter how fast and efficient the freezer, the texture of the fruit is broken down so a defrosted frozen strawberry never has the same texture as a fresh one. Raspberries, on the other hand, although they have a very high water content and delicate fibres, are relatively small in mass as they have a hole in the middle. Frozen really fast, the tiny ice crystals do little damage to the texture of the fruit and a well-frozen raspberry is almost indistinguishable from a fresh one. Nonetheless, in terms of pure preservation, freezing is by far the most efficient method available to us.

NOTE: With each recipe I have given the optimum freezer time for which the dish can be kept. After this time the food will start to deteriorate.

# STARTERS AND SOUPS

## Tomato Ice

*Serves 6*                                     *3 months*

This is a light and refreshing starter for the summer, but do remember to take it out of the freezer 30 minutes before you serve it or you will need a pickaxe to get into it.

> 1 kg/2 lb ripe tomatoes
> 2 handfuls parsley
> 1 teaspoon Worcestershire sauce
> 120 ml/4 fl oz dry white wine
> salt and pepper
> sprigs of mint or basil to garnish

Chop the parsley finely in the liquidizer or processor. Remove most of it and put in the tomatoes with the Worcestershire sauce and white wine. Purée them, then rub the mixture through a strainer. You will get a rather pale pink and fluffy liquid. Add the parsley and salt and pepper to taste, remembering that the seasoning will be slightly dulled in the freezing.

Pour into individual dishes or a container and freeze.

Serve in glass dishes or ramekins with a sprig of fresh mint or basil and lots of brown or white melba toast.

## Beef Tomatoes Stuffed with Bulgar Wheat and Chorizo

*Serves 6*                                     *3 months*

If you are going to serve the tomatoes hot, you can freeze them complete with stuffing, although the tomato casing will tend to disintegrate as it defrosts. If you want to serve them cold – or like your tomato to remain intact even if hot – make and freeze the stuffing separately and fill the fresh tomatoes just before you serve them. You can use sweet or hot chorizo sausage or a combination of the two.

> 6 large beef tomatoes, halved
> 2 tablespoons olive oil
> 225 g/8 oz leeks, cleaned and finely sliced, or sweet purple onions
> 175 g/6 oz potgourri or bulgar wheat
> 175 g/6 oz chorizo sausage, cut into small cubes
> 50 g/2 oz sunflower seeds
> salt and pepper

Remove the middles from the tomatoes and chop finely. Heat the oil in a heavy pan and lightly fry the leeks or onions until soft. Soften the potgourri or bulgar wheat with boiling water (according to the instructions on the package) and add to the pan with the sausage and the tomato middles and juices. If you are freezing the tomato filling alone and do not want to waste tomatoes, you can substitute a small can of Italian tomatoes, chopped and with most of their juice drained off, for the tomato middles. Cook the mixture together for about 10 minutes or until most of the liquid is absorbed. If the filling is to be frozen separately, do not add the sunflower seeds or adjust the seasoning until it is defrosted. If this dish is to be completed, add the sunflower seeds and adjust seasoning to taste. Pile the filling into the tomato shells.

The tomatoes can be served hot (put the filled tomatoes into a moderate oven (180°C/350°F/Gas Mark 4) for 10–15 minutes to warm the shells without cooking them); cold with a warm filling; or completely cold.

To freeze whole, stack in a well-sealed container and freeze. To freeze the filling alone, pack in a well-sealed bag or container.

Defrost whole tomatoes at room temperature to minimize the breaking up of the tomato shell and reheat in a moderate oven (180°C/350°F/Gas Mark 4) for 15–20 minutes. Defrost the filling at room temperature or in a microwave and complete the dish as above.

# Avocado and Mint Ice Cream

*Serves 6*                                            *1–2 months*

This is a good starter to make when avocados are cheap and fresh mint plentiful. It keeps its colour very well and looks lovely in glass dishes – or even wine glasses if you do not have 'sundae' dishes.

*4 small, very ripe avocados*
*8 sprigs fresh mint*
*juice of 2 lemons*
*150 ml/¼ pint double cream*
*salt (optional)*

Peel and stone the avocados, then put the flesh with the mint, stems and all, in a food processor or liquidizer. If you do not have either, chop the mint *very* finely and mix it into the puréed avocado. Add the lemon juice. Lightly whip the cream and fold it into the mixture. Taste and add a *little* salt if you feel it is necessary; for my palate it has enough flavour as it is.

Spoon the mixture into a container and freeze.

To serve, take the ice cream out of the freezer 20–30 minutes (depending on the weather) before you want to eat it. Spoon it into glasses and serve it with melba toast, crackers or fresh brown bread and butter.

# Cream of Chicken Soup with Roasted Peanuts

*Serves 6*                                            *6 months*

The flavour and crunch of nuts contrast well with the relative blandness of a chicken soup – a 'must' for peanut butter freaks.

*approx 450 g/1 lb chicken with bone (ideally part leg*
*   and part breast meat)*
*350 g/12 oz assorted vegetables, including onions,*
*   carrots and celery*
*bouquet garni*
*salt and pepper*
*550 ml/18 fl oz dry white wine*
*1.2 litres/2 pints water*
*15 g/½ oz butter or low fat margarine*
*100 g/4 oz dry roasted peanuts, chopped fairly small*
*   in a processor or liquidizer*

*15 g/½ oz flour*
*100 ml/3½ fl oz double cream*
*100 ml/3½ fl oz medium sherry*

Chop the vegetables roughly and put them with the chicken, bouquet garni, a little seasoning and the wine and water in a large saucepan. Bring to the boil, skim if necessary and simmer for 45 minutes or until the chicken is cooked. Discard the vegetables, reserve the stock and cool the chicken pieces slightly. Remove the chicken flesh from the bone and liquidize it with the stock. Melt the butter in the pan and lightly toss the peanuts in it. Add the flour, cook for a minute or two, then gradually add the puréed soup. Bring to the boil and cook for a couple of minutes to thicken slightly.

If the soup is to be frozen, it should be frozen at this stage in a well-sealed container.

To serve, defrost the soup at room temperature. If it separates, whisk it lightly with a birch whisk. Reheat gently, then add the cream and sherry – do not allow the soup to boil. Adjust the seasoning to taste and serve.

# Rhubarb Soup

*Serves 6*                                            *4–6 months*

This is a marvellous soup to serve in the springtime.

*450 g/1 lb young rhubarb, trimmed and roughly*
*   chopped*
*50 g/2 oz butter or low fat margarine*
*50 g/2 oz young leeks, cleaned and finely sliced*
*25 g/1 oz cooked lean ham, chopped small*
*50 g/2 oz fresh brown breadcrumbs*
*1.2 litres/2 pints chicken or light veal stock*
*150 ml/¼ pint dry white wine*
*salt*
*a couple of drops of Tabasco*
*juice of 1 small lemon*
*3–4 teaspoons sugar*
*150 ml/¼ pint double cream, lightly whisked*

Melt the fat in a saucepan, add the rhubarb, leeks and ham and stew them gently for 10 minutes or until the rhubarb is soft. Add the breadcrumbs, stock and wine, bring them to the boil and simmer for 15 minutes. Liquidize or purée the soup and return it to the pan. Add the salt, Tabasco, lemon juice and sugar to taste; how much of the last two you add will depend on how sweet the rhubarb and your own tooth is. However, take care not to oversalt before the soup is frozen.

If it is to be frozen, it should be frozen at this stage in a well-sealed container.

To serve, defrost the soup at room temperature and whisk lightly with a birch whisk if it separates. Reheat gently and serve with a blob of whipped cream in the middle of each bowl.

# Saffron Soup

*Serves 6*                                      *6 months*

If you want a vegetarian soup, substitute half white wine and half water for the chicken stock.

*1/2 teaspoon powdered saffron or 1 packet saffron threads*
*50 g/2 oz butter or low fat margarine*
*1 teaspoon ground turmeric*
*350 g/12 oz onions, roughly chopped*
*2 cloves garlic, peeled and roughly chopped*
*25 g/1 oz brown breadcrumbs*
*900 ml/1 1/2 pints chicken stock*
*60 ml/2 fl oz double cream*
*juice of 2 lemons*
*salt and pepper*

Melt the butter in a large pan, add the saffron and turmeric and stir until well mixed. Add the onions and garlic and cook gently until the vegetables are softened. Add the breadcrumbs and the stock, bring the mixture to the boil, simmer it for 20 minutes, then liquidize or purée it.

If the soup is to be frozen, it should be frozen at this stage in a well-sealed container.

To serve, defrost the soup at room temperature, then reheat gently. Add the cream and lemon juice and season to taste with salt and pepper. The soup is equally good hot or cold, although if cold, it may need to be thinned slightly with a little milk or chicken stock.

# Cream of Mushroom Soup

*Serves 6*                                      *9 months*

This can be made either by slicing the mushrooms (for a pale soup) or processing them (for a darker soup). I prefer a 'bitty' texture, but if you want a smooth cream, then process the soup after it is cooked.

*225 g/8 oz button or open mushrooms, wiped and thinly sliced or chopped in a processor*
*50 g/2 oz butter*
*1 large Spanish onion, peeled and very finely chopped*
*juice of 1 lemon*
*25 g/1 oz flour*
*300 ml/1/2 pint chicken, veal or vegetable stock*
*300 ml/1/2 pint milk*
*150 ml/1/4 pint dry white wine*
*salt and white pepper*
*150 ml/1/4 pint double cream*

Melt the butter in a heavy pan and gently cook the onion until it is transparent and starting to soften but not coloured. When the onion is soft, add the mushrooms and lemon juice and cook them together for a couple of minutes; again do not brown them. Add the flour, stir for a minute or two, then gradually add the stock, milk and white wine. The milk and wine may curdle slightly but don't worry – they will reamalgamate as they cook. Bring the mixture to the boil and simmer gently for 15 minutes. Season to taste with salt and freshly ground white pepper (if possible). If you want a puréed soup, put the mixture through a liquidizer or food processor, then return to the pan. Just before serving, add the cream and readjust the seasoning. Alternatively, add only half the cream and lightly whisk the rest. This can be dropped in dollops on the soup as it is served.

To freeze, cool completely once the soup is cooked (before you add the cream) and pack in well-sealed containers, leaving room for expansion.

Defrost at room temperature or in a microwave and reheat. Add the cream and adjust the seasoning. Serve as above.

*Saffron Soup and Red Cabbage and Apple Casserole (see page 109)*

# Curried Parsnip and Apple Soup

*Serves 6*                                          *6–8 months*

Because both the parsnips and the apples are sweet, the curry contrasts particularly well with them; this is somewhat of a party soup.

*450 g/1 lb parsnips, scrubbed and thinly sliced*
*225 g/8 oz cooking apples, peeled and chopped*
*25 g/ 1 oz butter*
*1 tablespoon vegetable oil*
*1 tablespoon curry powder*
*225 g/8 oz leeks*
*1.5 litres/2½ pints chicken stock or vegetable water*
*150 ml/¼ pint milk*
*150 ml/¼ pint dry white wine*
*salt and pepper*
*2 tart eating apples*

Melt the butter and oil in a heavy-based pan, stir in the curry powder, followed by the leeks, parsnips and cooking apples. Cook together gently without burning for 10–15 minutes or until the leeks are quite soft and the parsnips are beginning to soften. Add the stock, milk and wine, bring to the boil and simmer for 30–35 minutes or until the parsnips are quite cooked. Purée in a processor, liquidizer or *mouli légumes*. Reheat and adjust the seasoning to taste. Just before serving, add the two eating apples, peeled and finely chopped.

Freeze before adjusting the seasoning or adding the eating apple.

Defrost at room temperature or in a microwave. Reheat, adjust seasoning and add the apple before serving.

# Kidney Soup

*Serves 6*                                          *4–6 months*

This is a rich, dark brown, comforting soup that should be kept exclusively for cold, wet November evenings.

*350 g/12 oz lambs' kidneys, fresh or frozen, chopped small*
*75 g/3 oz butter*
*225 g/8 oz onions, chopped*

*2 cloves garlic, finely chopped*
*50 g/2 oz carrots, diced small*
*100 g/4 oz mushrooms (open if possible), chopped*
*4 parsley stalks*
*2 bay leaves*
*150 ml/¼ pint port*
*1.2 litres/2 pints water*
*50 g/2 oz brown breadcrumbs*
*2 teaspoons anchovy essence*
*6–10 peppercorns*
*salt*

Melt 50 g/2 oz of the butter in a heavy pan and fry the onions, garlic and carrots briskly until they are lightly browned and just softening. Add 225 g/8 oz of the kidneys and the mushrooms and continue to cook, rather more gently, for a couple of minutes or until the kidneys have stopped looking pink. Add the parsley stalks, bay leaves, port, water, breadcrumbs, anchovy essence and peppercorns, bring to the boil, cover and simmer gently for 45 minutes. Remove the bay leaves and purée the soup in a processor or liquidizer.

Meanwhile, lightly fry the remaining kidneys in the rest of the butter. Return the soup to the pan, add the kidney pieces and juice, reheat gently and season to taste with salt and a little more pepper if needed. If the soup is to be frozen, leave the final seasoning until it is defrosted.

To freeze, cool completely and pack in a well-sealed container.

Defrost at room temperature or in a microwave. Reheat and adjust seasoning to taste.

# Chilled Fennel Soup

*Serves 6*                                          *3–4 months*

Fennel is a bit like coconut; either you are passionate about it or you cannot stand the stuff. This is a soup for the passionate! For a vegetarian version, substitute white wine and water or fennel/celery water for the stock.

*450 g/1 lb fennel, roughly chopped*
*40 g/1½ oz butter or low fat margarine*
*2 onions, roughly chopped*
*25 g/1 oz root ginger, finely chopped, or 1 teaspoon dried ginger*
*900 ml/1½ pints chicken stock*

*150 ml/¼ pint dry white wine*
*150 ml/¼ pint milk*
*salt and pepper*
*50 g/2 oz ground almonds*
*150 ml/¼ pint double cream*
*watercress leaves to garnish (optional)*

Melt the butter in a pan and add the fennel, onions and ginger. Cook together very gently until the onion and fennel are soft. Add the stock, wine, milk and a little salt and pepper. Bring to the boil and simmer for about 30 minutes. Purée in a processor or liquidizer. I prefer the soup with little bits of fennel floating in it rather than a totally smooth purée; if you would rather have a purée, process it for somewhat longer and then strain the bits from the soup. Add the ground almonds and cream and adjust the seasoning to taste. You can serve it as it is or decorated with a few watercress leaves. The soup can also be served hot, but I find the flavours work better chilled.

It is better to freeze the soup after it has been puréed and before adding the almonds and cream, but it will come to no harm if everything has been added.

Defrost at room temperature or in a microwave.

# Cream of Cucumber Soup

*Serves 6*                                    *3–4 months*

People always think of cucumber as a raw vegetable, yet it cooks very well. Despite its high proportion of water, it retains its crunch after quite a long period in the pot.

*350 g/12 oz cucumber*
*25 g/1 oz butter or low fat margarine*
*225 g/8 oz leeks, cleaned and finely chopped*
*225 g/8 oz potatoes, scrubbed and diced (unless their*
*   skins are very coarse, in which case they should be*
*   peeled)*
*600 ml/1 pint milk*
*300 ml/½ pint water*
*300 ml/½ pint dry white wine*
*10 drops Tabasco*
*150 ml/¼ pint soured cream*
*juice of 1 lemon*
*salt and pepper*

Melt the butter in a large pan and add the leeks and 225 g/8 oz of the cucumber, roughly chopped but with its skin left on. Cook them very gently until the leeks are quite soft. Add the potatoes, milk, water, wine, Tabasco, lemon juice and a little salt. Bring to the boil and simmer gently for about 30 minutes or until the potatoes are cooked. Purée in a processor, liquidizer or *mouli légumes*. Return the soup to the pot and add the soured cream and the rest of the cucumber, finely chopped or diced but with its skin left on. Cook for a couple of minutes, then adjust the seasoning to taste and serve.

It is better to freeze the soup once it is cooked and to add the cream and cucumber dice when it is defrosted, but it will come to no great harm if frozen all together.

Defrost at room temperature or in a microwave and reheat. The soup is also good cold.

NOTE: Do not allow the soup to boil after the soured cream has been added.

# Iced Blue Cheese Soup

*Serves 6*                                    *2 months*

This is very rich but also very delicious in small quantities and served well chilled.

*175 g/6 oz Danish Blue cheese*
*4 large spring onions, cleaned and roughly chopped*
*a large handful of parsley, roughly chopped*
*300 ml/½ pint soured cream*
*90 ml/3 fl oz white wine*
*juice of 1–2 lemons*
*freshly ground black pepper*

Put the cheese, spring onions and parsley in a food processor and purée. Add the soured cream, wine and some of the lemon juice. Purée again and then add more lemon juice and black pepper to taste. Serve well chilled with melba toast or brown rolls.

Freeze in well-sealed containers, leaving room for expansion.

Defrost at room temperature. The mixture may separate, in which case you need merely return it to the processor. If it is too thick, thin it down with a little whole or skimmed milk.

# Celery, Bacon and Walnut Soup

*Serves 6*                                    *6 months*

I was making stuffing with these classic stuffing ingredients when it occurred to me that they would make a good soup – they do!

*25 g/1 oz butter or margarine*
*175 g/6 oz onions, very finely chopped*
*100 g/4 oz bacon, very finely chopped*
*225 g/8 oz celery, washed, strings removed and very*
  *finely chopped*
*300 ml/½ pint dry white wine*
*1.5 litres/2½ pints chicken stock*
*50 g/2 oz walnuts, finely chopped but not pulverized*
*salt and pepper*

Melt the butter or margarine in a heavy-based pan and very gently cook the onions, bacon and celery until the vegetables are quite soft. Add the wine and the stock, bring the mixture to the boil and simmer for 30 minutes. Add the walnuts, cook for a further couple of minutes, then adjust the seasoning to taste.

If the soup is to be frozen, it is better to add the walnuts and seasoning once it is defrosted. To freeze, cool the soup completely, then pack in well-sealed wax or polythene containers, leaving room for expansion.

Defrost at room temperature or in a microwave and reheat. Add the walnuts and adjust the seasoning to taste before serving.

# Gazpacho

*Serves 6*                                    *1 month*

A genuine Spanish gazpacho is a thin and rather oily cold tomato soup – I find this freezes and tastes better. It is worth making and freezing if there is a glut of cheap tomatoes.

*1 kg/2 lb ripe tomatoes, roughly chopped*
*2 cloves garlic*
*240 ml/8 fl oz double cream*
*juice of 1–2 lemons*
*salt and pepper*
*25–50 g/1–2 oz each chopped celery, green pepper*
  *and ham*

Liquidize or process the tomatoes with the garlic, then rub through a sieve. Add the cream, lemon juice and salt and pepper to taste. Chill well, then serve in bowls with the celery, pepper and ham as garnish.

If you want to freeze the soup and keep it for a long time, it is better to freeze the liquidized tomatoes on their own, the garlic may develop a slightly 'off' taste after a few months. In this case, you will need to repurée it on defrosting with the garlic to get the flavours well amalgamated.

If it is only to be frozen for a short period, liquidize the tomatoes with the garlic but do not add the cream, lemon juice or seasoning until it is defrosted.

NOTE: If you do not add the garlic to this soup, it will keep in the freezer for up to 9 months.

# Clear Onion and Mushroom Soup

*Serves 6*                                    *5–6 months*

This must be one of the world's simplest soups, yet, as long as you leave the onions and mushrooms to really sweat, it is also one of the best. It is a soup where I do not think you can successfully replace the butter as the sweating medium without losing flavour.

*350 g/12 oz onions, finely sliced*
*350 g/12 oz open mushrooms, chopped small*
*40 g/1½ oz butter*
*450 ml/¾ pint dry white wine*
*1.2 litres/2 pints chicken or veal stock or water or*
  *onion stock*
*salt and pepper*

Melt the butter in a heavy pan, add the onions and mushrooms and cook very slowly until they are both quite soft. Add the wine and stock, bring to the boil, season lightly and simmer for 30–35 minutes. Adjust seasoning to taste and serve.

Cool completely to freeze.

Defrost at room temperature or in a microwave and reheat.

*Cream of Cucumber Soup* (see page 13), *Braised Rolls of Beef* (see page 66) *and Stovie Pot* (see page 108)

# PÂTÉS AND TERRINES

## Chicken Liver and Tomato Pâté

*Serves 6*            *2–3 months*

The whisky in this pâté makes an interesting change from the more usual brandy.

> *225 g/8 oz chicken livers*
> *25 g/1 oz butter or low fat margarine*
> *2 rashers streaky or fat bacon, very thinly sliced*
> *4 cloves garlic, crushed or finely chopped*
> *1 onion, finely chopped*
> *2 tablespoons tomato paste*
> *60 ml/2 fl oz whisky*
> *salt and pepper*

Melt the butter in a large frying pan and gently fry the bacon, garlic and onion until it is soft but not browned. Add the chicken livers and cook for a couple of minutes only – the livers should still be just pink in the middle. Take the mixture off the heat, add the tomato paste and then purée it in a liquidizer or a food processor. Add the whisky and salt and pepper to taste. Spoon the pâté into a soufflé dish or ramekin dishes (lined with cling film if it is to be frozen) and chill.

If it is to be frozen, cover the pâté and freeze, then remove from the dish and pack as usual.

To defrost, remove the pâté from the freezer, peel off the plastic cling film and return the pâté to its dish. Defrost at room temperature.

Serve with plenty of hot brown toast.

## Chicken Liver and Curd Cheese Pâté

*Serves 6*            *2 months*

This is a variation on a traditional chicken liver pâté and is slightly less rich; I found it in a southern American cookbook.

> *175 g/6 oz chicken liver, chopped*
> *40 g/1½ oz butter*
> *75 g/3 oz onions, finely chopped*
> *175 g/6 oz curd cheese*
> *3 teaspoons red wine vinegar*
> *3 teaspoons Worcestershire sauce*
> *2 teaspoons mushroom ketchup*
> *salt and pepper*

Melt the butter in a pan and gently cook the onions until they are soft but not burnt. Add the liver and cook until still slightly pink. Turn into a food processor or liquidizer and add the cheese and seasonings. Purée the mixture, then adjust the seasonings to taste. Serve with brown toast.

Freeze the pâté when totally cold in well-sealed containers.

Defrost at room temperature or, with care, in a microwave and serve as above.

## Terrine of Chicken and Walnuts

*Serves 6*            *3 months*

I have been using this recipe so long that I cannot remember where it originally came from. It freezes beautifully, comes out a very pretty colour and is equally successful as a starting course or as a cold dish on its own.

> *½ chicken*
> *approx 600 ml/1 pint good chicken stock (or white wine and water)*
> *225 g/8 oz piece of green streaky bacon*
> *175 g/6 oz pie veal, roughly minced*
> *50 g/2 oz shelled broken walnuts (whole are expensive and unnecessary)*
> *½ teaspoon salt*
> *8 peppercorns, roughly crushed*
> *1 small clove garlic, crushed*
> *1 tablespoon brandy*

Poach the chicken in the stock or wine and water until cooked. Cool it slightly, then remove the flesh and chop it into reasonably small pieces. Reduce the stock by boiling fast for about 10 minutes.

Boil the bacon in unsalted water for about 20 minutes until cooked. Cool and then dice it. Mix the chicken in a bowl with the bacon, raw veal, walnuts, salt, crushed peppercorns, garlic and brandy. Add 75 ml/2½ fl oz of the reduced stock and mix it well in.

Grease a terrine dish (or line it with greaseproof paper if the dish is to be frozen) and spoon in the mixture. Cover and bake it in a moderate oven (180°C/350°F/Gas Mark 4) in a *bain-marie* for 75 minutes. Remove the terrine from the oven, cool it slightly and weight it for at least 12 hours. When it is absolutely cold, turn it out and slice it to serve.

To freeze, pack it tightly in polythene bags.

Defrost at room temperature.

# Terrine of Duck

*Serves 6*                                          *2–3 months*

If you have served roast duck for a dinner party (and cannot face picking at the carcase for the following night's supper), use up all the uncarvable bits in a terrine, which will keep for several days in the fridge or freeze successfully.

> *450 g/1 lb duck, cut in small pieces*
> *8–10 slices streaky bacon, thinly cut*
> *25 g/1 oz butter or half butter and half duck fat*
> *1 medium onion, finely chopped*
> *100 g/4 oz mushrooms (preferably dark ones)*
>   *including stalks, chopped*
> *2 tablespoons good brown gravy*
> *2 tablespoons apple purée or sauce*
> *2 tablespoons sweet Madeira or sweet sherry*
> *salt and pepper*
> *a pinch of allspice (optional)*

Lay out the slices of bacon in the bottom and up the sides of a terrine or loaf tin. Lay half the duck meat over the bacon. Meanwhile, melt the fat and lightly fry the onion and mushrooms until they are just softening, then spoon the mixture over the duck meat. Lay the rest of the duck evenly over the vegetables. Gently heat the gravy, apple purée and Madeira or sherry together (do not boil) and season with salt, pepper and a pinch of allspice. Pour this mixture evenly over the terrine.

Cover the dish and cook it in a *bain-marie* for 30 minutes in a moderate oven (180°C/350°F/Gas Mark 4). Remove from the oven, cool and weight overnight. Turn the pâté out and either serve it sliced with fresh brown bread or toast or with a salad.

To freeze, wrap it well in greaseproof paper (not aluminium foil) and pack it in a well-sealed bag.

Defrost as slowly as possible in a fridge or at room temperature, then turn out onto kitchen paper towel. Terrines tend to get rather 'wet' in the freezer and should be dried off once they are defrosted. Serve as above.

# Spinach and Mushroom Pâté

*Serves 8*                                          *3 months*

Although this is a vegetarian recipe, it should appeal to non-vegetarians who find the traditional fish- and meat-based pâtés unmanageably rich.

> *450 g/1 lb fresh spinach*
> *225 g/8 oz leeks, trimmed and finely sliced*
> *40 g/1½ oz butter*
> *225 g/8 oz open mushrooms with their stems, cleaned*
>   *and roughly chopped*
> *40 g/1½ oz pumpkin or sunflower seeds*
> *75 g/3 oz brown breadcrumbs*
> *1 egg*
> *salt and pepper*

Wash the spinach, remove the coarsest of its stems and cook it in the water that clings to its leaves – about 8–10 minutes on a hob; 3–4 minutes in a microwave. Drain the spinach thoroughly, squashing out any excess liquid with a spoon, and chop it roughly.

Meanwhile, soften the leeks in the butter, then add the mushrooms and cook both together for 3–4 minutes. Add the chopped spinach, pumpkin or sunflower seeds, breadcrumbs and the egg. Mix the whole lot thoroughly together and season

*Smoked Fish Pâté and Pork and Bean Pot* (see page 81) *served with salad*

to taste with salt and black pepper. Pack the mixture into a loaf tin, a loose-bottomed cake tin or a soufflé dish – if you want to be sure of getting it out easily, it would be wise to line the dish with foil or greaseproof paper. Cover and bake in a moderate oven (180°C/350°F/Gas Mark 4) for 30 minutes. Take it out of the oven, let it cool slightly, then weight it and allow it to cool completely. Turn it out and serve it with brown toast or crackers.

To freeze, wrap the cooled pâté tightly and freeze.

Defrost at room temperature and serve as above.

## Smoked Fish Pâté

*Serves 6*                                    *6 months*

All smoked fish pâtés freeze well and are so easy to make that it is worth always keeping some in the freezer; they can be used as an emergency starter or on oatcakes as a snack with drinks.

> *225 g/8 oz smoked mackerel, trout, eel or kipper*
> *175 g/6 oz soft butter*
> *75 g/3 oz cream or curd cheese*
> *salt and freshly ground black pepper*
> *juice of 1–3 lemons*
> *75 g/3 oz fine brown breadcrumbs (optional)*

Remove the skin and any bones from the fish and flake the flesh into a mixing bowl with the butter and cheese. Beat (preferably in an electric mixer) until they are well amalgamated, then season to taste with salt, pepper and lemon juice – how much you need will depend on your own taste. If you find the mixture too rich, beat in the brown breadcrumbs to reduce the richness slightly.

Freeze the pâté in one or several small containers so that you can get out small quantities if needed.

Defrost at room temperature or in a microwave *with care*, as it is all too easy to turn this to liquid.

# Ajwar (Red Pepper Pâté)

*Serves 6*                    *1 month*

Ajwar is a Yugoslavian pâté made with the red peppers so beloved in south-eastern Europe. Purists will skin the peppers by submerging them in hot oil until they blister, and look askance at the addition of aubergine, let alone brown bread. However, skinning the peppers is a slow and fiddly business which I feel is scarcely justified by the marginal improvement in the flavour, and the pâté is so rich in its native form that a little 'dilution' does not go amiss.

*6 thick slices aubergine*
*approx 3 tablespoons olive or sunflower oil*
*2 large red peppers, deseeded and roughly chopped*
*3 large cloves garlic*
*2 thick slices wholemeal brown bread*
*salt and pepper*

Fry the aubergine slices in the oil until they are just brown on each side. Put all the ingredients –

fried aubergine, peppers, garlic and bread – in a food processor or liquidizer and purée them. The pâté should not be totally smooth when puréed, but have the texture of a country terrine. Season to taste with salt and pepper, but if it is to be frozen do not be too heavy with the salt as the flavour of both the garlic and the salt will be exaggerated by freezing. Serve with fresh brown bread, brown toast or as a dip with crudités.

Pack in a container to freeze. If you want to freeze the pâté for longer than 1 month, do not add the garlic until after it is defrosted, as so heavy a concentration will give the pâté a slightly 'off' flavour.

Defrost at room temperature or in a microwave.

*Ajwar and Chicken and Almond Mould (see page 44)*

# A Terrine of Salmon

*Serves 6*                                      *3 months*

If you have fresh salmon, it seems a shame to do anything with it but eat it 'straight'. However, if there is some left over you could try this as a way of using it up.

>    *450 g/1 lb cooked salmon*
>    *50 g/2 oz butter*
>    *100 g/4 oz shallots or spring onions, very finely chopped*
>    *225 g/8 oz mushrooms, wiped and sliced*
>    *a handful of parsley, chopped*
>    *salt and pepper*
>    *2 eggs*
>    *a little ground mace and ground nutmeg*
>    *15 g/½ oz anchovy fillets, mashed in a little white wine*
>    *watercress or lemon slices to garnish*

Melt half the butter in a pan and gently cook the shallots or spring onions until they begin to soften. Add the mushrooms and cook briskly for a couple of minutes. Remove from the heat, stir in the parsley, season lightly and stir in 1 egg.

Meanwhile, mash the salmon and season it well with pepper, ground mace and nutmeg, then stir in the other egg. Lay half the salmon in the bottom of a loaf tin or soufflé dish (lined with foil if you are dubious about getting it out) and smooth it out. Lay the mushroom and onion mixture over the salmon and then the final layer of salmon. Melt the remaining butter, stir in the mashed anchovy fillets and pour the mixture over the terrine. Cover and cook it, in a *bain-marie* if possible, in a moderate oven (180°C/350°F/Gas Mark 4) for 30–35 minutes. Take it out of the oven and weight lightly to cool. To serve, turn the pâté out onto a serving dish and decorate it with watercress or lemon slices.

To freeze, turn the pâté out onto foil or greaseproof paper and wrap it in a neat parcel. Freeze in a well-sealed bag.

Defrost as slowly as possible to prevent disintegration and serve as above.

# Terrine of Chicken and Crab

*Serves 6*                                      *2 months*

The green strips of spinach or beans through the pink pâté look very pretty for a lunchtime dish with salads, as a terrine before a dinner, or even for an exotic picnic.

>    *225 g/8 oz cooked chicken, finely minced*
>    *225 g/8 oz crab meat*
>    *25 g/1 oz butter*
>    *25 g/1 oz flour*
>    *150 ml/¼ pint chicken stock*
>    *150 ml/¼ pint dry white wine*
>    *150 ml/¼ pint double cream*
>    *juice of 2 lemons*
>    *25 g/1 oz brown breadcrumbs*
>    *1 large egg*
>    *salt and pepper*
>    *a large pinch of mace*
>    *a few drops of Tabasco*
>    *450 g/1 lb fresh spinach, trimmed, or 225 g/8 oz green beans, trimmed*

Mix the chicken with the crab meat. Melt the butter and add the flour, cook for a minute or two, then gradually add the chicken stock, wine and cream. Cook gently until the sauce thickens, then add the lemon juice. Mix the sauce into the crab and chicken, add the breadcrumbs, egg and season well with the salt, pepper, mace and Tabasco.

Blanch the spinach in boiling water for a couple of minutes, then drain thoroughly, or cook the beans until just tender.

Spoon half the chicken mixture into the bottom of a terrine dish. Spread the spinach or beans over the mixture, then spread over the remainder of the chicken and crab. Cover and cook in a moderately cool oven (160°C/325°F/Gas Mark 3) for 40 minutes or until terrine is set. Cool completely, then turn out and slice.

Freeze the terrine, before slicing, wrapped well in plastic cling film and sealed in a bag.

Defrost as slowly as possible and slice to serve.

# Terrine of Crab, Mushroom and Liver

*Serves 6*                                    *2 months*

When I had finished testing pâtés for this book I was left with a fridge full of assorted bits so, being too mean to throw them out, I threw them all into the food processor instead and shoved the result in the freezer. When I came across it a month later and defrosted it somewhat dubiously, I discovered that it was probably the best of all the pâtés I had made!

*175 g/6 oz brown or white or mixed crab meat*
*25 g/1 oz butter*
*1 medium onion, roughly chopped*
*225 g/8 oz mushrooms (preferably open ones),*
*  roughly chopped*
*50 g/2 oz chicken livers*
*50 g/2 oz brown breadcrumbs*
*1 egg yolk*
*salt and pepper*

Melt the butter in a pan and gently cook the onion, mushrooms and chicken livers until the vegetables are soft and the livers firm. Put them all into a processor or liquidizer and blend until they are finely chopped but not puréed. Add the crab meat, breadcrumbs, egg yolk and seasoning to taste. Turn the mixture into a loaf tin or small soufflé dish, cover it and cook it in a moderate oven (180°C/350°F/Gas Mark 4) for 30 minutes. Remove and weight lightly to cool. When quite cold, turn out and serve with plenty of hot brown toast or oatcakes.

To freeze, wrap in greaseproof paper or foil and pack in a well-sealed bag.

Defrost as slowly as possible on kitchen paper towel to mop up the liquid that will leak out of the pâté. You may have to replace the paper a couple of times and, like all such pâtés, it will do its best to fall apart on you. This does not affect the flavour but makes it a little harder to handle.

# Terrine of Sole and Spinach

*Serves 6*                                    *3 months*

Although, like most terrines and pâtés, this goes a little 'wet' on defrosting, it is such a useful thing to have in the freezer that it is worth freezing it anyhow. It is an old Catercall favourite and has appeared on more buffet tables than I can remember!

*450 g/1 lb lemon sole (with bones and skin)*
*2 lemons*
*salt and pepper*
*450 g/1 lb freshly-cooked or frozen leaf spinach*
*salt, pepper and nutmeg*
*20 g/¾ oz gelatine*
*90 ml/3 fl oz medium sherry*

Fillet the fish and make some stock from the bones and skin (see page 152). Put the fish in a pan with one of the lemons, sliced, and the strained fish stock. Cover and cook in a moderate oven (180°C/350°F/Gas Mark 4) or over a low heat for 15–20 minutes. Remove the fish and flake it and season to taste. Reserve 90 ml/3 fl oz of the stock.

Meanwhile, drain the spinach *very* thoroughly and season it well with salt, pepper and nutmeg. Soften half the gelatine in the juice of the other lemon, add the reserved stock and melt the gelatine in it. Cool and stir into the fish. Put half the fish mixture into the bottom of a loaf tin or soufflé dish and smooth it off. Put it into the fridge to chill and set. Meanwhile, melt the rest of the gelatine in the sherry and add this to the spinach. When the first layer of fish is set, spoon a layer of spinach over it, smooth off and chill. Repeat with another layer each of fish and spinach. When the whole thing is thoroughly chilled and set, turn it out onto a serving dish, or if it is to be frozen, onto greaseproof paper.

To freeze, wrap it in the paper and put in a bag.

Defrost as slowly as possible to prevent disintegration – you will need to 'mop up' some of the juices with kitchen paper towel. Turn onto a serving dish, decorate and serve.

# COCKTAIL SNACKS AND APPETIZERS

## Cheese Sables

*Makes 20–30 biscuits*                    *2 months*

These are delicious little savoury biscuits – ideal to have in the freezer in case of an unexpected drinks visitor. However because of the high proportion of fat, they are *very* fragile – and very more-ish.

> *75 g/3 oz cold butter*
> *75 g/3 oz plain flour*
> *75 g/3 oz finely grated, strong-flavoured cheese (a good Cheddar is ideal)*
> *salt and pepper*
> *1 egg, beaten*

Rub the butter into the flour and then mix in the grated cheese and a little seasoning and form into a ball. Leave in a cool place for at least 10 minutes, especially if the weather is hot. Flour a board and roll the mixture out thinly – approximately 5 mm/ ¼ inch thick. Cut out biscuits with a cutter or a glass – you can try to make straws but because of the pastry's shortness straws tend to break; I find that small rounds work best. Brush the bisuits with beaten egg and bake them in a moderately

hot oven (190°C/375°F/Gas Mark 5) for about 10 minutes. However, you must watch them like a hawk as they burn all too easily. Cool on a rack.

Freeze in boxes to prevent breakages.

Defrost at room temperature – they will only take 5 minutes if spread out.

## Chicken Satay

*Serves about 30*          *6 months*

The chicken pieces in their sauce are delicious, but if you have sauce over, it is even better as a dip.

> *1 medium chicken (approx 1.5–2 kg/3–4 lb)*
> *25 g/1 oz ground almonds*
> *1 tablespoon shredded ginger root*
> *1 teaspoon each ground coriander, ground turmeric and dark brown sugar*
> *300 ml/½ pint coconut milk (see note)*
> *2 tablespoons good vegetable oil*
> *approx ½ teaspoon chilli powder*
> *2 medium onions, very finely chopped*
> *225 g/8 oz peanut butter*
> *approx 1 teaspoon pale brown sugar*
> *approx 1 tablespoon soy sauce*
> *juice of ½ lemon*

Remove the flesh from the chicken and cut into strips weighing approximately 15 g/½ oz each. Mix the almonds, ginger, spices and dark brown sugar. Add the coconut milk, mix well and use this to marinate the chicken pieces in for about 2 hours. You can freeze the chicken in the marinade if you think you will have time to cook it later. If you wish to cook it now, transfer it, with the marinade, to an ovenproof dish, cover and cook for 40 minutes in a moderate oven (180°C/350°F/Gas Mark 4). Meanwhile, heat the oil in a pan with the chilli powder and cook the onions gently until they are quite soft. Take off the heat and add the peanut butter and all the other ingredients to taste. If it is to be used at once, mix in the cooked marinade from the chicken pieces to make a thick sauce. Spear the chicken pieces on cocktail sticks and arrange them in a dish with a bowl of the sauce in the middle.

*Chicken Satay, Old English Meatballs (see page 24), Mini Corn Fritters (see page 25) and Asparagus Rolls (see page 24)*

If the satay is to be frozen, freeze the cooked chicken in the marinade in a well-sealed container and freeze the sauce separately.

Defrost at room temperature or in a microwave (do not microwave the sauce as you do not want to melt the butter). Mix the marinade with the sauce (you may need to heat it slightly to get the sauce thin enough to mix properly) and serve as above.

NOTE: The coconut milk is made by simmering 75 g/3 oz desiccated coconut in 300 ml/½ pint milk for 20 minutes. Allow to cool, then strain to remove the coconut.

# Asparagus Rolls

*Makes about 30 rolls*                    *2 months*

I do not personally think that asparagus rolls freeze particularly well as the asparagus tends to go soggy. However, if you are addicted to them and you want to prepare them ahead of time, it is perfectly possible to do. You could also use fresh asparagus for a really gourmet touch, but I would be inclined to serve the rolls fresh and maybe substitute a fairly thick Hollandaise for the butter.

> *1 small loaf fine grained, unsliced brown bread*
> *100–175 g/4–6 oz soft butter*
> *1–2 large cans (400 g/14 oz) asparagus tips, drained*
> *salt and freshly ground black pepper*
> *parsley to garnish*

Chill or partially freeze the loaf, then slice it as thinly and evenly as you can and remove the crusts. Butter the bread thoroughly, making sure that you get the butter right out to the edge of the slice of bread. Lay a spear of asparagus at one side of the slice (or make it up with two if there is not one long enough), shake over some salt and pepper and roll up the roll, pressing the edges well together. Trim any extra bread off the end of the roll if the asparagus tip is not visible. Depending on the shape and size of the loaf you may wish to cut the roll in half. Serve at once piled on a dish or laid end up so that the green is visible and decorate with parsley. Remember to keep them covered with wet kitchen paper towel and tightly wrapped in cling film until they are served to prevent the bread drying up.

Freeze the rolls in a well-sealed container.

Defrost slowly sitting end up on kitchen paper to absorb the melting liquid, but covered with cling film to prevent the top drying out. Serve as above.

# Old English Meatballs

*Makes 40 balls*                    *6 months*

This is a fruity and spicy ball which makes a change from the standard sausage flavour.

> *450 g/1 lb minced lamb, beef, pork or veal*
> *15 g/½ oz butter*
> *1 medium onion, minced*
> *50 g/2 oz raisins or soaked currants*
> *½ tart eating apple, peeled and grated*
> *1 teaspoon sea salt*
> *1 teaspoon ground cinnamon*
> *½ teaspoon ground black pepper*
> *½ teaspoon ground ginger*
> *a large pinch of ground cloves*
> *50 g/2 oz brown breadcrumbs*
> *1 large or 2 small eggs*
> *seasoned flour*
> *butter and oil for frying*

Melt the butter and gently cook the onion until it is quite soft. Add it to the minced meat with the fruits, seasoning, spices and breadcrumbs. Mix them all well together, then add the egg to bind the mixture. Roll the mixture into small balls, approximately 15 g/½ oz each, toss them in seasoned flour and fry them gently in butter and oil until they are browned on the outside and cooked through. It is as well to fry one and taste it to make sure that the seasoning is right before you commit yourself to the whole bowl.

Cool on a rack, then freeze in a well-sealed bag.

Defrost at room temperature or in a microwave and reheat to crisp up. They can be served hot or cold, with or without a dip.

# Smoked Salmon Pinwheels

*Serves about 30*          *1–2 months*

This is a more exotic version of the Anchovy Pinwheels (page 27). Tuna fish can be used in place of the salmon.

> *1 small loaf good quality but fairly fine grained,*
>   *unsliced brown bread*
> *approx 100 g/4 oz soft butter*
> *350–450 g/³⁄₄–1 lb sliced smoked salmon*
> *juice of 1–2 lemons*
> *freshly ground black pepper*
> *lemon butterflies or parsley to garnish*

Chill the loaf in the fridge or freezer, then slice it as thinly and evenly as you can; remove the crusts. Butter each slice fairly generously, making sure that you cover all the edges. Lay a piece of smoked salmon on each slice, cutting it so that it covers as much of the bread as possible. Sprinkle with lemon juice and black pepper and roll up. If they are to be used at once, chill them thoroughly before slicing the rolls across (you should get between 4 and 8 pinwheels per slice, depending on the shape of the loaf) and piling them in a dish. Decorate with lemon butterflies or parsley and make sure you cover the rolls with wet kitchen paper towel and tightly wrapped cling film until you are ready to serve them.

Freeze the complete rolls tightly packed in well-sealed containers.

Defrost at room temperature – not in a microwave or you will melt the butter. Slice before they are quite defrosted and serve as above.

# Mini Corn Fritters

*Makes about 20 fritters*          *6 months*

Fritters do freeze quite well, provided that you always remember to crisp them up in an oven before serving them – and freezing does at least ensure that both you and the house will not smell like a fish and chip shop when you serve them!

> *1 medium can (325 g/11 oz) sweetcorn, drained, or*
>   *fresh cooked or frozen sweetcorn*
> *2 teaspoons soft brown sugar*
> *3 eggs, beaten*
> *50 g/2 oz melted butter*
> *4 tablespoons grated Parmesan or other well-*
>   *flavoured hard cheese*
> *salt and pepper*
> *oil for deep-frying*

Mix the sweetcorn thoroughly in a bowl with the sugar, eggs, butter, cheese and seasoning. Heat the oil to approximately 190°C/375°C and lower in the corn batter in small teaspoonfuls. Fry the fritters for 2–3 minutes or until they are crisp and golden. Remove with a slotted spoon and drain on kitchen paper towel. Serve immediately on cocktail sticks by themselves or with a dip.

If they are to be frozen, allow them to get quite cold, then open freeze. When frozen, pack in a well-sealed container; they can get broken in a freezer if packed in bags.

Defrost at room temperature rather than in a microwave, which will make them even soggier than they already are. Lay out on an oven tray and reheat in a moderate oven (180°C/350°F/Gas Mark 4) for 5–10 minutes or until the outsides are crisp. Serve as above.

# 'Seedy' Pastry Squares

*Makes 30–40 squares or triangles*      *3 months*

If you make a really good shortcrust pastry (see page 161) or puff pastry and sprinkle the top of it liberally with seeds, it can turn into a very simple but delicious cocktail snack.

> *approx 225 g/8 oz shortcrust or puff pastry*
> *1 egg, beaten*
> *3–4 tablespoons poppy seeds, aniseeds, chopped*
>   *sunflower seeds, sesame, etc.*
> *a little fine sea salt*

Roll out the pastry reasonably thinly and brush it lightly with the beaten egg. Sprinkle your seeds, mixed with a little salt, liberally over the pastry, then cut it into small squares, triangles or rounds. If they are to be used at once, bake them in a moderately hot oven (190°C/375°F/Gas Mark 5) for 10–15 minutes, taking great care that they do not burn. Serve warm.

If they are to be frozen, open freeze them on a tray, then pack in a well-sealed container.

They can be cooked straight from frozen, again taking care they do not burn. Serve as above.

*Cheese Sables* (see page 22), *Devils on Horseback, Anchovy Pinwheels and 'Seedy' Pastry Squares* (see page 25)

# Devils on Horseback

*6 months*

This is a classic cocktail savoury and freezes excellently. If you want to be more exotic, you can substitute mussels for the prunes, but if they are to be frozen, they must be fresh ones. You can also replace the prunes with chicken livers (again they should be fresh not frozen if the snack is to be frozen) or mushrooms – although the latter are much better if made fresh. Do not use canned prunes as they are too soft to hold together, but if you are using dried, try to make sure that they are the soft ones, or soak them for a couple of hours first.

> 1 large, softened and destoned prune per devil, or 1 mussel, chicken liver or mushroom (half will be enough if they are large) per devil
>
> 1 slice thinly cut, derinded bacon per devil

Wrap the prune or whatever you are using tightly in the bacon and secure with a cocktail stick. It is better to freeze the devils uncooked as they will need to be crisped on defrosting, whether cooked or uncooked.

Open freeze them on a tray, then pack into well-sealed bags. (If you have wrapped them really tightly, you may be able to avoid skewering them until they are defrosted which will make them much easier to pack.)

Defrost at room temperature or in an oven – if you have not skewered them you should do so when they are half defrosted. Lay them out on a baking dish and cook for 10–15 minutes in a moderately hot oven (190°C/375°F/Gas Mark 5) or until the bacon is cooked and crisped and the filling is hot and (if it is anything except the prune) cooked. Serve hot.

# Anchovy Pinwheels

*Serves about 30*                                    *1–2 months*

Like all pinwheels, these should be frozen whole,
then sliced on defrosting. It does not pay to keep
them too long in the freezer as the bread
eventually dries up – make them a couple of
weeks ahead for a party you know you are going
to have and they will be fine.

> 1 small loaf good quality, unsliced white bread
> 1 small can (50 g/2 oz) anchovies, drained and
>   thoroughly chopped
> approx 225 g/8 oz soft butter
> parsley or watercress to garnish

Put the bread in the freezer for 30–45 minutes
until it just starts to freeze – it will be much easier
to cut – then slice it as thinly and evenly as you
can and remove the crusts.

Meanwhile, mix the anchovies with the butter.
Exactly how many you use will depend on how

strong you want your pinwheels to be; start with
approximately half the can and taste it on a bit of
bread until you get it right. Butter the slices with
the mixture fairly generously, making sure that
you take the butter right out to the edge of the
bread, then roll up each slice. If they are to be
used immediately, put them into the fridge or
freezer to get really well chilled before slicing each
pinwheel across – you should get between 4 and 8
slices, depending on the size and shape of the
loaf. Pile them in a dish or on a wooden board
and decorate with parsley or watercress. Make
sure you keep them covered with a piece of wet
kitchen paper towel and tightly wrapped plastic
cling film until just before you want to serve them
or they will dry out.

To freeze, pack the unsliced rolls tightly in a well-
sealed container.

Defrost at room temperature – not in a microwave
or you will melt the butter. Before they are quite
defrosted, slice and serve as above.

# FISH AND SHELLFISH

## Cod, Cream and Caper Pie

*Serves 6*                                    *1–2 months*

Now that it has become expensive to buy, cod is being appreciated for the excellent fish that it is. Also, as it is relatively firm-fleshed, it freezes well. Including cream in the sauce raises it from the everyday to the 'gourmet' level.

> *750 g/1½ lb fresh or frozen cod fillet or steak*
> *240 ml/8 fl oz dry white wine*
> *240 ml/8 fl oz water*
> *3–4 slices lemon*
> *65 g/2½ oz butter*
> *225 g/8 oz onions, peeled and very finely chopped*
> *40 g/1½ oz flour*
> *150 ml/¼ pint double cream*
> *3–4 tablespoons capers, drained and roughly chopped*
> *salt and pepper*
> *hard-boiled yolks of 6 eggs*
> *1 kg/2 lb potatoes, peeled*
> *approx 150 ml/¼ pint milk or milk and cream mixed*

Poach the fish in the wine and water, with the lemon slices, for about 15 minutes on a hob or 4–5 minutes in a microwave – do not let it overcook. Meanwhile, melt the onions in 40 g/1½ oz of the butter until they are quite soft. Add the flour, cook for a minute or two, then gradually add the liquid from cooking the fish and cook together for a couple of minutes. Add the cream and the capers – exactly how many capers you add will depend on how keen you are on capers. Season to taste with salt and pepper. Break the fish into large flakes and gently mix it into the sauce with the hard-boiled egg yolks, halved. Spoon the mixture into a pie dish (lined with foil or plastic cling film if it is to be frozen) and set aside.

Meanwhile, steam or microwave the potatoes, then mash them with 15 g/½ oz of the butter and as much creamy milk as is needed to make a smooth purée. Season them with salt and white pepper. Spoon or pipe (if you want to give the pie a really 'fancy' look) the potato carefully over the fish and dot the top of the potato with the remaining butter. Reheat the pie in a moderate oven (about 30 minutes at 180°C/350°F/Gas Mark 4) or in a microwave. If you use a microwave, you may need to put the pie under a grill for a couple of minutes to brown the top.

Open freeze the pie, then remove it from the dish and seal tightly in a bag to store.

Defrost at room temperature or, carefully, in a microwave. Reheat as above.

## Pickled Mackerel

*Serves 6*                                    *2–3 months*

This dish is based on an eighteenth-century recipe by John Farley but has been such a success with twentieth-century 'consumers' that it has become another Catercall standby. The spicing is quite strong (although not as strong as in the original when it would have been necessary to keep the fish edible), so do not try it on people with tender taste buds. If on the contrary you have an iron-clad palate, you may wish to increase the quantities of spices. Serve as a starter or as a cocktail snack, when it will be enough for 20 people.

> *2 large, fresh mackerel, cleaned*
> *15 g/½ oz freshly ground black pepper*
> *1 teaspoon freshly ground nutmeg (if possible)*
> *a large pinch of mace*
> *1 teaspoon sea salt*
> *6 tablespoons olive or sunflower oil*
> *1 tablespoon red wine vinegar*

Cut the mackerel, bone and all, into slices about 2.5 cm/1 inch thick. Mix the spices and seasonings together and rub them well into the flesh of the fish – it helps to make small cuts in which the spices can lodge. Heat 3 tablespoons of the oil in a heavy-based pan and fry the mackerel slices on both sides until they are crispy and cooked through – but not burnt. Cool them.

If the mackerel is to be eaten immediately, it can now be boned and skinned. If it is to be used as a starter, lay the slices out on a dish. Mix the remaining oil with the vinegar and spoon over the fish. Serve it cold with very fresh, preferably hot, brown bread. If it is to be used as a cocktail snack, bone the slices but do not skin them. Carefully break each slice into about four pieces and impale each on a cocktail stick. Put them in a dish, then mix the remaining oil and the vinegar and spoon over the pieces.

If the mackerel is to be frozen, the slices should be packed in polythene bags (unboned, as they will hold together better) as soon as they have cooled and before they are dressed.

Defrost at room temperature or in a microwave. Finish off as above.

## Stuffed Squid

*Serves 6*                                      *2–3 months*

For those who are do not mind 'dealing with squid', this is a relatively cheap but exotic and delicious dish. You can serve the squid warm with buttery brown rice and a salad, or you can let them get cold, halve, quarter or slice them, impale them on sticks and serve them with a salad or as cocktail bits.

> 12–18 small squid
> 350 g/12 oz smoked ham, thinly sliced
> 2 large handfuls parsley, finely chopped
> 210 ml/7 fl oz olive, sunflower or corn oil
> 2 medium onions, peeled and finely chopped
> salt and pepper
> 3 eggs
> 3 tablespoons tomato purée
> 150 ml/¼ pint dry white wine
> 360 ml/12 fl oz water
> salt and pepper
> a few drops of Tabasco

Remove the tentacles and wings from the squid and chop these finely, reserving the bodies for stuffing. Mix the bits with the ham and the chopped parsley. Heat 3 tablespoons oil in a pan, add the onions and soften them gently. Add the ham mixture and cook them all together for a couple of minutes. Remove the mixture from the heat, season it well and, when it has cooled

slightly, mix in the eggs. Clean the bodies of the squid, stuff them with the ham mixture and secure them with a cocktail stick.

Heat the remaining oil with the tomato purée, wine and water in a pan, lower in the squid and poach them gently for 25–30 minutes. Season the the juices to taste with salt, pepper and a touch of Tabasco. (If the squid is to be frozen, do not season the sauce until it is defrosted.) Serve the squid as a casserole in their own juices with brown rice. Alternatively, remove the squid from the juices and allow them to cool. They can then either be halved or quartered and impaled on sticks to be served as cocktail snacks or served whole or sliced with a salad.

Freeze the squid in their cooking liquids.

Defrost at room temperature or in a microwave and serve as above.

## Scallops with Cream and Orange

*Serves 6*                                      *4 weeks*

You can make this with frozen scallops and serve it fresh, or with fresh scallops and then freeze it. You can even make it with frozen scallops and then freeze it!

> 6 large or 12 small scallops
> 180 ml/6 fl oz dry white wine
> grated rind and juice of 1 large orange
> 2 teaspoons wine vinegar
> 25 g/1 oz butter
> 8 spring onions, trimmed and finely chopped
> 15 g/½ oz flour
> 90 ml/3 fl oz double cream
> salt and pepper
> 4 tablespoons unhusked brown or white rice, cooked,
>    drained and kept warm

Put the scallops in a pan with the wine, orange rind and juice and the vinegar, bring to the boil and simmer gently for 2–3 minutes or until the scallops are cooked. Meanwhile, melt the butter in a separate pan and gently cook the spring onions for a couple of minutes. Add the flour, cook for a minute, then gradually add the cooking liquid from the scallops and the cream. Season the sauce to taste with salt and pepper.

*Stuffed Squid* (see page 29)

Make an edging of the rice in a warmed small dish or a scallop shell. Put one or two scallops in the middle of each dish or shell and spoon over the sauce. Serve at once.

The scallops can either be frozen in their sauce in a container, or they can be frozen in their shells surrounded by the rice. In either case they should be packed in well-sealed containers.

Defrost as slowly as possible and reheat either in a microwave or covered in a moderate oven (180°C/350°F/Gas Mark 4).

# Herrings and Pears in Oatmeal

*Serves 6*                                          *2–3 months*

This is a slight variation on the old dish of herring fried in oatmeal with mustard; it freezes remarkably well as long as you are careful not to dry it out when reheating.

6 herrings, cleaned, boned and cut in half
6 tablespoons porridge oats
4 tablespoons good quality wholegrain mustard
50–75 g/2–3 oz butter or low fat margarine
6 small or 4 large pears, peeled and quartered or cut
     in large wedges

Dry the herrings, then coat them on both sides in a paste made by mixing the porridge oats and mustard well together. Melt the butter or margarine in a heavy-based pan and gently fry the herrings on both sides until they are cooked but not falling apart. If you have room in the pan, add the pear sections and lightly fry them at the same time. If not, remove the fish to some kitchen paper towel and keep warm while you fry the pears in the remaining butter until they are lightly cooked but still crunchy. If the herrings are to be served immediately, transfer them to a warmed dish with the pears and serve with lots of fresh brown bread and butter.

If the herrings are to be frozen, pack them with the pears in a container and freeze as usual.

Defrost at room temperature or, carefully, in a microwave. Reheat, uncovered, in a moderate oven (180°C/350°F/Gas Mark 4) for about 20 minutes, but take care not to leave them long enough for the fish to dry out. Serve as above.

*Fish Quenelles* (see page 37)

*Herrings and Pears in Oatmeal*

# Rolled Fillets of Sole Stuffed with Spinach and Almonds

*Serves 6*                    *3 months*

This recipe is based on one from William Verral's *Complete System of Cookery* published in 1759. I would suggest that you freeze the fish rolls once cooked, but make the sauce when you defrost the dish before serving it.

> 6 large fillets of lemon sole (or any white fish)
> 25 g/1 oz butter
> 6 spring onions, finely chopped
> 50 g/2 oz lean bacon, finely chopped
> 50 g/2 oz ground almonds
> 50 g/2 oz brown breadcrumbs
> ½ teaspoon ground nutmeg
> ½ teaspoon white pepper
> 1 teaspoon sea salt
> 350 g/12 oz fresh spinach, cooked and chopped, or
>   225 g/8 oz frozen leaf spinach, defrosted
> juice of ½ orange and ½ lemon
> 1 egg
> 300 ml/½ pint good fish stock (see page 152)
> 15 g/½ oz plain flour
> 150 ml/¼ pint double cream
> ½ teaspoon dill weed
> watercress or orange slices to garnish

Melt half the butter and gently fry the spring onions and bacon until they are soft but not coloured. Turn them into a bowl and add the almonds, breadcrumbs, spice and seasonings. Stir in the spinach (which should be well drained) and fruit juices. Beat the egg and add that to the mixture. Lay the fillets out on a board and divide the mixture between them. Roll them loosely and place them in a baking tray. Pour over the stock, cover them and cook in a moderate oven (180°C/ 350°F/Gas Mark 4) for 30 minutes. If you are freezing the dish, you can do so at this point (see below).

If the dish is to be served at once, remove the fillets onto a rack and keep them warm. Meanwhile, melt the remaining butter in a pan, add the flour and cook for a couple of minutes. Gradually add the strained liquid from the fish, the cream and the dill. Season to taste. If the sauce is too thin, reduce it slightly by simmering gently for 5 minutes. Remove the fish onto a serving dish, spoon over the sauce and decorate the dish with watercress or slices of orange. Serve at once.

To freeze, remove the fillets from the stock and pack them in a well-sealed container. Freeze the stock separately. If you freeze the fillets in the stock, the expansion of the liquid tends to break up the fish even more than it is already and make it impossible to move without it falling apart!

Defrost as slowly as possible and reheat the fillets gently in a microwave or a moderate oven (180°C/ 350°F/Gas Mark 4), well covered. Meanwhile, defrost the stock, make the sauce and serve as above.

# Smoked Mackerel and Cockle Flan

*Serves 6*                    *2–3 months*

This has an excellent flavour and will tolerate being frozen, defrosted and reheated (sometimes more than once) with endless good humour. It can be used in fingers as a substantial cocktail snack; in small wedges as starting course; and in large wedges as a cheap buffet dish. Substitute mussels if cockles are hard to find.

> 225 g/8 oz smoked mackerel fillet
> 100 g/4 oz cockles (frozen will do fine)
> 15 g/½ oz butter
> 15 g/½ oz flour
> 150 ml/¼ pint milk
> 1 egg
> salt and freshly ground black pepper

> **Pastry**
> 150 g/5 oz wholemeal flour
> 50 g/2 oz butter
> 50 g/2 oz lard

Make the pastry by rubbing the fats into the flour and binding with a little cold water. Roll it out and line a 20-cm/8-inch flan case, then bake it blind.

Meanwhile, melt the butter in a pan, add the flour, cook for a minute or two, then gradually add the milk, stirring continually until you have a smooth sauce. Cook for another couple of minutes. Skin and mash the smoked mackerel in a bowl. Add the cockles, the sauce and the egg. Season to taste with salt and freshly ground black pepper and spoon into the pastry case. If you have pastry left over, you can use it to make a lattice-work on the top. Cook the flan in a moderate oven (180°C/350°F/Gas Mark 4) for 20–25 minutes.

Cool and freeze. Once frozen, you should be able to remove it from the dish for permanent storage, wrapped well in a polythene bag.

Defrost at room temperature or in a microwave, and serve either warm or cold.

# Turkish Prawn Pilaff

*Serves 4*                                   *3 months*

This is one of my mother's recipes which has appeared (very successfully) at every buffet party I can remember since I was a child! It is spicy and interesting, and is good cold or hot as a starter or main course. It also freezes very well.

*5–6 giant Pacific prawns or 100 g/4 oz peeled*
*  ordinary prawns*
*4 tablespoons olive or sunflower oil*
*1 small onion, peeled and finely chopped*
*2 small red peppers, finely chopped*
*1 clove garlic, finely chopped or crushed*
*4 heaped tablespoons long-grain patna rice*
*½ teaspoon ground allspice*
*½ teaspoon cumin seeds*
*1 heaped teaspoon dried mint or basil*
*2 tablespoons washed currants*
*salt*
*juice of 1–2 lemons*
*a handful of parsley, finely chopped*

Heat the oil in a large, flat pan and gently cook the onion, peppers and garlic until they are soft but not browned. Add the rice, spices and herbs, stir together for a few minutes, then add enough water to cover the rice. Bring the mixture to the boil and simmer with the pan uncovered for 10–15 minutes or until the rice is just cooked but not mushy. You may have to add a little more water if it dries up too fast. Add the prawns, currants and a generous sprinkling of salt. Cook for a couple more minutes, add the lemon juice and parsley and adjust the seasoning to taste. Serve warm or cold.

To freeze, cool completely and pack in well-sealed containers or bags.

Defrost at room temperature or in a microwave and reheat, well covered, in a moderate oven (180°C/350°F/Gas Mark 4) or microwave if it is to be served hot.

# Tuna Fish Loaf

*Serves 6*                                   *4–6 months*

This tuna fish loaf, which is excellent for lunch or buffet parties, is based on a recipe from Anna del Conte's Italian cookery book.

*200 g/7 oz can tuna fish in oil, drained and mashed*
*2 hard-boiled egg yolks*
*75 g/3 oz freshly grated Parmesan or, if not*
*  available, Cheshire or other crumbly cheese*
*75 g/3 oz brown breadcrumbs*
*a handful of finely chopped parsley*
*nutmeg, black pepper and a little salt*
*2 whole eggs*
*1 onion, halved*
*a few parsley stalks*
*150 ml/¼ pint wine vinegar*
*150 ml/¼ pint dry white wine*
*lettuce or watercress*
*3 tablespoons olive oil*
*juice of 1 small lemon*

Mash the hard-boiled egg yolks with the tuna, cheese, breadcrumbs and parsley. Season liberally with nutmeg and pepper and less generously with salt. Mix in the whole eggs. Form the mixture into a roll and lay it in a piece of clean muslin or a new kitchen cloth, fold it over and tie the ends. Place the roll in a pan or casserole and add the onion, parsley stalks, vinegar and wine. Add water to just cover the roll, bring to the boil, cover and simmer for 45 minutes. Remove the roll, place it between two plates and weight it while it cools. Serve the roll, thinly sliced, on a bed of lettuce or watercress and dressed with the oil and lemon juice.

Freeze the roll in one piece after it has cooled.

Defrost at room temperature or in a microwave, slice and serve as above.

# Sole or Grey Mullet with Plum and Chilli Sauce

*Serves 6*                                        *1–2 months*

Fish is usually better frozen uncooked, but if you think you may be pushed for time at the other end, fish dishes can be made up completely. If you do not anticipate being short of time, use seasonal plums or gooseberries to make batches of the sauce so that it will be available whenever you need it.

> *6 lemon sole or grey mullet*
> *25 g/1 oz butter*
> *1 small onion, finely chopped*
> *75 g/3 oz fresh or frozen (not canned) gooseberries*
> *3 red plums*
> *1 whole red chilli (fresh or dried), deseeded and finely*
> *  chopped*
> *1 teaspoon sugar (optional)*
> *slices of lemon*
> *a little white wine and water mixed*

Melt the butter in a small pan and gently cook the onion, gooseberries, plums and chopped chilli for 10–15 minutes until they are totally mushy. Purée them in a food processor or liquidizer and taste. If the sauce is too sour for your taste, add a little sugar, but only a little.

If you are using sole and the fish are to be frozen cooked, fillet the sole and roll up the fillets. Put them in an ovenproof dish, surround with lemon slices and just cover with the wine and water. Cover and bake in a moderate oven (180°C/350°F/Gas Mark 4) for 15–20 minutes or in a microwave for 3–4 minutes; they should just be cooked but no more.

If you are using mullet, the fillets will not roll so easily, so lay them out flat on the dish to cook. Line the dish in which you eventually expect to serve the fish with plastic cling film or foil and lay the cooked fillets in the bottom. Cover them with the sauce and freeze. Once frozen, the fish can be removed from the dish and packed for storage.

To defrost, peel the foil or plastic cling film off the fish and sauce while they are still frozen and drop them into the original dish. Defrost at room temperature. Reheat with great care, covered, in a low oven (150°C/300°F/Gas Mark 2) or a microwave. The texture of the fish is such that it will all too easily disintegrate.

If the fish has been frozen uncooked, defrost it at room temperature (spread out) and cook it as above. If possible, it is better to bone and fillet the fish after it has been cooked so as to retain the flavour of the bones. Lay the cooked fish in the serving dish and spoon over the sauce.

# Leek and Tuna Fish Pie

*Serves 4*                                    *6 months*

This is an excellent winter pie.

> *2 × 200 g/7 oz cans tuna fish*
> *1 small can (50 g/2 oz) anchovy fillets*
> *4 large leeks, finely sliced*
> *225 g/8 oz fresh spinach (if not available use frozen)*
> *150 ml/¼ pint dry white wine*
> *450 g/1 lb potatoes, scrubbed and very thinly sliced*
> *approx 50 g/2 oz butter*
> *freshly ground black pepper*

Drain the oil from the tuna and anchovy cans into a shallow pan and gently fry the leeks until they are soft but not burnt. Turn them into the bottom of a pie dish. If the pie is to be frozen, line the dish with foil. Chop the fresh spinach or thoroughly drain the frozen spinach and spread it over the leeks. Break up the tuna fish and chop the anchovy fillets, mix the two together and spread them over the top of the spinach. Pour over the wine and cover the pie with the very thinly sliced potatoes, arranged in rounds. Dot it with half the butter and bake it, covered, in a moderate oven (180°C/350°F/Gas Mark 4) for 30 minutes. Take out of the oven, uncover and dot the potatoes with the rest of the butter. Return the pie to the oven, uncovered, for a further 15–20 minutes to brown the potatoes. (If the pie is to be frozen, you may prefer to leave the final cooking and browning until it is defrosted.) Grate over some fresh black pepper (you should not need any more salt because of the anchovies) and serve at once.

*Sole with Plum and Chilli Sauce, Tuna Fish Loaf (see page 33) and Rolled Fillets of Sole Stuffed with Spinach and Almonds (see page 32)*

To freeze, cool completely and open freeze. Remove from the dish and pack in a well-sealed bag to store.

Remove the foil and turn the pie back into its dish. Defrost at room temperature or in a microwave and reheat in an oven or microwave. Serve as above.

# Fish Cakes

*Serves 6*                                            *3 months*

These are slightly more exotic than the standard fish cake and are good on their own or with a dipping sauce – although the sauce should not be too strong or it will drown the flavour of the fish. You can increase or decrease the amount of chilli depending on how hot you like your food.

> *450 g/1 lb fresh cod, haddock or other well-flavoured*
>   *white fish*
> *100 g/4 oz onions, chopped*
> *½–1 fresh chilli, deseeded and finely chopped*
> *2 tomatoes, roughly chopped*
> *approx 350 g/12 oz brown breadcrumbs*
> *2 eggs*
> *salt and pepper*
> *1–2 teaspoons soy sauce*
> *25–50 g/1–2 oz butter or low fat margarine*

Put the fish with the onions, chilli and tomatoes in a food processor or liquidizer and blend them thoroughly together. Add 100 g/4 oz of the breadcrumbs, the eggs, seasoning and soy sauce and blend again until well amalgamated. The mixture will be quite soft, so it may be easier to chill it for a while before making it into cakes.

To make the cakes, form tablespoonfuls of the mixture into flat cakes and coat them thoroughly in the rest of the breadcrumbs. Melt the butter in a flat pan and fry the cakes gently for 3–4 minutes each side until cooked through and lightly browned on each side. Serve at once.

Freeze the cakes before cooking them (unless they have been made with frozen fish, in which case they must be cooked before they are frozen), in well-sealed containers layered with foil or greaseproof paper.

Defrost at room temperature and fry as above. If

they are already cooked, reheat them gently in a moderate oven (180°C/350°F/Gas Mark 4).

# Smoked Trout Mousse

*Serves 6*                                            *2 months*

The delicate flavour of the smoked trout keeps well in the freezer as long as you do not leave it for too long. As the texture of the mousse is quite soft, it should be served well chilled.

> *2 smoked trout, skinned and boned*
> *3 tablespoons good mayonnaise*
> *generous 15 g/½ oz gelatine*
> *juice of 1–2 lemons*
> *2 whole eggs plus 2 egg whites*
> *150 ml/¼ pint double cream*
> *sea salt and freshly ground black pepper*
> *watercress or lemon slices to garnish*

Mash the flesh of the trout, making sure you have removed all the bones. Mix in the mayonnaise thoroughly. Soften the gelatine in the juice of 1 lemon and melt it in a bowl over hot water, then cool it by plunging the bowl into cold water. Once the gelatine mixture is roughly the temperature of the trout, mix it in well. Separate the eggs and mix the yolks well into the trout, then lightly whisk the cream and fold it into the mixture. Season with the salt and pepper, taste and add a little more lemon juice if you would like it sharper. Put the bowl in the fridge until the mousse is just starting to set. Remove it from the fridge, whisk the whites until they hold their shape and fold them into the mousse. Pour the mixture into a soufflé dish or a mould and chill until it is set. Decorate the top with watercress or lemon, or turn the mould out and decorate. Serve with fresh brown toast.

If the mousse is to be frozen, line the dish with plastic cling film and open freeze once it is set. Do not freeze before it is set as premature freezing can have an adverse affect on the gelatine. Once frozen, turn out of the dish and store in well-sealed bags.

Remove the plastic cling film and put the mousse back into its dish. Defrost as slowly as possible to maintain its texture. Decorate and serve as above.

# Kedgeree

*Serves 6*          *6 months*

Although not many people now eat kedgeree for breakfast, it still makes a delicious supper or Sunday brunch dish – and freezes well.

> *350 g/12 oz smoked haddock fillets*
> *6 tablespoons long-grain rice*
> *1 small onion*
> *100 g/4 oz butter*
> *175 g/6 oz raisins*
> *1–2 teaspooons strong curry powder*
> *1 hard-boiled egg*
> *juice of 1 lemon*

Poach the fish for 10 minutes in gently boiling water, then drain well and flake it. Cook the rice in boiling water for about 11 minutes or until it is cooked but not mushy. Drain it and run a little more boiling water through it to separate the grains. Chop the onion finely and cook it gently in 25 g/1 oz of the butter until soft, but do not allow to brown. Pour boiling water over the raisins and leave them to soak for 10 minutes before draining.

Use either a double saucepan or boiler or an ovenproof or microwave dish with a lid; if the kedgeree is to be frozen, line the dish with foil. Put the fried onion in the bottom of the dish and cover with the raisins and then the flaked fish. Melt the rest of the butter and mix it with the curry powder to make a paste. Mix this well into the rice and spoon it over the fish. If it is to be cooked on the hob or in the oven, cover the dish first with a cloth and then the lid so that it is well sealed. Cook for 25 minutes in the double saucepan or boiler or in a slow oven (150°C/300°F/ Gas Mark 2), or for 5–7 minutes in a microwave on full power. To serve, heat a flat dish and turn the kedgeree out so that the fish, raisins, etc. are uppermost. Finely chop the hard-boiled egg and sprinkle it over the top with the lemon juice. Serve at once.

Freeze the dish after it has been amalgamated and before it is cooked. Open freeze the kedgeree, then turn it out and pack in well-sealed bags.

Defrost enough to remove the foil and drop the kedgeree back into its original dish. Defrost at room temperature or in a microwave and then continue to cook and serve as above.

# Fish Quenelles

*Serves 6*          *3 months*

These are thought to be the height of *haute cuisine*, but with the help of a food processor are incredibly simple to make. You can make them more exotic by including crab meat or coating them with a lobster sauce – but they taste excellent made of cod and coated with a tomato sauce.

> *450 g/1 lb fresh cod fillet or steaks, or 225 g/8 oz fresh*
> *cod and 225 g/8 oz mixed brown and white crab*
> *meat*
> *180 ml/6 fl oz double cream*
> *2 egg whites (for plain cod), or 3 egg whites (for cod*
> *and crab mixture)*
> *salt and pepper*

Remove any skin and bones from the fish and put it, with the cream, egg whites and seasoning, in the bowl of a food processor and process until it is totally puréed. Remove from the bowl and, if you have time, chill for 1 hour before cooking – this makes the quenelles hold together slightly better. Fill a large flat pan with water and heat until it is just simmering. Take a small tablespoonful of the mixture, smooth it into an oval and place it gently in the water. Fill the pan with quenelles and poach them very gently. When they are cooked, they will automatically turn over – this will take between 5 and 10 minutes. Leave them for another couple of minutes, then remove them carefully with a slotted spoon and drain on kitchen paper towel for a minute or two. If they are to be served immediately, move them onto a warmed serving dish and spoon over the tomato sauce (see page 154).

To freeze, cool the quenelles completely, layer them in a flat container interleaved with foil or greaseproof paper, then pack them in well-sealed bags.

Defrost as slowly as possible, then reheat gently, well covered, in a moderately cool oven (160°C/ 325°F/Gas Mark 3) or in a microwave, and serve as above.

# Baked Bass Provençale

*Serves 4*                                              *3 months*

Bass is such a well-flavoured, firm fish that it freezes very happily. The same treatment can be applied to fresh mackerel.

*1 bass (750 g–1 kg/1½–2 lb), complete with head and*
  *tail*
*4 tablespoons olive oil*
*225 g/8 oz onions, roughly chopped*
*1 large clove garlic, crushed or finely chopped*
*1 medium red pepper, finely sliced*
*2 medium courgettes, wiped and sliced*
*4 tomatoes, peeled and roughly chopped*
*salt and pepper*

Heat the oil in a large, heavy-based ovenproof pan – ideally it should be large enough to hold the fish without trouble. Add the onions, garlic and red pepper and cook gently until they are beginning to soften. Add the courgettes and tomatoes, season lightly and cook gently for a further 10 minutes or until the vegetables are quite soft. Adjust the seasoning to taste. Lay the cleaned fish on the vegetables, cover the pan tightly and bake the fish for about 30 minutes in a moderate oven (180°C/350°F/Gas Mark 4), or it can be cooked in a microwave – it should take 7–8 minutes.

If you have cooked the fish in an oven-to-table dish, it can be served immediately, although you will then have to skin and bone it as you serve it. Alternatively, transfer the fish to a warm plate where you can skin and bone it, then serve the fillets on a bed of the provençale vegetables. This dish can be accompanied by a green vegetable or brown rice.

To freeze, cool the fish and vegetables without skinning the fish, then transfer them to a freezer container, making sure that the fish is entirely surrounded by the vegetables.

Defrost at room temperature or in a microwave. Transfer the fish and vegetables to a serving dish and reheat them gently. Serve as above.

*Preparing Baked Bass Provençale*

*Scallops with Cream and Orange* (see page 29) *served with rice, fresh pasta and green salad*

# Crab, Ginger and Almond Soufflé

*Serves 6*                                        *14 days*

This soufflé can be made several days before you need it and stored in the freezer. It will not be quite as fluffy as if it were freshly made, but it does save all that last minute whisking. However, it will take almost twice as long as an ordinary soufflé to cook.

> *350 g/12 oz crab meat, mixed brown and white*
> *50 g/2 oz butter*
> *6 spring onions, finely chopped*
> *25 g/1 oz fresh ginger root, peeled and finely chopped*
> *2 tablespoons flour*
> *150 ml/¼ pint white wine*
> *300 ml/½ pint milk*
> *juice of 1½–2 lemons (depending on size)*
> *25 g/1 oz ground almonds*
> *salt and pepper*
> *5 egg yolks*
> *7 egg whites*

Melt the butter in a large pan and lightly fry the onions and ginger root until soft but not coloured. Add the flour, stir and cook for a couple of minutes, then gradually add the wine, milk and lemon juice and cook until the sauce thickens. Add the crab meat and ground almonds, mix well and season to taste with salt and pepper. Remove from the heat, cool slightly and stir in the egg yolks. Whisk the egg whites until they form soft peaks. Stir one-third of the whites into the soufflé mixture, then lightly fold in the rest. Scrape the mixture, into a soufflé dish – it should three-quarters fill it – and put it straight into a moderate oven (180°C/350°F/Gas Mark 4) for 30–35 minutes or until it is well risen and browned on top.

To freeze the soufflé, put the dish straight into the freezer and open freeze. If it is to be kept for more than 24 hours, pack the dish in a well-sealed bag once it is frozen.

Cook from frozen (allowing 10 minutes out of the freezer for the dish to thaw slightly), but allow approximately double the cooking time.

# Smoked Fish Sausages

*Serves 6*                                        *3 months*

These are excellent for a finger buffet or cocktail party (when they will serve 20 people) as they ring the changes on the standard sausagemeat ball. They are also good as a starter and are best served hot with a mayonnaise or other dip.

> *100 g/4 oz smoked haddock fillets*
> *100 g/4 oz smoked mackerel fillets, skinned*
> *juice of 2 lemons*
> *100 g/4 oz fresh brown breadcrumbs*
> *1–2 large handfuls parsley, finely chopped*
> *2 eggs*
> *freshly ground black pepper*
> *75–100 g/3–4 oz medium oatmeal or porridge oats*
> *butter or low fat margarine for frying*

Cook the smoked haddock in a microwave for about 4 minutes or in a pan in enough boiling water to cover for about 10 minutes; cool and skin it. Put the haddock with the mackerel fillets and lemon juice in a food processor and mash. If you do not have a processor, mash the fish thoroughly with a fork. Add the breadcrumbs, parsley and eggs and mix thoroughly. Season to taste with freshly ground black pepper – you should not need any salt because of the natural saltiness of the smoked fish. Form the mixture into whatever size sausages or cakes you want and roll them in the oatmeal or porridge oats. Fry the sausages gently in butter or low fat margarine until they are lightly browned all over (about 5 minutes). Drain for a minute on kitchen paper towel and serve warm with a mayonnaise or other dip.

To freeze, cool the sausages completely and pack in well-sealed containers.

Defrost at room temperature or in a microwave and reheat gently in a moderate oven (180°C/350°F/Gas Mark 4) for about 15 minutes. They can also be reheated from frozen.

# Seafood Pancakes

*Serves 4*                                    *2 months*

8 medium-sized pancakes (see page 162), warmed
50 g/2 oz butter
4 shallots or 8 spring onions, very finely chopped
100 g/4 oz button mushrooms, finely sliced
juice of 1 large lemon
50 g/2 oz flour
360 ml/12 fl oz milk or 180 ml/6 fl oz milk and
   180 ml/6 fl oz fish stock
350 g/12 oz cooked, shelled seafood (mussels, cockles,
   prawns, scallops, crab meat or any combination)
150 ml/¼ pint double cream
salt and pepper
lemon slices or watercress to decorate

Melt the butter in a pan and gently cook the shallots or onions until soft. Add the mushrooms with the lemon juice and continue to cook for a few minutes. Add the flour, stir together for a minute, then gradually add the milk or milk and fish stock. Bring the mixture to the boil and simmer until the sauce thickens. If the dish is to be eaten at once, add the seafood and cook everything for a couple of minutes to heat through thoroughly. Add the cream and season to taste with salt and pepper. Lift the seafood and vegetables, with a little of the sauce, out of the pan with a slotted spoon and use them to fill the pancakes. Place the pancakes in a warmed serving dish, pour over the remains of the sauce, decorate with slices of lemon or watercress and serve.

If the pancakes are to be frozen, add the cream and seasoning to the sauce and allow it to cool before adding the seafood. Fill the pancakes while cold and lay them in a foil container or in a serving dish lined with foil and pour over the sauce. Open freeze, then cover, if they are in a container, or remove from the dish and pack in a well-sealed bag if they were in a serving dish.

Defrost at room temperature or in a microwave (having turned the pancakes back into the serving dish) and heat, covered, in a moderate oven (180°C/350°F/Gas Mark 4) or a microwave. Serve decorated as above.

# Smiley Moules

*Serves 6*                                    *3 months*

I have no idea where this recipe originally came from, but it makes an excellent quick and exotic dish. It is particularly useful for frozen mussels, as the sauce is powerful enough to compensate for any loss of flavour or texture in mussels that have been deprived of their shells before freezing.

450 g/1 lb mussels out of their shell, either fresh,
   cooked or frozen
20 roasted almonds
4 cloves garlic, peeled and roughly chopped
1 onion, peeled and roughly chopped
1 teaspoon sugar
1 large teaspoon Anise or Anisette
90 ml/3 fl oz brandy
1 small can (200 g/7 oz) tomatoes
1 dried red chilli
salt and pepper
3 tablespoons olive oil

Put all the ingredients except the mussels and the olive oil in a liquidizer or a food processor and process until you have a reasonably smooth purée. Heat the oil in a heavy-based pan, add the liquidized sauce, heat through, then add the mussels and heat briskly – they should not be allowed to boil. Serve at once with brown rice or wholemeal brown bread.

To freeze, liquidize the sauce and freeze in well-sealed containers.

Defrost at room temperature or in a microwave and heat as above, adding the mussels just before serving.

# POULTRY AND GAME

## Chicken with Leek, Grapefruit and Orange

*Serves 6*            *4–6 months*

This light chicken dish is excellent when you want something hot but not too heavy. It is better, if possible, to add the almonds once the dish is defrosted.

> *1.5–2 kg/3–4 lb roasting chicken*
> *50 g/2 oz butter*
> *1 kg/2 lb trimmed leeks, finely sliced*
> *2 pink grapefruits*
> *150 ml/¼ pint fresh orange juice*
> *150 ml/¼ pint medium-sweet white wine*
> *300 ml/½ pint chicken stock*
> *salt and pepper*
> *50 g/2 oz browned, flaked almonds*

Melt the butter in a heavy casserole, not much bigger than the chicken, and briskly fry the bird on all sides until it is golden brown. Remove the chicken, reduce the heat and add the leeks. Cook the leeks gently until they are quite soft but not burnt. Segment the 2 grapefruits over the pan so as not to waste any juice and squeeze any remaining juice out of the carcase of the fruit. Mix the leeks and grapefruit well together, then place the chicken on top. Add the orange juice, wine and stock, mixed together and lightly seasoned. Cover the pan tightly and simmer gently for 45–60 minutes or until the chicken is cooked and tender. Adjust the seasoning to taste, sprinkle over the almonds, which have been browned either in the oven or fried in a little butter, and serve at once with rice or puréed potatoes and a green vegetable.

To freeze, remove the dish from the heat once the chicken is cooked, without adding the almonds, cool it completely and freeze.

Defrost at room temperature or in a microwave Reheat gently in a moderate oven (180°C/350°F/ Gas Mark 4) for about 30 minutes. Adjust the seasoning to taste and sprinkle on the almonds before serving.

## Chicken Braised with Ginger and White Grapes

*Serves 6*            *4–6 months*

This chicken dish has a distinctly Oriental feel about it. It is better to leave adding the grapes until the last moment if possible.

> *6 chicken joints (breasts or legs according to*
>    *preference)*
> *50 g/2 oz butter or low fat margarine*
> *50–75 g/2–3 oz fresh ginger, peeled and finely sliced*
> *300 ml/½ pint dry white wine*
> *300 ml/½ pint chicken stock*
> *salt and pepper*
> *450 g/1 lb white grapes (the large, slightly scented*
>    *ones if possible), peeled and pipped*

Melt the butter in a heavy-based casserole or pan and gently fry the ginger slices for 5 minutes without letting them burn. Scoop them out with a slotted spoon, increase the heat slightly and fry the chicken joints briskly until they are golden on all sides. Return the ginger to the pan and add the wine and stock with a little seasoning. Bring to the boil and simmer gently for 35–45 minutes or until the the chicken is cooked. Add the grapes and cook for a further 3–4 minutes. Adjust the seasoning to taste and serve at once with steamed brown rice and a green vegetable, such as *haricots verts*.

If the dish is to be frozen, remove from the heat once the chicken is cooked, before adding the grapes. Cool completely and freeze.

Defrost at room temperature or in a microwave. Reheat gently, add the grapes, adjust the seasoning and serve as above.

*Chicken Braised with Ginger and White Grapes served with brown rice and haricots verts*

# Chicken and Almond Mould

*Serves 6*                                    *3–4 months*

This is an excellent dish for a buffet party: it looks good turned out of a ring mould with its centre filled with watercress. It is unusual, and, because it is rich, it goes a long way.

> *225 g/8 oz cooked chicken, finely chopped*
> *100 g/4 oz long-grain Patna rice*
> *300–450 ml/½–¾ pint chicken stock*
> *50 g/2 oz ground almonds*
> *2 teaspoons ground ginger*
> *180 ml/6 fl oz soured cream*
> *salt and pepper*
> *1 bunch watercress (optional)*

Simmer the rice in the chicken stock until it is cooked but still firm. Drain off any excess liquid and return the rice to the pan. Add the chicken, almonds, ginger and cream. Stir well together and cook for a couple of minutes to get the flavours and textures well amalgamated. Season to taste with salt and pepper. Spoon the mixture into a ring or ordinary shaped mould and chill. If the mould is to be frozen, line the dish with plastic cling film. When it is quite cold, it can be turned out on a dish and decorated with watercress, parsley or any other green salad ingredients.

Freeze in its mould and turn out once frozen.

Defrost at room temperature or in a microwave and serve as above.

# Gingered Chicken Drumsticks

*Serves 6*                                    *6 months*

Chicken drumsticks are always useful to have in the freezer for a quick lunch or picnic or as an instant barbecue.

> *6 chicken drumsticks, their skins well pricked with a*
> *    fork*

> **Marinade**
> *2 tablespoons grated fresh ginger root, or 1*
> *    tablespoon ground ginger*
> *2 cloves garlic, crushed*
> *juice of 1 lemon*
> *2 tablespoons olive oil*

Mix the marinade ingredients well, then rub thoroughly into the drumsticks. Leave them to soak in the marinade, skin side down, for 6–12 hours, then bake them on a rack in a moderate oven (180°C/350°F/Gas Mark 4) for about 20 minutes or until they are browned, crisp and cooked through. Alternatively, you can cook them on a barbecue.

To freeze, cool the drumsticks completely, then pack in well-sealed, heavy-gauge bags.

Defrost at room temperature, in a microwave, or from frozen in the oven. Reheat to crisp in a moderate oven (180°C/350°F/Gas Mark 4) for 15 minutes or on a barbecue.

# Chicken and Courgette Pie

*Serves 6*                                    *4–6 months*

The courgettes and herby cheese contrast well in looks and taste with the white chicken meat – it could almost class as a 'party' pie.

> *1.5–2 kg/3–4 lb roasting chicken*
> *600–900 ml/1–1½ pints water or white wine and*
> *    water mixed*
> *1 onion, carrot, stick celery, parsley stalk, etc.*
> *50 g/2 oz butter*
> *450 g/1 lb courgettes, wiped and sliced*
> *40 g/1½ oz flour*
> *300 ml/½ pint milk*
> *300 g/10 oz Boursin or other herbed cream cheese*
> *a large handful of chopped parsley*
> *salt and pepper*
> *150 g/6 oz shortcrust pastry*
> *1 egg, beaten*

Put the chicken in a pan and cover it with water or white wine and water mixed. If available, add an onion, carrot, piece of celery, parsley stalk, etc. Bring to the boil and simmer gently for 45–60 minutes or until the chicken is cooked. Remove the chicken and cool it, reserving the stock. When the chicken is cold enough, remove the flesh in reasonable-sized pieces.

Meanwhile, melt the butter in a heavy-based pan and gently fry the courgette slices until they are just beginning to turn colour. Add the flour, stir well and cook for a couple of minutes. Gradually add 600 ml/1 pint of the chicken stock and the milk. Stir and cook together until the sauce thickens. Add the cheese, the chopped parsley and seasoning to taste. Finally, add the chicken pieces and mix well into the sauce. Spoon the mixture into a pie dish; if it does not fill it, support the middle with a pie support or a couple of egg cups. Roll out the pastry and top the pie using the trimmings for decoration. Brush generously with the beaten egg and bake in a moderately hot oven (190°C/375°F/Gas Mark 5) for 25–30 minutes or until the pastry is cooked and golden. Serve at once.

If the pie is to be frozen, this can be done before the pastry top is put on, making it easier to freeze.

Defrost at room temperature or in a microwave and reheat in a conventional moderate oven (180°C/350°F/Gas Mark 4) – not a microwave – to crisp the pastry and heat the filling.

# Chicken with Orange and Water Chestnuts

*Serves 6*                                    *9 months*

This is a refreshing summer chicken dish which freezes well, as the water chestnuts retain their crunch when frozen.

> *6 chicken joints*
> *50 g/2 oz butter*
> *400 g/14 oz can water chestnuts*
> *juice of 3 oranges*
> *salt and pepper*

Melt the butter in a heavy-based pan and gently fry the chicken joints until they are lightly browned on both sides. Add the water chestnuts, thickly sliced, with 150 ml/¼ pint of their juice, and the orange juice. Season lightly, cover the pan and simmer gently for 35–40 minutes or until the chicken is cooked through. Serve at once with brown rice and a green vegetable.

To freeze, cool completely, then pack in a well-sealed container.

Defrost at room temperature or in a microwave and reheat, covered, in a moderate oven (180°C/350°F/Gas Mark 4) for about 30 minutes, or in a pan or microwave. Adjust the seasoning and serve as above.

# Chicken Hotch Potch

*Serves 6*                                    *6 months*

This recipe started life as an easy dish for an elderly person living on their own, but it is so easy – and actually tastes so good – that I did not see why everyone should not share it! It is also good for slimmers since there is no frying involved. If it is to be frozen, it is better if you leave adding the rice until it is defrosted. You can use chicken portions instead of a whole chicken – the cheaper joints are perfectly acceptable. You can also replace any of the vegetables with your favourites, but do not add 'softer' vegetables, such as cauliflower, until later on in the cooking.

> *1.5–2 kg/3–4 lb chicken*
> *3 onions or 3 large leeks, cleaned and roughly sliced*
> *3 sticks celery, 3 carrots and 3 parsnips*
> *2 teaspoons mixed dried herbs, or 2 tablespoons chopped mixed fresh herbs*
> *salt and pepper*
> *1.8 litres/3 pints water or mild chicken stock or 1.5 litres/2½ pints water and chicken stock and 300 ml/½ pint dry white wine*
> *200 g/7 oz can Italian tomatoes or sweetcorn (optional)*
> *6 tablespoons brown rice or wholemeal pasta shapes*

Put the chicken with the vegetables, herbs and a good shake of seasoning into a large pot and pour in the liquid. Cover the pan, bring it to the boil and simmer for 45–90 minutes, depending on whether you are using joints or a whole bird. The flesh should be falling off the bone by the time it is cooked. About 20 minutes before you think it is ready, add the tomatoes or sweetcorn (if you are using them) and the rice or pasta. Once the chicken and the rice are cooked, adjust the seasoning to taste and serve. You should be able to serve the hotch potch like an Irish stew – a small bowl of soup first followed by the chicken and vegetables.

If the dish is to be frozen, do not add the tomatoes, sweetcorn or rice but remove it from the heat before it is completely cooked, cool the whole thing and freeze it in a well-sealed container leaving room for expansion.

Defrost at room temperature or in a microwave and return to its pot. Bring back to the boil, and finish as above.

*Boned Stuffed Chicken* (see page 48)

# Poussin Stuffed with Cream Cheese and Herbs

*Serves 6*                                    *9 months*

Depending both on the size of the poussin and how many other courses you are having, you will need to allow a half or a whole poussin per person. For visual effect, buy small birds and allow a whole bird per person – they are rather impressive!

*6 small poussin*
*175 g/6 oz grated Parmesan (fresh if possible)*
*3 large handfuls fresh parsley, chopped*
*50–75 g/2–3 oz butter, softened*
*9 rashers bacon, chopped*
*175 g/6 oz curd cheese*
*50 g/2 oz fresh wholemeal breadcrumbs*
*300 ml/½ pint dry white wine*
*juice of 2 oranges*

Carefully lift the skin off the breasts of the poussin with your fingers. Mix the Parmesan and parsley with as much of the butter as you need to make a reasonably workable paste and divide it between the birds. Spread the stuffing evenly over the breast meat and under the skin. Grill, fry or microwave the chopped bacon until it is crisp, then mix it with the curd cheese and breadcrumbs. Divide this stuffing between the cavities of the birds.

Put the birds in an ovenproof casserole and pour in the wine and orange juice. Cover the casserole and cook in a moderate oven (180°C/350°F/Gas Mark 4) for 35–40 minutes. Remove the lid from the casserole and cook for a further 15 minutes or until the poussin are well browned and cooked through. Serve at once. The poussin are very rich, so serve them with lots of green vegetables or salads.

To freeze, cool completely and freeze in their juice in a well-sealed container.

Defrost at room temperature or in a microwave. Reheat in an open dish or casserole in a moderate oven (180°C/350°F/Gas Mark 4) for about 20 minutes – this will recrisp and brown the skin – and serve as above.

*Poussin Stuffed with Cream Cheese and Herbs*

# Boned Stuffed Chicken

*3–6 months*

Provided you can face boning it, any bird can be stuffed to make a galantine which will freeze excellently and look very dramatic as the centrepiece for a buffet or dinner table. Since chickens are relatively cheap and universally acceptable, I am giving the recipe for chicken, but feel free to adapt it (and the stuffing ingredients) for turkey, pheasant, grouse, etc., according to your taste – and the number you have to feed!

> 2–3 kg/4–5 lb chicken or capon
> approx 1.5 kg/3 lb good sausagemeat or minced veal
> approx 225 g/8 oz dark meat from a game bird
> 225–350 g/8–12 oz well-flavoured liver and
>   mushroom stuffing (see below)
> 175 g/6 oz piece of black pudding, cut in half
>   lengthways
> 175 g/6 oz well-flavoured and coloured garlic or
>   chorizo sausage or salami, cut into large
>   matchsticks
> approx 20 pistachio nuts
> 4–6 hard-boiled egg yolks
> 50 g/2 oz softened butter

Lay the bird out on a board and completely bone it, pushing the meat from the legs and wings back into the body. Sew up the apertures, leaving just one big cut down the backbone, and any gashes in the skin to prevent the stuffing from falling out. Line the inside of the bird with a layer (about 2.5 cm/1 inch thick) of the sausagemeat or minced veal. Remember that when the bird is served it will be cut across and look like a pâté, so lay the dark game meat, liver and mushroom stuffing, black pudding, sticks of sausage or salami lengthways and sprinkle the pistachio nuts and the egg yolks throughout. Finish with a layer of sausagemeat. Remember also that the skin will have to meet to be sewn up, so do not get too enthusiastic and do try to keep the shape of the bird in mind as you stuff it. When it is full, pull the edges together and sew up firmly.

Place the bird in a well-buttered baking tray, sewn side down, and rub it well with softened butter. Cover it lightly with foil and bake it in a moderate oven (180°C/350°F/Gas Mark 4) for 20 minutes per 450 g/1 lb. About 30 minutes before it is done, remove the foil and baste the bird well so

that it has a good brown top. Cool and chill well before slicing.

Provided the bird is fresh, it can be frozen before it is cooked. If you have used a frozen bird or if you even suspect that it may have been frozen, the bird should be cooked before it is frozen. Wrap it well in polythene to freeze.

Defrost at room temperature or in a microwave with care.

# Liver and Mushroom Stuffing

> 25 g/1 oz butter
> 100–175 g/4–6 oz chicken livers, finely chopped
> 100–175 g/4–6 oz mushrooms, finely chopped
> 50 g/2 oz dark brown breadcrumbs (preferably rye)
> salt and pepper

Melt the butter in a pan and gently fry the liver and mushrooms together until the liver is firm and the mushrooms soft. Add the breadcrumbs, season generously and use as stuffing.

# A Speedy Coronation Chicken

*Serves 6*                                    *6 months*

This is somewhat of a cheat, both in terms of freezing and in relation to the original Cordon Bleu recipe, but my way makes an excellent, quick summer dish. You can cook the chicken ahead of time and store it in the freezer so that it only needs defrosting.

> 1 large or 2 small chickens
> stock ingredients (an onion, carrot, a few mushroom
>   and parsley stalks, bouquet garni, some black
>   peppercorns and a little white wine)
> 3–4 tablespoons mild curry paste
> 1–2 tablespoons smooth apricot jam
> 10–12 tablespoons home-made or good quality
>   bought mayonnaise
> salt and pepper
> a little boiling water
> watercress to garnish

Put the chicken(s) in a large pan with the stock ingredients and cover with water. Bring to the boil and simmer gently for 45–75 minutes (depending on the size of the chicken(s)) or until the meat is ready to fall off the bone. Remove them from the stock, cool the chickens and strain the stock. If the dish is to be served at once, make the sauce while the chickens are cooling. Gradually add the curry paste and apricot jam to the mayonnaise until you have got the right combination of flavours – some people like it hotter, some sweeter – and season to taste. You will probably need to 'let the sauce down' with a little boiling water; it should be a light coating consistency and not sticky. When the chicken is quite cold, pull it apart into bite-sized pieces and mix it into the sauce, making sure that each piece is thoroughly coated. Pile on a serving dish and decorate with watercress. It is good with a brown rice salad, which can also be made ahead!

If you are freezing the chicken, pull it apart in reasonably large pieces and pack it in a well-sealed container covered in the strained stock, leaving room for expansion. The sauce cannot be frozen because of the high mayonnaise content but it can be made up to a week in advance and stored in the fridge.

Defrost the chicken at room temperature or in a microwave, strain off the stock and use for soup, etc. Dry the chicken pieces, cut or pull them into bite-sized pieces and complete the recipe as above.

# Curried Chicken Pancakes

*Serves 4*                              *3 months*

> *8 medium-sized pancakes (see page 162)*
> *3 tablespoons good vegetable oil*
> *3 medium onions, peeled and finely chopped*
> *100 g/4 oz carrots, finely chopped*
> *1 green or red pepper, finely chopped*
> *2 tablespoons curry powder*
> *1 teaspoon turmeric*
> *1 teaspoon ground ginger*
> *225 g/8 oz cooked chicken meat, pulled or chopped*
> *  into small pieces*
> *50 g/2 oz raisins*
> *2 tablespoons chutney (whatever variety you prefer,*
> *  but if there are any very big lumps in it, make sure*
> *  they are chopped)*
> *360 ml/12 fl oz red wine or beer*
> *2 tablespoons curry paste, strong or mild depending*
> *  on how hot you like your curry*
> *1 large cooking apple, peeled and finely chopped*
> *450 ml/¾ pint water*
> *salt and pepper*

Heat 2 tablespoons of the oil in a large pan and gently cook 2 onions with the carrots and pepper until they all start to soften. Add the curry powder, turmeric and ginger, cook for a couple of minutes, then add the chicken, raisins, chutney and 180 ml/6 fl oz of the wine or beer. Bring to the boil, cover and simmer for 15 minutes.

Meanwhile, heat the rest of the oil in a separate pan and add the remaining onion. Cook until it begins to soften, then add the curry paste, the apple, the remaining 180 ml/6 fl oz of wine or beer and the water. Bring to the boil and simmer for about 10 minutes or until the apple is cooked. Season both the filling and the sauce to taste.

If the dish is to be served at once, warm the pancakes, then fill them with the chicken mixture and lay them in the dish. Just before serving, spoon over the sauce.

If the pancakes are to be frozen, fill them with the chicken filling and lay them in a foil container or pack them into a foil parcel and freeze. Freeze the sauce separately.

Defrost at room temperature or in a microwave. Reheat the pancakes, covered, in a serving dish in a moderate oven (180°C/350°F/Gas Mark 4) or in a microwave. Reheat the sauce separately and spoon it over just before serving.

*A Speedy Coronation Chicken* (see page 48) *and Tomato Rice Cakes* (see page 104)

# Coq au Vin Blanc

*Serves 6*                                           *6 months*

There must be as many recipes for Coq au Vin as there are for Boeuf Bourguignon, each claiming to be 'the original' recipe. However, a wine merchant friend of mine maintains that the best Coq au Vin is made with white rather than red wine – and he should know! You can use a large chicken, jointed, in place of the chicken joints, or if you prefer any particular part of the chicken use just that.

    *6 chicken joints*
    *3 tablespoons butter*
    *2 tablespoons olive oil*
    *100 g/4 oz unsalted bacon, diced*
    *225 g/8 oz button onions (about 20), peeled*
    *1–2 cloves garlic, finely chopped*
    *225 g/8 oz button mushrooms (about 20), wiped*

    *2 tablespoons seasoned flour*
    *2 bouquet garni*
    *salt and pepper*
    *approx 450 g/1 lb small new potatoes (about 20), steamed or boiled, drained and kept warm*
    *5 tablespoons brandy*
    *210 ml/7 fl oz full-bodied but not sweet white wine (Muscadet is quite good)*
    *90 ml/3 fl oz water*
    *1 level tablespoon soft butter*
    *1 level tablespoon flour*
    *plenty of fresh chopped parsley*

Melt the butter and oil in a heatproof casserole and briskly fry the bacon, onions and garlic until they are beginning to soften. Add the mushrooms and continue to cook until the vegetables are all golden but not burnt. Remove them with a slotted spoon and keep warm. Toss the chicken joints in the seasoned flour and sauté them in the butter and oil until they too are golden on both sides but not burnt. Return the vegetables to the casserole, add the bouquet garni and a little seasoning, cover the casserole and cook it in a moderate oven (180°C/350°F/Gas Mark 4) for 30–40 minutes or until the chicken is really tender. Remove the chicken and vegetables from the pot, arrange them in a serving dish with the potatoes and keep them all warm. Skim as much extra fat off the juices as possible. Warm the brandy in a ladle, pour it into the juices and light it. Let it burn for a minute or two, then pour in the wine and the water. Stir thoroughly to make sure you get any burnt bits off the bottom of the pan, then cook briskly for 5–10 minutes to reduce the quantity slightly. Mix the softened butter with the flour and add it a small piece at a time to the sauce. Cook until it thickens. Adjust the seasoning to taste and pour the sauce over the chicken and vegetables. Sprinkle liberally with chopped parsley and serve at once.

If the dish is to be frozen, it can either be frozen once the cooking of the chicken is completed, leaving the finishing of the sauce until it is defrosted (this is, ideally, better), or it can be frozen when the dish is complete – but in this case the potatoes should not be added until it is defrosted. In either case, cool completely and freeze in well-sealed containers.

Defrost at room temperature or in a microwave. If the dish was frozen halfway through, reheat the chicken and vegetables in the juices, then complete the recipe as above. If the dish was completed before freezing, reheat it in a microwave or a moderate oven (180°C/350°F/Gas Mark 4), add the potatoes, adjust the seasoning to taste and serve as above.

*Coq au Vin Blanc*

# Spiced Chicken with Yoghurt

*Serves 6*                                      *6 months*

This is the simple, but delicious, invention of one of my Catercall colleagues which she swore would not freeze – but it does.

> *1 large chicken or 6 chicken joints*
> *25–40 g/1–1½ oz fresh ginger root, peeled and*
>   *roughly chopped*
> *6 cloves garlic, peeled*
> *3 medium onions, peeled and roughly chopped*
> *2 handfuls fresh mint, or 1 tablespoon dried*
> *salt and pepper*
> *450 ml/¾ pint plain yoghurt*

Put the ginger, garlic, onions, mint, seasoning and yoghurt in a food processor or liquidizer and purée them. Put the chicken or chicken joints in an ovenproof casserole or dish and pour over the purée. Bake it, uncovered, in a moderate oven (180°C/350°F/Gas Mark 4) for 30–40 minutes if the chicken is in joints; 45–60 minutes if it is a whole bird – or until the chicken is cooked and ready to fall off the bone. Remove the dish from the oven. The sauce will have reduced into a creamy curd but may still be rather 'watery'. If so, remove it from the dish into a saucepan and simmer it gently until the 'water' has evaporated. Adjust the seasoning to taste. If the chicken is in joints, arrange them in a serving dish and spoon over the sauce; if it is whole, carve it, arrange the pieces on a serving dish and spoon over the sauce.

If the dish is to be frozen, remove it from the oven and cool it completely without reducing the sauce. Freeze in a well-sealed container.

Defrost at room temperature or in a microwave and reheat in a microwave or an oven in its sauce. If the sauce is 'watery', reduce and finish the dish as above.

# Turkey with Orange and Artichoke Heart Sauce

*Serves 6*                                      *6 months*

This recipe will do equally well with turkey or chicken, but since turkey is now available in small joints, it might make a pleasant change to vary the bird. The sauce can also be used to dress up the remains of a roast turkey – which always seems to leave you with such quantities of 'leftovers'!

> *750 g/1½ lb boneless turkey fillets or pieces*
> *stock ingredients (an onion, carrot, few mushroom*
>   *and parsley stalks, some black peppercorns and a*
>   *little white wine)*
> *25 g/1 oz butter*
> *225 g/8 oz onions, very finely sliced*
> *3 sticks celery, chopped small*
> *15 g/½ oz flour*
> *4 oranges*
> *225 g/8 oz artichoke hearts (freshly cooked, frozen or*
>   *canned), well drained and quartered*
> *salt and pepper*

Put the turkey pieces with the stock ingredients and about 600 ml/1 pint of water in a pan and bring them slowly to the boil. Simmer gently for 25–30 minutes or until the meat is just cooked, then remove the turkey and strain and reserve the stock.

Meanwhile, melt the butter in a pan and slowly cook the onions and celery until they are soft but not coloured. Add the flour and cook for a minute or two, then gradually add 450 ml/¾ pint of the reserved stock, the rind and juice of 2 oranges and the artichoke hearts. Cook everything together for a couple of minutes, then add the turkey pieces. Heat the dish through thoroughly and season to taste with salt and pepper. If the dish is to be used immediately, spoon it into a warmed serving dish and decorate with the remaining 2 oranges, neatly segmented.

To freeze, allow the mixture to cool completely, then freeze in a well-sealed container, allowing a little headroom for expansion.

Defrost at room temperature or in a microwave, reheat gently in a pan on the hob, in a microwave or in a moderate oven (180°C/350°F/Gas Mark 4), and serve decorated as above.

# Roast Duckling with Cucumber

*Serves 6*                    *6 months*

Cucumber is so wedded to salads in most people's minds that its virtues as a cooked vegetable go quite unnoticed! This recipe is based on an eighteenth-century dish – the 'freshness' of the cucumber helps to counteract the richness of the duck – and it keeps its crispness remarkably well in the freezer.

> *2 ducklings*
> *2 large onions, peeled and very finely chopped*
> *3 medium cucumbers, unpeeled but their seeds removed, and cut into fairly thick matchsticks*
> *300 ml/½ pint light red wine*
> *2 small cooking apples or tart eating apples*
> *25 g/1 oz butter*
> *25 g/1 oz flour*
> *300 ml/½ pint chicken stock*
> *salt and pepper*
> *2 bunches very fresh watercress*

Put the onions and cucumbers in a bowl with the red wine and leave to marinate for a couple of hours. Meanwhile, prick the ducks all over and put them on a rack above a baking tin. Halve the apples and push them into the cavity of the ducks. Roast the ducks in a moderate oven (180°C/350°F/Gas Mark 4) for 20 minutes per 450 g/1 lb.

To make the sauce, drain the vegetables and reserve the wine. Melt the butter in a pan and gently cook the onion until it is beginning to soften. Increase the heat and add the cucumber. Cook both briskly for a couple of minutes until they are lightly coloured but not burnt. Add the flour and cook for a couple more minutes, then gradually add the reserved wine and the stock. Season lightly and cook until the sauce thickens slightly. Remove the leaves from half of one of the bunches of watercress and chop them very finely and add to the sauce. Cook for a minute or two, then adjust the seasoning to taste.

If the dish is to be served immediately, remove the ducks from the oven, carve them and serve them decorated with the remaining watercress and accompanied by the sauce.

If the dish is to be frozen, do not add the watercress or final seasoning to the sauce. Carve the ducks and lay them in a well-sealed container. Spoon over the sauce, cover and freeze.

Defrost at room temperature but preferably not in a microwave so as to avoid overcooking the cucumber. Reheat gently in a pan over a low heat, a microwave or a moderate oven (180°C/350°F/Gas Mark 4), add the chopped watercress leaves to the sauce and adjust the seasoning to taste. Spoon the duck and sauce into a warmed serving dish, decorate with watercress and serve.

# Duck with Orange and Apple Sauce

*Serves 4–6*                    *9 months*

Depending on the size of the duck, this recipe will feed either four or six people – and since it is rich, if you give them plenty of vegetables you will probably stretch it to six anyway!

> *1 duck (2–2.5 kg/4–5 lb)*
> *1 small cooking apple*
> *1 medium onion*
> *1 stick celery*
> *1 tomato*
> *1 sprig parsley*
> *150 ml/¼ pint red wine*
> *300 ml/½ pint water*
> *salt and pepper*
> *2 oranges*
> *15 g/½ oz butter*
> *15 g/½ oz flour*

Prick the duck's skin thoroughly, fill its cavity with the cooking apple, peeled and roughly chopped, and roast it for about 1½ hours. Meanwhile, make some good stock from the giblets of the duck (reserving the liver), the onion, celery, tomato, parsley, wine, water and a little seasoning. Carefully peel the rind from the oranges, taking as little pith as possible. Cut it in thin matchsticks and blanch it for a couple of minutes in boiling water. When the duck is cooked, remove it from the rack and pour off as much of the fat from the juices in the roasting tin as you possibly can. (One of those separator jugs with an upper and lower spout are quite efficient at this.)

Melt the butter in a saucepan, add the duck liver, chopped small, and cook for a couple of minutes. Add the flour, stir well and cook for another minute or two, then add the juices from the pan, the apple from the middle of the duck, well mushed up, 300 ml/½ pint of the strained stock and the juice from the 2 oranges. Stir together well, bring to the boil and simmer for 5–10 minutes. Meanwhile, carve the duck and lay it in a warmed serving dish, removing as much or as little of the fatty (but crisp) skin as you want. Strain the sauce, return it to the pan, add the orange rind and reheat. Adjust the seasoning to taste and pour it over the duck. Serve at once with a green vegetable and really baby new potatoes, if they are available.

The duck can either be frozen whole and the sauce frozen separately or be frozen in its sauce.

To defrost, partially reheat, carve the duck and then complete reheating it in its sauce, or if frozen in the sauce, reheat in a moderate oven (180°C/350°F/Gas Mark 4) or a microwave in the sauce and serve as above.

*Rabbit with Mustard and Cheese*

# Rabbit with Mustard and Cheese

*Serves 4*                                    *6 months*

The combination of rabbit and mustard is a well known one; the addition of cheese is not so familiar. I have heard that it was a Scottish tradition but have not found any trace of it. For the squeamish, rabbit is now very easy to buy ready cut up and frozen. For those who really cannot stand the thought of rabbit, substitute stewing veal or even chicken.

*450 g/1 lb boneless, trimmed rabbit meat*
*25 g/1 oz butter*
*1 tablespoon olive or good vegetable oil*
*1 medium onion, roughly chopped*
*225 g/8 oz baby turnips, peeled and diced*
*2 tablespoons seasoned flour*
*1–2 tablespoons dry mustard (either English or one*
*   of the newer herbed mustards)*
*300 ml/½ pint good chicken or veal stock (see*
*   page 152)*
*100 g/4 oz well-flavoured hard cheese, grated*
*salt and pepper*

Melt the butter and oil in a large pan and gently cook the onion and turnips until they are just beginning to soften. Mix the seasoned flour with the mustard. Dry the rabbit pieces thoroughly, then toss them in the flour and mustard mixture. Add the rabbit to the vegetables with the remains of the flour and mustard. Fry them all briskly for a couple of minutes without burning, then add the stock. Bring gently to the boil, cover and simmer for 45–60 minutes or until the rabbit is tender. Alternatively, you can cook the stew, covered, in a moderate oven (180°C/350°F/Gas Mark 4) for slightly longer. When the meat is tender, add the cheese, cook for a couple of minutes to allow it to melt, then season to taste with salt and pepper. Serve at once with a good green vegetable.

If the stew is to be frozen, cool it once the meat is cooked but before the cheese is added. Freeze it in a well-sealed container, leaving room for expansion.

Defrost at room temperature or in a microwave and reheat in a pan on the hob, in a moderate oven (180°C/350°F/Gas Mark 4) or in a microwave. Add the grated cheese and finish as above.

*Iced Blue Cheese Soup* (see page 13) *and Duck with Orange and Apple Sauce* (see page 53)

# Grouse Casseroled with Port and Celery

*Serves 4*                              *4–6 months*

If you are a game enthusiast and have 'sources of supply' during the season, you may not want to eat all the birds that come your way immediately. They can, of course, be successfully frozen raw. However, most game birds are naturally quite dry, so freezing them in a liquid may produce a better result. This is equally good made with pigeon.

> *4 small or 2 large grouse*
>
> **Marinade**
> *4 rashers streaky or fat bacon, chopped*
> *6 shallots, peeled and finely chopped*
> *180 ml/6 fl oz port*
> *360 ml/12 fl oz claret*
> *salt and pepper*
>
> **Stuffing**
> *3 rashers streaky bacon, chopped*
> *6 shallots, finely chopped*
> *2–3 sticks celery, finely chopped*
> *40 g/1½ oz butter*
> *100 g/4 oz porridge oats*
> *salt and pepper*

Mix the chopped bacon, shallots, port and claret in a bowl just big enough to hold the birds, season lightly with salt and pepper and immerse the birds in the marinade for 1–4 hours.

Meanwhile, lightly fry the bacon, shallots and celery for the stuffing in the butter until they are softened. Add the porridge oats and again season *lightly*; the bacon may be salty so you do not want to overdo it, especially if the birds are to be frozen.

When you are ready to cook the birds, remove them from the marinade and stuff each with a quarter (or half) of the stuffing. Put them in an oven or heatproof casserole just big enough to hold them, pour over the marinade and cover tightly. Cook the birds in a moderate oven (180°F/ 350°C/Gas Mark 4) for an hour; 1¼ hours if you suspect they may be old. Alternatively, simmer them very gently on the hob for the same amount of time. When cooked, adjust the seasoning to taste and serve with plainly cooked vegetables as the sauce is very rich.

Freeze the birds in their juice in well-sealed containers, leaving room for expansion.

Defrost at room temperarure or in a microwave. Reheat gently to serve.

# Venison Braised with Port and Redcurrants

*Serves 6*                              *6 months*

Like most game, venison can benefit from freezing as it helps to break down what can be rather tough fibres. If you are not sure of the age or quality of the meat you are getting, it is probably better to braise it rather than to try roasting or baking it.

> *1 kg/2 lb venison, well trimmed and cubed*
> *4 rashers bacon, chopped fairly small*
> *225 g/8 oz onions, finely chopped*
> *100 g/4 oz open mushrooms, finely chopped*
> *1 tablespoon fresh thyme, or 1 teaspoon dried*
> *600 ml/1 pint port*
> *25 g/1 oz butter*
> *25 g/1 oz flour*
> *300 ml/½ pint water*
> *225 g/8 oz redcurrants*
> *salt and pepper*

Put the venison, bacon, onions, mushrooms and thyme in a bowl and cover with the port. Leave to marinate for up to 24 hours. Remove the venison from the marinade and dry it on some kitchen paper towel. Heat the butter in a pan until sizzling and briskly fry the venison until brown all over. Reduce the heat and add the flour, stir for a couple of minutes, then add the marinade and the water. Bring to the boil, cover and simmer for 1½–2 hours or until the meat is really tender. Add the redcurrants, cook for a further 5 minutes, then season to taste. Serve with baked or creamed potatotes and a green vegetable or salad.

If the venison is to be frozen, cool it completely and freeze it in well-sealed containers before adding the redcurrants and the seasoning.

Defrost at room temperature or in a microwave, reheat gently and add the redcurrants and seasoning as above.

# A Dark Venison Stew

*Serves 4*                                    *3 months*

Venison is such a dark, rich meat anyhow that it seems worth going the whole hog and giving it a really dark, rich sauce. However, you do need something like baked potatoes to mop up the sauce and a nice green salad to bring you back to earth afterwards! Like all game, this dish freezes well but should not be left in the freezer too long. If you cannot get open mushrooms, you can use button mushrooms, but they are not so well flavoured.

> 1 kg/2 lb stewing venison, trimmed and cut in
>    large dice
> 2 onions, peeled and very finely chopped
> 3 bay leaves
> a bunch of fresh thyme and parsley (if available)
> 450 ml/¾ pint real ale or stout
> approx 25 g/1 oz seasoned flour
> 50 g/2oz butter
> 450 g/1 lb open mushrooms, quartered
> 1 tablespoon black treacle
> 25 g/1 oz dark brown sugar
> salt and pepper
> 50 g/2 oz whole cranberrries, frozen redcurrants or
>    raspberries (optional)

Trim the venison and marinate it, with the onions and the herbs, in the beer for 6–12 hours. Remove the venison, reserving the onions and marinade but discarding the herbs, and dry the meat on some kitchen paper towel. Toss it in the seasoned flour. Melt half the butter in a large pan and briskly cook the mushrooms until they are just wilting. Turn them into an oven or heatproof casserole. Melt the rest of the butter in the pan and briskly fry the venison pieces until they are lightly browned on all sides. Add any extra flour to the pan, then gradually add some of the marinade, making sure you get off all the bits stuck on the bottom of the pan. Cook for a minute or two until the sauce thickens, then add the treacle and sugar and, gradually, the rest of the marinade. Turn the whole lot into the casserole with the mushrooms, stir together and season lightly. Cover and cook gently on the hob or in a moderately cool oven (160°C/325°F/Gas Mark 3) for 1½–2 hours or until the venison is really tender. Adjust the seasoning to taste and add the fruit if you wish to use it – some people prefer to keep the rich flavour of the venison and beer unpolluted! Serve at once.

If the dish is to be frozen, cook it for slightly less time and do not adjust the seasoning or add the fruit until you defrost it. Allow the casserole to cool completely, then freeze it in a well-sealed container, leaving room for expansion.

Defrost at room temperature or in a microwave and reheat on the hob, in an oven or in a microwave, adjust the seasoning to taste and add the fruit if you wish to.

# Pheasant Braised with White Grapes

*Serves 6*                                    *6 months*

This is a very simple recipe which does not disguise the delicious flavour of young pheasants – although purists will say that doing anything except roasting them disguises the flavour!

> 3 small or 2 large pheasants, trussed
> 50 g/2 oz butter
> 12 spring onions, finely chopped
> 2–3 sprigs rosemary
> 450 ml/¾ pint dry white wine
> salt and pepper
> 225 g/8 oz seedless white grapes or larger white
>    grapes, pipped and halved

Fry the pheasants briskly on all sides in the butter in a heavy casserole until they are well bronzed all over. Add the onions, reduce the heat and continue to fry more gently until the onions soften. Add the rosemary, wine and a little salt and pepper, cover the casserole and cook gently on the hob or in a moderate oven (180°C/350°F/Gas Mark 4) for 1 hour. Remove from the oven, take out the rosemary, add the grapes and cook on the hob for a further 5 minutes. Adjust the seasoning to taste and serve.

Freeze in well-sealed containers once the pheasant is cooked and before adding the grapes or adjusting the seasoning.

Defrost at room temperature and reheat in a casserole or in a microwave. Add the grapes and adjust the seasoning before serving.

# Jugged Hare

*Serves 5–6*                                    *3 months*

Jugged hare is not one of my favourite dishes, but the one I was served by my Catercall partner's Mum even I had to admit was delicious. She was a great supporter of Mrs Beeton whose recipe she used. However, she subsituted wholemeal dumplings for the veal forcemeat in the original recipe, as she thought the dish was quite rich enough already. Although she never froze her hare, I have and it freezes very well.

> *approx 2 kg/4 lb hare, skinned, cleaned and the flesh*
>   *cut into pieces about the size of an egg*
> *75 g/3 oz butter*
> *1 medium onion, peeled and stuck with cloves*
> *12 peppercorns*
> *½ teaspoon salt*
> *bouquet garni*
> *1 tablespoon lemon juice*
> *900 ml/1½ pints good, hot beef stock (see page 152)*
> *150 ml/¼ pint port*
> *25 g/1 oz flour*

Heat 50 g/2 oz of the butter in a large pan and briskly fry the hare pieces until well browned on all sides. Turn the hare into an ovenproof casserole or a wide-necked jar, if you have one. Add the onion, peppercorns and salt, bouquet garni, lemon juice, hot beef stock and half the port. Cover the casserole or jar, place it in a *bain-marie* and cook it in a moderate oven (180°C/350°F/ Gas Mark 4) for 3 hours or until the hare is really tender. About 30 minutes before it is ready to serve, knead the rest of the butter with the flour and add it with the rest of the port to the hare. When the hare is ready, adjust the seasoning to taste and serve it with redcurrant jelly and wholemeal dumplings (see page 97).

To freeze the hare, do not adjust the seasoning and cool the dish entirely. Freeze it in a well-sealed container, leaving room for expansion.

Defrost at room temperature or in a microwave and reheat on a hob, in a moderate oven (180°C/ 350°F/Gas Mark 4) or a microwave. Adjust the seasoning to taste and serve as above.

# Casseroled Pigeon with Apple and Spices

*Serves 6*                                    *3 months*

Pigeons can be dry and tough, so I usually casserole them to be on the safe side. Freezing will help to break down the toughness a bit but will also increase the gamey flavour if left frozen for more than three months.

> *6 pigeons, cleaned and dried but not trussed*
> *100 g/4 oz brown breadcrumbs*
> *6 cloves garlic, finely chopped*
> *1 teaspoon each dried thyme, marjoram and savory*
> *2 teaspoons chopped parsley*
> *50 g/2 oz plump dried apricots, roughly chopped*
> *100 g/4 oz cooking apples, peeled and roughly*
>   *chopped*
> *salt and pepper*
> *2 eggs*
> *½ teaspoon ground ginger*
> *½ teaspoon ground nutmeg*
> *juice of 1 orange*
> *300 ml/½ pint red wine*
> *1.2 litres/2 pints strong brown stock*
> *6 slices brown wholemeal toast or fried bread*
>   *(optional)*

Mix the breadcrumbs with the garlic, herbs, fruit and seasoning in a bowl, add the eggs and mix the whole lot well together. Divide the stuffing in six and fill the birds. Truss their legs neatly to keep the stuffing in. Put the pigeons in a heavy-based pan just big enough to hold them. Mix the spices with the orange juice, add this to the wine and stock and pour over the pigeons. Cover, bring to the boil and simmer very gently for 2–2½ hours – by which time even the toughest of pigeons should be tender! If they are to be frozen, do not cook them quite so long to allow for extra cooking when they are defrosted. Adjust the seasoning to taste and serve the birds on the bread, or with baked potatoes or rice, with their juices.

To freeze, cool completely, then freeze in well-sealed containers with their juices, leaving room for expansion.

Defrost at room temperature or in a microwave and reheat in an oven, microwave or on the hob. Adjust seasoning and serve as above.

# MEAT

## Chilli Pancakes

*Serves 4*                    *6 months*

8 medium-sized pancakes (see page 162)
1 tablespoon good vegetable oil
1 medium onion, chopped
100 g/4 oz carrots, diced
2–3 small dried chillies, deseeded and chopped
225 g/8 oz minced beef
2 tablespoons flour
1–2 teaspoons cayenne pepper
3 tomatoes, roughly chopped
2 tablespoons tomato purée
300 ml/½ pint beer and 150 ml/¼ pint beef stock, or
  450 ml/¾ pint beef stock
450 g/1 lb cooked kidney beans (you can use canned
  beans quite successfully)
salt and pepper

Heat the oil in a pan and briskly fry the onion, carrots and chilli until they are lightly coloured. Increase the heat and add the meat, fry it rapidly until it is browned, then reduce the heat and add the flour mixed with the cayenne pepper. Stir together for a few minutes, then add the tomatoes, tomato purée and the liquid. Bring to the boil and simmer for 15–20 minutes. Add the beans and simmer for a further 5 minutes, then adjust the seasoning to taste. Remove the meat, vegetables and beans from the pot with a slotted spoon and use them to fill the pancakes; lay them in a serving dish. Reduce the remaining sauce slightly by boiling it briskly, then pour it over the pancakes and serve.

If the pancakes are to be frozen, lay them in a foil container, a foil package or a dish lined with foil. The sauce can be frozen separately or poured over them to freeze.

Defrost at room temperature or in a microwave and reheat, covered, in a moderate oven (180°C/350°F/Gas Mark 4) or a microwave. If the sauce was frozen separately, reheat it in a pan or microwave and pour over just before serving.

## Poor Man's Beef Stroganoff

*Serves 6*                    *6 months*

If it is cooked long and slowly, the beef should be as tender as fillet – and a great deal cheaper!

1 kg/2 lb braising beef, well trimmed and cut into fat
  matchsticks
15 g/½ oz butter
2 tablespoons olive, sunflower or corn oil
1 bunch spring onions, cleaned and finely chopped
2 tablespoons paprika
150 ml/¼ pint red wine
150 ml/¼ pint beef consommé
2 tablespoons creamed horseradish
150 ml/¼ pint soured cream
salt and pepper

Heat the butter and oil in a heavy-based pan and fry the beef briskly until it is lightly browned all over. Take it off the heat and add the onions and paprika, stir well together, then add the wine and consommé. Bring the pan back to the boil, cover it and simmer gently for 70–95 minutes; if you prefer you can cook it in a moderate oven (180°C/350°F/Gas Mark 4) for 70–95 minutes or in a microwave for 20–30 minutes. The beef should be tender without disintegrating. If the dish is to be frozen, it is better to freeze it at this stage and to complete the sauce on defrosting. The completed dish will freeze, but you risk the sauce separating on defrosting.

To complete the sauce, mix the horseradish with the soured cream and add to it 150 ml/¼ pint of the juices from cooking the meat. Drain off the rest of the juices and set them aside. Add the cream mixture to the meat and reheat gently. Season to taste and add more of the cooking juices to thin the sauce or reduce its richness if you want to. Serve with steamed brown rice and a green vegetable or salad.

Freeze the dish, at whichever stage, in a well-sealed container, leaving room for expansion.

Defrost at room temperature or in a microwave and reheat as above.

# A Victorian 'Beef Cake'

*Serves 6*                                    *3 months*

The Victorians used such enormous joints of meat for their family meals that they were permanently stuck with the problem of using up leftovers. This recipe is only one of the many devised for such purposes. You can use either cooked or fresh meat for the 'cake' which turns out like a pâté and is excellent for a cold lunch, buffet party or a picnic. It can also be served warm, but tends to fall apart! Do not freeze for too long as the spices will become overpowering.

*450 g/1 lb minced beef, either cooked or raw*
*175 g/6 oz beef suet, fresh or packaged*
*100 g/4 oz onions, finely chopped*
*50 g/2 oz mushrooms (flat ones if possible), finely chopped*
*50 g/2 oz dark brown breadcrumbs (rye crumbs are ideal if you can get them)*
*½ teaspoon each sea salt, ground mace and ground cloves*
*a large pinch of cayenne pepper*
*1 tablespoon each Worcestershire sauce and mushroom ketchup*
*60–90 ml/2–3 fl oz beef stock or red wine*

Mix the beef in a bowl with the suet, onions, mushrooms and breadcrumbs. Mix the spices with the sauces in a cup, then add 60 ml/2 fl oz of the stock or wine. Mix this thoroughly into the beef mixture. If it seems too dry (you want it moist but not runny), add a little more stock or wine. Spoon the whole mixture into a loaf tin or casserole dish and smooth the top. You may wish to line the dish with foil to make it easier to get out when cooked. Cover it and cook it in a moderate oven (180°C/350°F/Gas Mark 4) for 1–1½ hours – depending on whether you are using cooked or raw meat. If possible, cook the cake in a *bain-marie* as this helps to retain its moistness. Take the cake out of the oven and weight it lightly to cool. When it is completely cold, loosen the edges and turn it out onto a serving dish or foil or greaseproof paper.

Serve it with good salads or pack it tightly in greaseproof paper and put it in a well-sealed bag to freeze.

Defrost as slowly as possible to prevent disintegration and serve as above.

# Beef and Corn Hash Pie

*Serves 6*                                    *6 months*

This is what most cookery books would call a 'hearty pie' – but it is unusual and freezes well.

*550 g/1¼ lb good quality minced beef*
*2 medium onions, finely chopped*
*a handful of chopped fresh parsley, or 1 tablespoon dried*
*2 tablespoons chopped fresh mixed herbs, or 2 teaspoons dried*
*100 g/4 oz brown breadcrumbs (if possible, rye breadcrumbs)*
*salt and pepper*
*150 ml/¼ pint red wine*
*60 ml/2 fl oz water*
*1 tablespoon Worcestershire sauce*
*450 g/1 lb fresh or frozen corn kernels, lightly mashed, or 400 g/14 oz can creamed corn*
*1 medium green pepper, finely chopped*
*4 large spring onions, finely chopped*
*1 egg, lightly beaten*
*225 g/8 oz wholemeal shortcrust pastry (see page 161)*

Mix the beef, onions, herbs and breadcrumbs in a bowl and season them generously. Add the wine, water and Worcestershire sauce and mix thoroughly. Spread half the mixture in the bottom of a pie dish (lined with foil if it is to be frozen). Meanwhile, mix the corn with the pepper and spring onions and half the egg, spread this over the beef and top with the rest of the meat mixture. Cover the dish with foil or a lid and cook for 30 minutes in a moderate oven (180°C/350°F/Gas Mark 4) or for 10 minutes in a microwave. Remove and cool slightly. Top the pie with the pastry, decorate with the trimmings, brush with the rest of the egg and return it to a slightly hotter oven (190°C/375°F/Gas Mark 5) for 25–30 minutes or until the pastry is cooked and golden.

The pie can be frozen either before or after it is topped with the pastry. Open freeze, then remove the pie from the dish and pack in a well-sealed bag.

Defrost at room temperature or in a microwave and finish as above.

# Steak and Kidney Pie

*Serves 6*                                    *6 months*

This is a real old favourite which freezes well with or without its lid. If you are feeling energetic, make lots of the filling and freeze it for future use.

*750 g/1½ lb stewing steak*
*450 g/1 lb ox or pigs' kidney*
*2–3 tablespoons well-seasoned flour*
*350 g/12 oz button or flat mushrooms*
*225 g/8 oz white or wholemeal shortcrust pastry (see page 161)*
*1 egg, beaten*

Trim the steak and cut it into reasonable-sized cubes, then toss it in the seasoned flour. Trim the kidney, cutting out all the middle, cut it into cubes and toss in the flour. Remove the stems from the mushrooms (save them for soup), wipe and halve or quarter them if necessary and mix them with the meats. Tip the whole lot into a pie dish, sprinkle over the rest of the flour and two-thirds fill the dish with cold water. Cover it with foil or a lid and cook it in a moderately cool oven (160°C/325°F/Gas Mark 3) for about 1 hour or until the steak is tender. Take it out of the oven halfway through the cooking and stir to make sure the flour is well mixed in. Top the pie with the pastry (supporting the middle if the dish is rather large for the filling), decorate the top with the pastry trimmings and brush with the beaten egg. Cook in a moderately hot oven (190°C/375°F/Gas Mark 5) for 25–30 minutes or until the crust is cooked and lightly browned. The pie can be eaten hot with vegetables or cold with baked potatoes and a salad.

If you are freezing in bulk, allow the mixture to cool completely, then pack in convenient–sized servings (175–225 g/6–8 oz per person) in well-sealed foil or plastic containers and freeze. You can also freeze the pie in its dish topped with pastry, either uncooked or cooked; if the latter, take care not to burn the pastry when reheating it.

Defrost at room temperature or in a microwave, spoon the mixture into a pie dish and continue as above, or reheat the completed dish in a moderate oven (180°C/350°F/Gas Mark 4).

# Spiced and Casseroled 'Rump of Beef'

*Serves 6*                                    *6–9 months*

This recipe is based on a dish in Joan (Oliver's wife) Cromwell's recipe book which was published in 1660. The spices give it a slightly smoky, unusual flavour while the casserole roasting keeps it deliciously moist. It would be a good dish for either a microwave or a slow cooker.

*a generous 1 kg/2 lb topside of beef*
*1 teaspoon each aniseeds and fennel seeds*
*2 teaspoons coriander seeds*
*1 teaspoon each dried thyme and whole cloves*
*½ teaspoon cinnamon*
*1 teaspoon each freshly ground black pepper and sea salt*
*600 ml/1 pint dry white wine*
*300 ml/½ pint good, jellied beef stock (see below)*

Lightly pound the aniseeds, fennel seeds and coriander seeds, then mix them with the rest of the spices, seasoning and the wine. Put the beef in a glass or china bowl and pour over the marinade. Cover the bowl and leave it in a fridge or larder (a larder is better) for 24 hours. Remove the beef to a casserole just big enough to hold it. Strain the marinade and mix 300 ml/½ pint of the strained marinade with the beef stock. Pour the mixture over the beef and cover the pot. Cook in a moderately cool oven (160°C/325°F/Gas Mark 3) for 2–3 hours or until the beef is really tender. (If you are going to freeze the dish, reduce the cooking time slightly to allow for further cooking when the meat is defrosted.) Serve in the pot with its juices and accompany with baked potatoes. Incidentally, if there is any left over, the beef is also excellent cold.

To freeze, cool completely and freeze in its juices in a well-sealed container.

Defrost at room temperature or in a microwave, reheat gently in its juices and serve as above.

NOTE: If jellied beef stock is not available, you can use concentrate, although the flavour is really too strong; it would be better to use chicken stock.

# Casseroled Beef from Meaux

*Serves 6*                                              *3 months*

Like most casserole dishes, this beef with Meaux
mustard seems to improve in the freezer. Olives,
however, do not freeze well so it is better to add
them after defrosting, just before you serve the
dish.

> *1 kg/2 lb braising beef, trimmed and cubed*
> *225 g/8 oz onions, peeled and finely sliced*
> *450 ml/³/₄ pint red wine*
> *2 tablespoons Meaux or other good French mustard*
> *25 g/1 oz butter*
> *225 g/8 oz button mushrooms, wiped and their stalks*
>   *removed*
> *100 g/4 oz black olives, stoned*
> *salt and pepper*

Put the beef in a bowl with the onions and the
wine well mixed with the mustard; marinate it for
up to 12 hours. Remove the meat and onions from
the marinade, drain them, then dry them on
some kitchen paper towel. Melt half the butter in
a heavy pan and briskly fry the beef until it is

lightly browned. Transfer it to an oven or
heatproof casserole. Fry the onions lightly in the
same pan until just coloured and then transfer
them to the casserole. Finally, melt the rest of the
butter in the pan and toss the mushrooms lightly
in it; transfer to the casserole. Add the marinade,
cover the pot and cook in a moderate oven (180°C/
350°F/Gas Mark 4 ) or over a very low heat, for
about 2 hours or until the meat is really tender.
Add the olives, then season to taste with salt and
pepper and serve.

If the casserole is to be frozen, do not add the
olives or the seasoning, but cool and then freeze
in a container or polythene bag.

Defrost at room temperature or in a microwave.
Reheat, add the olives, then season to taste before
serving.

*Cumberland Mutton Pie (see page 76), Casseroled Beef from
Meaux and Barbecued Spareribs (see page 84)*

# Pickled Beef

*Serves 20*                                    *3 months*

This is a genuine Old English winter recipe but is
really not worth doing unless you use a large
joint. The potassium nitrate is obtainable from
most chemists.

> *approx 5 kg/10 lb silverside of beef*
> *7 litres/12 pints water*
> *2.5 kg/5 lb coarse salt*
> *50 g/2 oz potassium nitrate (saltpetre)*
> *a large sprig each bay, rosemary, parsley and thyme*
> *20 peppercorns*
> *10 cloves*
> *600 ml/1 pint red wine*
> *300 ml/½ pint red wine vinegar*

If possible, persuade your butcher to salt your
beef for you. If you have to do it yourself, dissolve
the salt and the saltpetre in the water in a
porcelain or enamel container (not plastic or
metal) and submerge the beef in it, making sure it
is all under water. Leave it for 5–8 days in a cold
larder or fridge.

Drain the beef and discard the brine. Put the
herbs under the beef in a pot just big enough to
hold it. Add the peppercorns, and stick in the
cloves, then pour over the wine and vinegar. Fill
the pot with water, bring to the boil and simmer
very gently for 3–4 hours. Remove the beef from
the pot and weight it overnight while it cools. The
beef can then be reheated to serve hot with a
sauce made from the stock, which should be
cooled, skimmed of fat and reduced, or served
cold, in which case the stock can be turned into
soup.

To freeze, wrap the beef tightly in a polythene
bag, or freeze in a container in the cooking juices,
skimmed of their fat.

Defrost at room temperature.

# London Pie

*Serves 6*                                       *6 months*

A very old friend of mine always used to serve this up-market version of shepherd's pie on a cold night in the dead of winter – there is nothing better! But she could never tell me why it was called 'London' pie. It freezes excellently and, if you are desperate for time, can even be made with instant potatoes. You can also substitute pork for the beef if you wish.

> *750 g/1½ lb good quality minced beef*
> *2 medium onions, finely chopped*
> *2 heaped tablespoons sultanas or raisins (optional)*
> *1 cooking apple or 2 large, tart eating apples, peeled and chopped fairly finely*
> *3 tablespoons tomato purée*
> *150 ml/¼ pint chicken or beef stock*
> *salt and pepper*
> *a generous dash of Worcestershire sauce*
> *1.25 kg/2½ lb potatoes, boiled or steamed*
> *a little butter, milk or cream*
> *75 g /3 oz grated well-flavoured cheese*

Mix the meat with the onions, sultanas or raisins, and apple in an ovenproof dish. (If the pie is to be frozen, you can line the dish with some foil so it can be turned out when it is frozen.) Mix the tomato purée with the stock, season it with salt, pepper and Worcestershire sauce and pour it over the beef. Cover the dish with foil or a lid and cook it in a moderate oven (180°C/ 350°F/Gas Mark 4) for 30 minutes or in a microwave for about 10 minutes.

Meanwhile, cook the potatoes and mash with some butter, milk or cream. Season them and mix in half the cheese. When the meat is cooked, spoon the potato over it, sprinkle over the rest of the cheese and return the dish to the oven for 15 minutes or until the cheese is melted and browned. Serve at once.

If this is to be frozen, do not return it to the oven once the potato and cheese have been added but allow it to cool completely, then open freeze. Remove the pie from the dish and pack in a well-sealed bag.

To defrost, remove the foil lining and drop the pie back into its dish while it is still frozen. The pie can be heated from frozen, about 1 hour in a moderate oven (180°C/350°F/Gas Mark 4), or defrosted at room temperature or in a microwave and reheated before serving. If necessary, brown the top under a moderate grill.

# Oxtail Stew

*Serves 6*                                    *4–6 months*

Oxtails are so cheap and make such a wonderful rich, meaty stew – provided they are cooked long and slowly enough – that it is worth making a really big batch and keeping a stock of it for a cold winter. For the flavour's sake, it pays to blanch and skim the tails before you start on the stew.

> *1.5 kg/3 lb oxtails, cut into 5–8-cm/2–3-inch pieces*
> *75 g/3 oz lard*
> *350 g/12 oz onions, roughly chopped*
> *3 rashers bacon, roughly chopped*
> *175 g/6 oz carrots, scrubbed and diced*
> *175 g/6 oz parsnips, scrubbed and diced*
> *225 g/8 oz open black mushrooms or button mushrooms, halved or quartered*
> *1 heaped tablespoon flour*
> *450 ml/¾ pint red wine*
> *1.5 litres/2½ pints beef, veal or chicken stock*
> *salt and black peppercorns*
> *parsley stalks*
> *2–3 bay leaves*

Put the oxtails in a large pan, cover them with cold water and bring rapidly to the boil, removing any scum that rises. Boil for 5 minutes, continuing to remove any scum, then drain and dry each piece thoroughly.

Heat the lard in a heavy-based casserole until it is almost smoking, then add the oxtail pieces and fry them briskly until they turn golden all over. Reduce the heat slightly, add the onions, bacon, carrots and parsnips and continue to fry until they too are well coloured. Add the mushrooms and cook for another couple of minutes, then stir in the flour. Cook for another minute or two, add the wine and stock, stirring well to remove any burnt bits off the bottom of the pan. Season with salt and a small handful of black peppercorns, add the parsley stalks and bay leaves and cover the pot tightly. Cook it slowly either on the hob or in a low oven (150°C/300°F/Gas Mark 2) for 2–3 hours or until the meat is falling off the bone. Take it out of the oven and cool completely, then chill. Once the stew is quite cold, the fat will rise to the top and can be removed with a spoon or knife. If it is to be eaten at once, reheat the stew and adjust the seasoning to taste before serving with baked or mashed potatoes.

To freeze, once you have removed the fat, spoon the stew into a container and freeze.

Defrost at room temperature or in a microwave, then reheat and adjust seasoning to taste before serving as above.

## Casseroled Beef with Walnuts and Celery

*Serves 6*                                   *4–6 months*

The walnuts add an unexpected crunch to an otherwise traditional beef casserole.

> 750 g/1½ lb lean chuck steak, cut into large cubes
> 50 g/2 oz butter
> 2 tablespoons olive or vegetable oil
> 1 tablespoon seasoned flour
> 15–18 button onions, peeled
> 1 clove garlic, finely chopped
> 180 ml/6 fl oz red wine
> salt, pepper and bouquet garni
> approx 600 ml/1 pint beef stock
> ½ head celery, finely chopped
> 175 g/6 oz broken walnuts

Melt 25 g/1 oz of the butter with the oil in a heavy based pan or casserole. Toss the meat in the seasoned flour and fry it briskly in the fat until well coloured. Remove the meat, add the onions and garlic and fry them for a couple of minutes until they begin to turn colour. Return the meat to the pan, add the wine, stir well to remove any burnt bits from the bottom of the pan, then add the salt, pepper and bouquet garni and enough beef stock to just cover the meat. Cover the casserole and simmer it for 1–1½ hours or until the meat is really tender.

Meanwhile, lightly fry the celery in the remaining butter until it starts to soften, then add the walnuts. Cook both for a couple of minutes and add them to the casserole. Continue to cook for a further 5 minutes, adjust seasoning to taste and serve. Baked potatoes and spinach, green beans or broccoli go well with this.

If the dish is to be frozen, do not add the celery and walnuts before freezing. Cook the casserole until the meat is tender, then cool completely and freeze.

Defrost at room temperature or in a microwave. Reheat gently, then fry the celery and walnuts and add as above.

## Paprika Beef with Brandy and Sweetcorn

*Serves 6*                                   *6 months*

This is a 'full bodied' casserole which freezes excellently.

> 1 kg/2 lb braising beef, trimmed and cubed
> 50 g/2 oz butter
> 2 medium onions, peeled and finely chopped
> 2 cloves garlic, crushed or finely chopped
> 2 teaspoons paprika
> 25 g/1 oz seasoned flour
> 2 tablespoons brandy
> 1 tablespoon fresh thyme, chopped, or 1 teaspoon dried
> 2 bay leaves
> 225 g/8 oz tomatoes, peeled and chopped small
> 300 ml/½ pint dry white wine
> 225 g/8 oz sweetcorn, freshly cooked, frozen or canned and drained
> 120 ml/4 fl oz double cream
> salt and pepper

Melt the butter in a large pan and gently cook the onions and garlic until they are soft but not coloured. Mix the paprika with the seasoned flour and toss the beef cubes thoroughly in it. Add the meat to the onion and garlic and fry briskly until lightly coloured all over. Draw off the heat and cool slightly, then add the brandy and light it. Once the flames have died, add the herbs, tomatoes and the wine, making sure that you scrape any burnt bits off the bottom of the pan. Bring to the boil, cover and simmer gently for 40–50 minutes or until the beef is really tender. If the dish is to be frozen, it should be cooled, the bay leaves removed, and frozen at this point. If it is to be served immediately, remove the bay leaves, add the sweetcorn, heat through for a couple of minutes, then add the cream and adjust the seasoning to taste. Serve at once, decorated with the bay leaves, with lots of brown rice or baked potatoes.

To freeze, cool completely once the beef is cooked and freeze in a well-sealed container, leaving room for expansion.

Defrost at room temperature or in a microwave and reheat gently in a pan on the hob or in a microwave. Add the sweetcorn and cream, adjust the seasoning to taste and serve as above.

# Francatelli's Braised Beef à la Polonaise

*Serves 10*                                          *3 months*

Like the pickled beef, it is not worth making this dish with a small piece of beef. However, once it is cooked there is no reason why it should not be halved and frozen in two pieces to feed four and six. The dish works equally well hot or cold; cold it makes a spectacular centre for a buffet table.

> *1.5 kg/3 lb topside of beef in one piece, plus the bones*
>     *(if available)*
> *75 g/3 oz piece of bacon, cut into 3 strips*
> *2 small onions, stuck all over with cloves*
> *1 carrot, scrubbed and roughly chopped*
> *a large bunch of herbs, including bay leaves and*
>     *parsley stalks*
> *60 ml/2 fl oz brandy*
> *150 ml/¼ pint medium sherry*
> *900 ml–1.2 litres/1½–2 pints good beef stock or a*
>     *combination of beef consommé and water*
> *100 g/4 oz cooked beetroot, diced small*
> *salt and pepper*

Cut the meat almost through in three places and put a layer of bacon in each cut. Tie the beef carefully back into its original shape with some string. Place the onions, carrot, herbs and any bones you have in the bottom of a heatproof casserole just big enough to hold the beef. Add the brandy and sherry and bring just to the boil. Add the beef, then sufficient stock or consommé and water to just cover the meat. Cover the casserole and simmer very gently on a low heat or cook in a moderately cool oven (160°C/325°F/Gas Mark 3) for 2–3 hours or until the meat is really tender. Cool the meat in the juice.

Remove the meat from its juices and dry. Take 900 ml/1½ pints of the cooking juices and strain them into a pan with the beetroot. Bring to the boil and reduce by almost half. Adjust seasoning to taste.

To serve hot, reheat the beef gently, well covered, in the oven or in a microwave, then slice it fairly thickly and serve it on a bed of hot red cabbage salad with the sauce spooned over the top. To serve cold, just slice the beef and lay it over the cabbage, then mask with the sauce. (For Braised Red Cabbage Salad, see page 95.)

The beef can either be frozen when it has finished cooking, in which case it should be frozen in the cooking juices and the sauce made when it is defrosted. Alternatively, the whole dish can be finished before freezing, in which case the beef should be tightly wrapped in a polythene bag and the sauce frozen separately. The cabbage salad will also freeze well.

Defrost at room temperature (minimum 12 hours).

# Braised Rolls of Beef

*Serves 4–6*                                          *6 months*

The rolls, when cut, should look rather attractive on the dish. Since the dish is rich, it will be plenty for six – provided they do not have too gargantuan appetites!

> *450 g/1 lb lean braising beef or rump steak, sliced*
>     *horizontally into thin strips (you should get*
>     *between 4 and 6 reasonable strips)*
> *sea salt and freshly ground black pepper*
> *175 g/6 oz freshly minced pork*
> *generous pinches of marjoram and oregano*
> *¼ teaspoon allspice*
> *60 ml/2 fl oz medium sherry*
> *350 g/12 oz mushrooms*
> *4–6 rashers back bacon*
> *50 g/2 oz butter or low fat margarine*
> *2 tablespoons oil*
> *300 ml/½ pint red wine*
> *300 ml/½ pint good beef stock or beef consommé*
> *1 level tablespoon flour*
> *a handful of chopped fresh parsley*

*Francatelli's Braised Beef à la Polonaise*

Lay out the strips of beef and sprinkle with salt and pepper. Mix the pork with the herbs, spices and sherry and spread it over the beef strips. Slice approximately 100 g/4 oz of the mushrooms and lay them down the middle of each strip. Roll the strip carefully lengthways, trying to keep as many of the innards inside as possible, then roll each beef roll in a rasher of bacon and secure with string or a cocktail stick.

Melt half the fat and oil in a heavy-based pan and briskly fry the rolls until lightly browned all over. Add the wine and stock, cover the pan and simmer gently for 1 hour. Alternatively, the beef can be cooked in a moderate oven (180°C/350°F/ Gas Mark 4) for the same amount of time.

When the beef is cooked, slice the remaining mushrooms finely. Cook them lightly in the rest of the butter and oil. Add the flour, stir and cook for a couple of minutes, then gradually add the strained juices from the pan to make the sauce. Adjust the seasoning if necessary. Remove the rolls, slice them neatly so that the different layers are visible, and lay them on a warmed serving dish. Spoon the mushrooms over the slices, pour over the sauce and sprinkle with the parsley. Serve with new potatoes and a green vegetable.

If the dish is to be frozen, freeze the beef rolls in their juices once they are cooked and cooled.

Defrost at room temperature or in a microwave, then finish as above.

# Kibbee

*Serves 4*                                                    *6 months*

I found the original of this recipe in an American cookery book compiled by the good ladies of the Louisville Junior League – there was no indication as to where it got its strange name! However, it freezes well and tastes delicious.

> *450 g/1 lb good quality minced beef*
> *175 g/6 oz cracked or bulgar wheat*
> *50 g/2 oz butter*
> *2 onions, finely chopped*
> *1 clove garlic, crushed or finely chopped*
> *2–3 sprigs fresh mint, chopped, or 2 teaspoons dried*
> *2 teaspoons ground cumin*
> *salt and freshly ground black pepper*
> *100 g/4 oz broken walnuts or pecan nuts*
> *2 tablespoons tomato purée*
> *a generous shake of Worcestershire sauce*
> *150 ml/¼ pint red wine*

Soak the wheat in enough boiling water to cover it generously for 3–4 minutes, then drain it and set it aside. Meanwhile, melt half the butter in a pan and lightly fry one of the onions and the garlic until they are soft and lightly coloured. Mix in the mint, cumin and some seasoning, then mix the whole lot into the cracked wheat.

Meanwhile, melt the rest of the butter in another pan and fry the remaining onion briskly with the beef and the nuts until all are well browned. Mix in the tomato purée, Worcestershire sauce and seasoning to taste, then add the red wine and mix again. Lay the beef in the bottom of an ovenproof casserole or microwave dish. (If you are going to freeze it, line the dish with foil or greaseproof paper so you can extract it from the freezer.) Spread the cracked wheat over the beef in a smooth layer. Cover the casserole tightly and either cook it in a moderate oven (180°C/350°F/Gas Mark 4) for 45–50 minutes or in a microwave on full power for 8–10 minutes. Serve warm or cold (but not chilled) with a good green salad.

To freeze, cool completely, then open freeze. Once frozen, you should be able to get it out of the dish. Store in a well-sealed bag.

To defrost, remove the wrapping and drop the kibbee back into its dish. Defrost at room temperature or in a microwave and warm through to serve.

# Marinated Loin of Veal or Pork

*Serves 6*                                                    *4 months*

Since veal is so horrendously expensive, you can easily substitute pork in this recipe. The result can be eaten either hot or cold.

> *1 kg/2 lb loin of veal or pork, with the bone*
> *a large handful of parsley*
> *8 spring onions*
> *a handful of fresh herbs (rosemary, sage, thyme, etc.)*
> *20 coriander seeds*
> *salt and black pepper*
> *600–900 ml/1–1½ pints milk*
> *100 g/4 oz mushrooms, finely chopped*
> *juice of 2 oranges*

Remove the bone from the meat and use it (together with an onion, carrot, few mushroom and parsley stalks and a little white wine) to make some good stock (see page 152).

Chop half the parsley finely with the spring onions and herbs. Mix them with the coriander seeds, salt and pepper and spread them over the meat. Roll and tie the loin neatly. Put it in a bowl which just fits it and cover it with milk. Leave it for 12–24 hours, covered, in the fridge.

When you are ready to cook it, put the remains of the parsley, chopped, in a pan, with the mushrooms, orange juice and 300 ml/½ pint of the stock from the bones. Drain off the milk marinade and add it to the pan, then put in the roll of veal. Bring the pan to the boil and simmer, covered, for 30 minutes per 450 g/1 lb. When the meat is done, take it out and keep it warm if it is to be served hot, or allow to cool it if it is to be served cold. Continue to cook the sauce uncovered until it has reduced to a thick, granular sauce with little lumps of mushroom and parsley. Adjust the seasoning to taste. It sounds slightly unattractive but actually both looks and tastes delicious! Slice the meat and serve it accompanied by the sauce.

If the roll is to be frozen, cool the meat in the sauce before it is reduced, then freeze them together in a well-sealed container, leaving room for expansion.

Defrost at room temperature or in a microwave. If the dish is to be served hot, reheat the meat in the sauce and then reduce the sauce as above; if it is to be served cold, merely defrost both, then reduce the sauce and allow it to cool before serving.

## Casseroled Veal with Mushrooms in Soured Cream

*Serves 6*                          *6 months*

This is a recipe that has truly stood the test of time – and is always to be found in Catercall's freezers. It is better to add the cream on defrosting in case it curdles on you.

*1.5 kg/3 lb lean stewing or pie veal, well trimmed*
*salt and pepper*
*50 g/2 oz butter or low fat margarine*
*2 tablespoons olive or sunflower oil*
*1 medium onion, finely chopped*
*225 g/8 oz button mushrooms, wiped and halved or*
   *quartered*
*½ teaspoon paprika*
*1 tablespoon flour*
*150 ml/¼ pint white wine*
*240–300 ml/8–10 fl oz soured cream*

Rub the veal well with the seasoning. Meanwhile, heat the fat in a large pan and gently cook the onion until just soft, then add the mushrooms and cook for a further minute or two. Mix the paprika and flour, stir it into the pan, cook for a minute, then add the wine and the veal. Cover the pan, bring it to the boil and simmer gently for 1–1½ hours or until the veal is tender. It can also be cooked in a moderate oven (180°C/350°F/Gas Mark 4) for the same time or in a microwave for about 30 minutes. When the meat is cooked, add the cream and adjust the seasoning to taste. The veal is particularly good with green or white noodles.

To freeze, cool the casserole completely once the veal is cooked and before adding the cream, and freeze in well-sealed containers.

Defrost at room temperature or in a microwave. Reheat gently (in a pan, oven or microwave), add the cream and adjust the seasoning to taste before serving.

## Escalopes of Veal with Spinach and Anchovies

*Serves 6*                          *4 months*

The use of anchovies to season meat is an eighteenth-century habit – but one which adds a much more interesting flavour than just mere salt! If you do not want to go to the expense of using veal escalopes, you could substitute chicken or turkey breasts, beaten flat.

*6 escalopes of veal*
*a little seasoned flour*
*50 g/2 oz butter*
*12 spring onions*
*175 g/6 oz fresh spinach, washed and finely chopped*
*a small handful of fresh mixed herbs, or ½ teaspoon*
   *dried*
*6 anchovy fillets, finely chopped*
*300 ml/½ pint good chicken or veal stock*
*240 ml/8 fl oz double cream*
*a little salt and white pepper*

Make sure the escalopes are well flattened, then dust them in the seasoned flour. Melt the butter in a large pan and fry the escalopes reasonably briskly until they are golden but not burnt on both sides. Remove them from the pan and add the onions, spinach, herbs and anchovies. Cook them together for a couple of minutes, then add the stock and return the escalopes to the pan. Cover the pan and gently cook the escalopes for 5–10 minutes, depending on thickness. Remove the lid, add the cream, stir for a couple of minutes, then adjust the seasoning to taste – you should not need any more salt but might want a little pepper. Serve at once with rice or new potatoes.

If the dish is to be frozen, cool and freeze it in a well-sealed container once the meat is cooked but before you add the cream.

Defrost at room temperature or in a microwave, reheat in the sauce, then add the cream and adjust the seasoning as above.

*Escalopes of Veal with Spinach and Anchovies* (see page 69) *and Carrot Soufflé* (see page 109)

*Terrine of Chicken and Crab* (see page 20) *and Rolled Breast of Veal with Allspice*

# Rolled Breast of Veal or Lamb with Allspice

*Serves 6*                                    *4 months*

The breast is always the cheapest part of any animal and, as long as it is well defatted, can be delicious. This roll can be served hot or cold and works as well with lamb as it does with veal.

> *1 kg/2 lb boned breast of veal or lamb with most of the fat removed*
> *4 tablespoons brown breadcrumbs*
> *grated rind and juice of 2 oranges*
> *2–3 tablespoons chopped parsley*
> *4 spring onions, finely chopped*
> *1 teaspoon chopped fresh sage, or ½ teaspoon dried*
> *½ teaspoon chopped rosemary leaves, fresh or dried*
> *salt and pepper*
> *1 tablespoon allspice*
> *25 g/1 oz soft butter*

Lay out the meat flat on a board. Mix together the breadcrumbs, orange rind, parsley, spring onions and herbs. Add a little salt and pepper and a generous pinch of the allspice, then work them, with half the butter, into a paste. Spread this over the meat and roll and tie it neatly. Melt the rest of the butter and allspice, with the orange juice, in a pan just big enough to hold the meat. Add the meat, cover the pan and pot roast it gently for 20 minutes per 450 g/1lb. Serve it at once with a good green vegetable, such as spinach or beans, and the juices from the bottom of the pan. If it is to be served cold, remove it from the pan and cool it completely before slicing and serving.

To freeze, remove the roll from the pan, cool it and freeze it in a well-sealed plastic bag. If you expect to serve it hot, freeze the pan juices separately.

Defrost at room temperature or in a microwave. If it is to be served hot, reheat in a pan with the juices; if it is to be served cold, just slice and serve with bread or a salad.

# Stuffed Breast of Veal with Spinach and Sausagemeat

*Serves 6*                              *8 months*

This is a very cheap but rather effective dish for a cold buffet. You can use a fairly large breast to make a big joint which can be cut up and frozen in small pieces for greater convenience. It can also be served hot, although it does not look quite so effective.

> *1.5–2 kg/3–4 lb breast of veal*
> *salt and pepper*
> *juice of 1–2 lemons*
> *50 g/2 oz butter or low fat margarine*
> *2 spring onions, finely chopped*
> *225 g/8 oz fresh spinach, washed, or 100 g/4 oz*
>   *frozen leaf spinach, defrosted and well drained*
> *a large handful of parsley, chopped*
> *225 g/8 oz good quality sausagemeat*
> *1 egg*
> *a large pinch each of nutmeg, thyme and savory*
> *1 tablespoon flour*
> *2 tablespoons olive or vegetable oil*

Trim the veal of as much fat as possible, lay it out on a board and sprinkle it lightly with salt, pepper and lemon juice. Meanwhile, melt half the fat in a pan and lightly sauté the onions until soft, then add the spinach and cook for 4–5 minutes. Remove from the heat and add the parsley, sausagemeat and egg and season with salt, pepper and herbs. Mix well together and spread over the veal. Roll the veal lengthways into a long sausage and tie it neatly. Sprinkle it with the flour. Roast the veal in a moderate oven (180°C/350°F/Gas Mark 4) for 1½ hours, basting every now and then with the oil and the remains of the butter. Once cooked, allow the meat to cool completely and chill before slicing to serve. It is particularly good with a crisp green salad with lots of peppers or chicory.

To freeze, cool the meat completely and then pack in one or several pieces in well-sealed bags.

Defrost at room temperature or in the fridge (if you use a microwave, you may have to rechill it) and slice to serve as above.

# Veal Chops with Gooseberries and Cucumber

*Serves 4*                              *6 months*

In Eliza Acton's *Modern Cookery*, published in 1845, this recipe is called a 'Spring Stew of Veal'. I have altered it slightly to accomodate chops and a freezer, but otherwise it is substantially as Miss Acton gave it. It would work equally well with pork chops, or even chicken joints.

> *4 veal chops, trimmed of most of their fat*
> *2 tablespoons seasoned flour*
> *40 g/1½ oz butter*
> *6–8 spring onions, trimmed and chopped*
> *1 small lettuce, finely sliced or chopped*
> *approx 25 green gooseberries (frozen will do but not*
>   *canned as they will have been sweetened)*
> *600 ml/1 pint good chicken or veal stock*
> *a bunch of assorted fresh herbs or 2 bouquet garni*
> *½ large cucumber, skin on but deseeded and cut into*
>   *matchsticks*
> *salt and pepper*

Coat the chops thoroughly in the seasoned flour. Heat the butter in a large pan and fry the chops fairly briskly with the spring onions until the chops are golden on each side but not burnt. Add any flour left over, the chopped lettuce, gooseberries, stock and herbs and stir together. Bring gently to the boil and simmer for 15 minutes. Add the cucumber matchsticks and continue to simmer for a further 5–10 minutes or until the chops are cooked. Remove the bouquet garni or any stalks of herbs, adjust the seasoning and serve at once. The dish goes well with well-steamed spring vegetables, such as carrots, baby potatoes or cauliflower.

If the chops are to be frozen, remove the herbs once they are cooked but do not season any further. Cool completely, then freeze in their sauce in a well-sealed container.

Defrost at room temperature or in a microwave. Reheat gently in a pan or a microwave in the sauce, adjust the seasoning to taste and serve as above.

# Cassoulet

*Serves 6*                    *4–6 months*

Everyone has their own version of a French country cassoulet, although the main ingredient must be haricot beans; feel free to add or substitute as the mood moves you. However, if it is to be frozen, you should remember to add slightly more liquid than otherwise.

> 750 g/1½ lb shoulder of lamb, cubed
> 350 g/12 oz dried haricot beans
> 8 rashers streaky bacon
> 2 carrots, scrubbed and sliced
> 2 onions, stuck with 6 cloves, plus 2 large onions, roughly chopped
> 4 cloves garlic, halved
> peppercorns and sea salt
> 75 g/3 oz butter
> 225 g/8 oz garlic sausage, diced
> 2 tablespoons tomato purée
> 750–900 ml/1¼–1½ pints veal or chicken stock
> 100 g/4 oz brown breadcrumbs

Soak the beans in cold water for a minimum of 4 hours, then drain and discard the water. Line a casserole big enough to hold all the ingredients with the bacon rashers. In a bowl mix together the beans, carrots, onions stuck with cloves, 2 cloves garlic, 6-8 peppercorns and a little salt. Spoon this mixture into the pot with the bacon, just cover it with water and bake it, covered, in a moderately cool oven (160°C/325°F/Gas Mark 3) for 2 hours. Meanwhile, melt 50 g/2 oz of the butter in a heavy-based pan and brown the garlic sausage and the lamb. Stir in the chopped onion, the rest of the garlic, the tomato purée and the stock. Bring to the boil and simmer gently for 30 minutes. Turn the meat mixture into the bean pot, stir all well together and return to the oven for another 30 minutes. Taste and adjust seasoning if necessary, then sprinkle a thick layer of breadcrumbs over the top. Dot with the remaining butter and return to the oven, uncovered, for 20–25 minutes until the crumbs are crisp. Serve at once.

If the cassoulet is to be frozen, cool it, turn it into a container and freeze before adding the topping.

Defrost at room temperature or in a microwave, top with the breadcrumbs and butter and reheat in a moderately hot oven (190°C/375°F/Gas Mark 5) for 30–45 minutes.

# Noisettes of Lamb with a Spinach and Redcurrant Purée

*Serves 6*                    *6 months*

Noisettes of lamb tend to be horrifically expensive, so you may prefer to use cutlets – the flavour is exactly the same. It is better to freeze the meat raw and to cook it when it is defrosted – it may lose out slightly on flavour, but cooked noisettes or cutlets without a sauce can become tough in the freezer.

> 12 small noisettes or cutlets of lamb
> 1.5 kg/3 lb fresh spinach, washed and shaken
> 225 g/8 oz open or button mushrooms, roughly chopped
> 100 g/4 oz butter
> juice of 6 oranges
> 225 g/8 oz redcurrants (fresh or frozen)

Put the spinach and mushrooms with 75 g/3 oz of the butter, the orange juice and 100 g/4 oz of the redcurrants in a large pan and cook them gently for 5 minutes.

If the lamb is to be eaten immediately, melt the rest of the butter in a frying pan and lightly brown the noisettes or cutlets on both sides. Place them on top of the vegetables, cover the pan and cook them gently for about 30 minutes or until the lamb is done. Remove the lamb from the pan and keep warm.

If the dish is to be frozen, do not cook the noisettes at this stage but simmer the vegetables on their own for 30 minutes. Purée the vegetables in a processor or liquidizer. Return the purée to the pan and cook it for a few minutes to reduce it slightly. Add the remaining redcurrants, cook for another couple of minutes and then season to taste. Serve the noisettes coated with and accompanied by the purée.

To freeze, cool the vegetables completely, then freeze in a well-sealed, container. Pack the noisettes in well-sealed, heavy-guage bags with as much air extracted as possible.

Defrost the meat and vegetable purée at room temperature or in a microwave. Grill or fry the noisettes for 5–7 minutes on each side, depending on thickness – they should remain pink inside. Meanwhile, reheat the purée in a pan or microwave and serve the lamb as above.

# Gigot D'Agneau Bedouin

*Serves 6*                                   *6 months*

This exotic-sounding leg of lamb has all the flavours of the East – you feel it should almost be garnished with sheeps' eyes! Ideally, you should stuff the lamb, then freeze it uncooked, leaving the roasting until you actually want to serve it. However, if you are concerned about time at the other end, you can cook it successfully and reheat it once cooked, as long as you do the reheating with care. Do not use frozen lamb unless you are going to cook the dish before freezing.

> *approx 2 kg/4 lb fresh leg of lamb*
> *a large bunch of fresh herbs (thyme, mint, rosemary, bay leaf, parsley, etc.) or a selection of dried herbs*
> *175 g/6 oz fresh brown or white breadcrumbs*
> *25 g/1 oz flaked almonds*
> *25 g/1 oz sultanas*
> *75 g/3 oz stoned, chopped dates (fresh if possible)*
> *½ level teaspoon ground oregano*
> *½ teaspoon black pepper*
> *2 level teaspoons ground coriander, or 2 small sprigs fresh coriander, finely chopped*
> *1 level teaspoon ground cumin*
> *1½ level teaspoons sea salt*
> *grated rind and juice of 1 lemon*
> *1 large egg*
> *150 ml/¼ pint milk*
> *75 g/3 oz melted butter*
> *1 tablespoon seasoned flour*
> *2 tablespoons runny or slightly warmed thick honey*
> *watercress or sprigs of rosemary to garnish*

Bone the lamb and put the bone together with the bunch of herbs in a pan containing approximately 600 ml/1 pint water. Bring them slowly to the boil, skim off any scum that rises to the surface, cover and leave them to simmer for 45–60 minutes.

Meanwhile, mix the breadcrumbs with the almonds, sultanas, dates, herbs, seasoning and lemon rind. Beat the egg, add the lemon juice, milk and melted butter and mix the liquid into the dry ingredients. Make sure that all are well amalgamated, adding a little more milk if the stuffing is too dry. Remove the lamb from the stock and pack with the stuffing. Tie it neatly to prevent the stuffing escaping.

If it is to be frozen uncooked, it should now be wrapped in foil and frozen in a well-sealed bag.

If it is to be cooked before freezing, dust the joint with seasoned flour and spoon over the honey. Weigh the joint, then put it into a baking dish with a generous 2.5 cm/1 inch of water in the bottom and bake it for 20 minutes in a preheated moderately hot oven (190°C/375°F/Gas Mark 5). Reduce the heat to 180°C/350°F/Gas Mark 4 and continue to cook for about a further 45 minutes. It should be cooked for no more than 20 minutes per 450 g/1 lb altogether.

If it is to be served immediately, remove the lamb from the baking tin and keep warm. Strain the herby stock and add it to the juices in the bottom of the baking dish scraping any residue off the bottom of the dish. Return the sauce to a saucepan and season to taste with salt and pepper; you may also wish to add a little redcurrant jelly, although the honey drippings from the roast will normally make it quite sweet enough. You should have approximately 450 ml/¾ pint of sauce; if there is too much, reduce it by simmering gently, uncovered, for a further 10–15 minutes.

Decorate the stuffed lamb with fresh watercress or fresh rosemary sprigs and serve at once accompanied by the sauce. You could also accompany it with a brown rice pilaff, although all it really needs is a good green salad to contrast with the richness of the lamb and sauce.

If the lamb is to be frozen cooked, put the joint in a container. Amalgamate the stock with the baking juices as above but do not complete the seasoning or reduce them. Pour them around the lamb in the container. Allow to cool completely, then pack in a well-sealed bag to freeze. If the lamb is being frozen uncooked, strain the stock and freeze it separately.

Defrost both cooked and uncooked lamb as slowly as possible to avoid drying out and to allow the flavours to develop. If the lamb was frozen uncooked, continue the recipe as above. If it was frozen cooked, transfer the joint to a baking dish or a microwave dish, with the juices, and reheat gently – in both cases the dish should be covered to prevent the joint drying out. Once reheated, remove from the juices and keep warm. Complete the sauce and serve as above.

# Lamb or Pork Kebabs with Yoghurt and Turmeric

*Serves 6*                                    *4 months*

450 g/1 lb lamb or pork fillet
2 cloves garlic, finely chopped
9–12 spring onions, finely chopped
50 g/2 oz fresh ginger root, peeled and finely chopped
2 teaspoons turmeric
juice of 2 lemons
3 tablespoons plain yoghurt
2 tablespoons sesame, nut or olive oil
1 teaspoon soy sauce
salt and pepper
½ yellow pepper, cut into large squares, or 1–2
  cooking apples

Cut the meat into reasonable-sized chunks. Mix all the ingredients except the yellow pepper or apples in a bowl, add the meat and leave to marinate for 2–6 hours.

When ready to cook, remove the meat from the marinade and thread it onto skewers or kebab sticks alternately with the yellow pepper or pieces of apple. (If using apples, after peeling cut them into slices, then dip immediately in lemon juice to stop them from discolouring.) Cook under a hot grill or on a charcoal barbecue for 5–7 minutes, basting periodically with the remains of the marinade. The lamb needs to be frizzled on the outside but can be pink inside; the pork must be cooked through. Serve the kebabs with lots of brown rice.

If you are to freeze the kebabs, do so in their marinade.

Defrost at room temperature or in a microwave.

# Country Lamb Casserole

*Serves 6*                                    *4–6 months*

Lamb is so expensive these days that it is nice to find something simple and tasty to do with it that will not break the bank!

1 kg/2 lb stewing lamb
50 g/2 oz butter or low fat margarine
225 g/8 oz onions, roughly chopped
225 g/8 oz carrots, scrubbed and sliced

*Kebabs with Yoghurt and Turmeric*

225 g/8 oz parsnips, scrubbed and sliced
½ head celery, chopped
225 g/8 oz mushrooms with their stalks (open if
  possible), roughly chopped
2 tablespoons seasoned flour
approx 600 ml/1 pint veal or chicken stock
salt and pepper
90 ml/3 fl oz medium sherry

Melt the butter in an ovenproof casserole and briskly fry the onions, carrots, parsnips and celery until they are lightly browned all over. Add the mushrooms and cook for a further couple of minutes. Meanwhile, trim the lamb of any excess fat or gristle and toss it in the seasoned flour. Add it to the pan and fry until bronzed. Add enough stock to just cover the meat and a little seasoning. Bring to the boil and simmer gently for 45–60 minutes or until the lamb is really tender. Add the sherry, cook for a further 5–10 minutes, adjust the seasoning to taste and serve with baked or mashed potatoes and/or a green vegetable.

To freeze, cool completely before adjusting the seasoning and pack in a well-sealed container, leaving room for expansion.

Defrost at room temperature or in a microwave, reheat gently, adjust the seasoning and serve.

# Cumberland Mutton Pie

*Serves 8*                                    *6 months*

These pies have been made for centuries in the hills and dales of the Lake District of England, where in winter you can be cut off for weeks from any sources of fresh food other than what is in your larder. The high proportion of mincemeat (in the original there would have been two layers of mincemeat to each layer of meat) would help to keep the meat fresh, while the hot water crust pastry lasts well. Since hot water crust tends to go slightly soggy in the freezer, I have substituted a well-cooked shortcrust pastry, but if the pie is not to be frozen and you want to keep nearer the flavour of the original, you can use hot water crust pastry. Ideally the pie should be cooked when defrosted to keep the pastry as fresh as possible. However, it can be cooked before freezing and be crisped up in an oven on defrosting, provided it is done with care.

> 750 g/1½ lb cooked lamb or mutton, finely chopped
> 450 g/1 lb shortcrust pastry (see page 161), or 600 g/
>    1¼ lb hot water crust (see page 161)
> 100 g/4 oz green bacon (in the piece), diced
> 100 g/4 oz onions, finely chopped
> 2 teaspoons dried rosemary leaves or 2 sprigs fresh
>    leaves, chopped
> 1 teaspoon dried sage leaves or 2 sprigs fresh leaves,
>    chopped
> 1 teaspoon sea salt
> ½ teaspoon ground black pepper
> ½ teaspoon ground nutmeg
> 225 g/8 oz fruit mincemeat
> 1 egg, beaten
> 210 ml/7 fl oz good jellied mutton or chicken stock

Make the pastry and use two-thirds of it to line a 25-cm/10-inch loaf tin. If you are using hot water crust, keep the rest of the pastry warm. If the pie is to be frozen and your loaf tin does not have removable sides, you may want to line it with foil.

Meanwhile, fry the bacon and onions in the fat that runs from the bacon until both are lightly coloured. Mix them into the lamb along with the herbs and seasonings. Lay one half of the mixture in the bottom of the loaf tin. Cover this with the mincemeat and then the rest of the lamb mixture. Top the pie with the rest of the pastry, leave a small hole in the middle through which to pour the stock and decorate it with the trimmings.

If the pie is to be frozen uncooked, open freeze it at this point. Once frozen, remove it from the tin and pack it in a well-sealed bag.

If it is to be eaten immediately or frozen cooked, brush the top of the pie with the beaten egg and cook it for 40–50 minutes in a moderately hot oven (190°C/375°F/Gas Mark 5) or until the pastry is cooked and lightly coloured. If you are using hot water crust, it is worth removing the pie carefully from the tin about 15 minutes before it is finished and returning it to the oven to make sure that the sides and bottom get properly cooked – this should not be necessary with shortcrust.

If it is to be eaten at once, remove the pie from the oven and pour the stock through a funnel into the hole in the top of the pie. Leave it to get completely cold before removing it from the tin and serve cold, but not chilled, with a salad.

If the pie is to be frozen cooked, do not pour the stock into it but allow it to cool completely, then freeze. Once frozen, you can remove it from the tin and pack as above. Freeze the stock separately.

Return the pie to the tin and defrost at room temperature. If the pie was frozen uncooked, brush with the beaten egg and complete as above. If it was frozen cooked, reheat it for 20–30 minutes in a moderate oven (180°C/350°F/Gas Mark 4), then pour in the stock and complete as above.

NOTE: You can freeze the whole pie, stock and all, but it will be impossible to keep the pastry really crisp – but then some people like soggy pastry!

# Lamb Korma

*Serves 6*                                    *2–3 months*

This is an anglicized version of one of the most popular of Indian dishes. It freezes well, although you need to take care to defrost it slowly so that the sauce does not separate.

> 1.5 kg/3 lb boned leg of lamb, cubed
> ½ teaspoon ground cardamom
> 1 teaspoon ground cumin
> 1½ teaspoons ground turmeric
> 300 ml/½ pint plain yoghurt

*2 tablespoons butter*
*100 g/4 oz desiccated coconut*
*300 ml/½ pint milk*
*4–6 tablespoons olive or good vegetable oil*
*350 g/12 oz onions, finely chopped*
*2 cloves garlic, finely chopped*
*1 teaspoon ground ginger*
*½ teaspoon dry English mustard*
*¼ teaspoon each black pepper, cinnamon and*
  *cayenne pepper*
*a pinch of ground cloves*
*2 medium tomatoes, peeled, seeded and diced*
*salt*
*1 tablespoon lemon juice*

Mixed the cardamom, cumin and turmeric thoroughly into the yoghurt, then submerge the lamb in the marinade, cover it and set it aside for at least 1 hour. Melt the butter in a pan, then add the coconut and the milk, bring to the boil and simmer gently for 15 minutes. Strain the milk and set it aside.

Heat half the oil in a large pan and briskly cook the lamb with its marinade for about 5 minutes, stirring continuously. Heat the remaining oil in a separate pan and sauté the onions and garlic until they are soft and lightly coloured. Remove from the heat and add the remaining spices. Stir them well together and return to the heat for a couple of minutes. Add the onion mixture to the lamb with the tomatoes, the coconut milk and a little salt. Bring to the boil and simmer gently until the lamb is tender and the sauce thick – it will probably take about 30 minutes. If the Korma is to be served at once, add the lemon juice and adjust the seasoning to taste. If the sauce is too thin, it can be thickened with a little more coconut. Serve with lots of brown or white rice.

If the Korma is to be frozen, cool it completely before adjusting the seasoning and freeze it in a well-sealed container.

Defrost slowly to prevent the sauce separating. Reheat gently in a pan or a microwave, add the lemon juice and adjust the seasoning to taste before serving as above.

# Bobotie

*Serves 6*                    *4–6 months*

Bobotie is a South African dish whose unexpected ingredients turn into the most delicious cross between a pie and a quiche; a third cousin to a moussaka. Leftovers, if there are any, are also good cold.

*450 g/1 lb cooked lamb*
*2 slices thick wholemeal bread*
*600 ml/1 pint milk*
*50 g/2 oz butter*
*2 onions, finely chopped*
*3 tablespoons mild curry powder*
*juice of 3 lemons*
*2 teaspoons dark brown sugar*
*salt and pepper*
*3 eggs*
*100 g/4 oz toasted nibbed almonds*
*100 g/4 oz raisins*

Soak the bread in half the milk for a couple of minutes, then mince it roughly with the cooked lamb in a mincer or food processor. Melt half the butter in a pan and lightly fry the onions with the curry powder. Mix the lemon juice, sugar, salt, and pepper and 1 egg in a bowl. Add the onion mixture, then the bread and meat and mix them all well together. Spoon them into an ovenproof dish; if the Bobotie is to be frozen, line the dish with foil. Mix the remaining eggs and milk, with the almonds and raisins and pour them over the meat mixture, allowing the liquid to soak well in and making sure that the fruit and nuts are evenly spread over the top. Dot with the remaining butter and bake, uncovered, in a moderate oven (180°C/350°F/Gas Mark 4) for 30 minutes or until the top is lightly browned and puffed. Serve with lots of boiled rice and home-made chutney – although the Bobotie has so much flavour that it scarcely needs the chutney.

To freeze, cool completely, then open freeze. Remove from the dish and pack to store.

To defrost, peel off the foil and drop back into its dish. Defrost at room temperature or in a microwave and reheat in a moderate oven (180°C/350°F/Gas Mark 4) for 20–30 minutes. Serve as above.

# Stuffed Leg of Lamb

*Serves 6*                    *3–6 months*

I have based the stuffing for this dish on a
Victorian recipe for lamb stuffed with oysters; but
I have been a little kinder to your purses! If you
find the flavour of the mussels too strong with the
lamb, you could substitute mushrooms or
artichoke hearts.

*1 small leg of lamb (approx 1 kg/2 lb)*
*a large handful of fresh spinach or a cabbage lettuce,*
*    roughly chopped*
*2 rashers bacon, chopped*
*1 medium onion, finely chopped*
*1 stick celery, finely chopped*
*100 g/4 oz cooked mussels (frozen will do very well)*
*salt and pepper*
*15 g/½ oz butter*
*1 tablespoon olive or sunflower oil*
*150 ml/¼ pint red wine*

Bone the lamb. Mix the spinach or lettuce, bacon,
onion, celery and mussels thoroughly together
and season them lightly. Use about one-third of
the mixture to stuff the lamb and tie it neatly.
Melt the butter and oil in the bottom of a heavy-
based, ovenproof casserole and add the rest of the
vegetable mixture. Cook it gently for a few
minutes until it begins to soften, then add the
wine. Place the leg of lamb on top of the vegetable
mixture (mirepoix) and roast in a moderate oven
(180°C/350°F/Gas Mark 4) for 15 minutes per 450 g/
1 lb. Remove from the oven, allow to rest for 5–10
minutes, then carve and serve with the mirepoix.

To freeze, cool completely, then pack in a well-
sealed container with the vegetables.

Defrost at room temperature, return to an
ovenproof dish with the vegetables under the
lamb and reheat in a moderate oven (180°C/350°F/
Gas Mark 4) for 20–30 minutes.

*Bobotie with chutney (see page 77)*

*Preparing Stuffed Leg of Lamb*

# Navarin of Lamb

*Serves 6*                                          *6 months*

At Catercall we have been using this traditional French recipe for navarin for years as it freezes so well. It is better to add the peas and potatoes when you defrost it. Shoulder of lamb is excellent for this recipe.

>   *1 kg/2 lb good stewing lamb, boned and trimmed*
>   *2 tablespoons lard*
>   *2 Spanish onions, quartered*
>   *3 cloves garlic, finely chopped*
>   *2 tablespoons flour*
>   *½ teaspoon sugar*
>   *salt and pepper*
>   *6 small turnips, scrubbed and diced*
>   *bouquet garni*
>   *4 tablespoons tomato purée*
>   *300 ml/½ pint chicken or veal stock*
>   *12 button onions*
>   *100 g/4 oz unsmoked bacon, diced*
>   *12 small new potatoes, well scrubbed*
>   *100 g/4 oz fresh peas or frozen petits pois*
>   *a small bunch of parsley*
>   *grated rind of 1 lemon*

Melt the lard in a heavy-based casserole and add the quartered onions and garlic. Cook until they are starting to soften, then increase the heat and add the trimmed lamb. Cook briskly together until they are lightly browned, then add the flour and stir well for a couple of minutes. Add the sugar and season generously, then add the turnips, bouquet garni, tomato purée and the stock. Stir everything well together, cover the pot and simmer gently on the hob or cook in a moderate oven (180°C/350°F/Gas Mark 4) for an hour or until the lamb is tender. Remove the lamb and vegetables with a slotted spoon and set aside. Leave the juices to get completely cold, then remove any fat that has risen to the top. Strain the juices into a clean casserole (or container if it is to be frozen) and add the lamb and vegetables. Blanch the button onions and bacon briefly in boiling water, then sauté them in the bacon fat until they are lightly coloured and add them to the casserole. If the navarin is to be eaten at once, add the potatoes and return the casserole to the oven for a further 35 minutes or until the potatoes are cooked. About 10 minutes before they are done, add the peas if they are fresh; if they are frozen, add them 5 minutes before the end. Adjust the seasoning to taste and serve the navarin in its casserole sprinkled generously with chopped parsley and grated lemon rind.

If it is to be frozen, freeze it in a well-sealed container as soon as you have added the onions and bacon.

Defrost at room temperature or in a microwave. Reheat in a clean casserole and finish as above.

# Broiled Leg or Collops of Pork

*Serves 4*                                          *6 months*

This dish is based on a seventeenth-century recipe I discovered when I was researching ideas for a book on Samuel Pepys' cookery. The original is very spicy and a little too dry to freeze well.

>   *½ small leg of pork (1–1.5 kg/2–3 lb), sliced into*
>     *thick 'collops' or chops, or 4 thick pork chops*
>   *4 teaspoons fresh thyme, or 2 teaspoons dried*
>   *4 teaspoons fresh sage, or 2 teaspoons dried*
>   *2 teaspoons sea salt*
>   *1 teaspoon freshly ground black pepper*
>   *50 g/2 oz butter*
>   *25 g/1 oz dark brown sugar*
>   *2 tablespoons wine or cider vinegar*
>   *2 tablespoons wholegrain mustard*
>   *300 ml/½ pint chicken or veal stock*

Chop the herbs and mix well together with the salt and pepper. Coat the meat thoroughly in the mixture on both sides, then 'broil' the meat briskly for a couple of minutes on each side in a hot frying pan or under a very hot grill. Meanwhile, melt the butter and sugar in a heavy pan, then add the vinegar and mustard. Mix well, add the stock, cook together for a minute or two, then add the pork. Cover and simmer for 20–25 minutes. Adjust seasoning to taste and serve with baked or mashed potatoes.

To freeze, cool completely before adjusting seasoning and freeze in a well-sealed container.

Defrost at room temperature or in a microwave and reheat for 30 minutes in a moderate oven (180°C/350°F/Gas Mark 4) or for 6–8 minutes in a microwave.

# Pork and Bean Pot

*Serves 6*                                    *3–4 months*

You can use belly of pork or bacon for this bean pot, which makes it cheap but still very flavoursome. You could also substitute lentils for mung beans if you preferred, although they tend to go a bit mushy, and any cheap 'plonk' will do!

*450 g/1 lb belly of pork or bacon, cubed*
*25 g/1 oz butter or low fat margarine*
*3 onions, roughly chopped*
*8 carrots, roughly chopped*
*3 cloves garlic, finely sliced or crushed*
*350 g/12 oz mung beans*
*900 ml/1½ pints red wine*
*450 ml/¾ pint water*
*a handful of peppercorns*
*3–4 sprigs parsley*
*2 bay leaves*
*salt*
*approx 1 tablespoon Worcestershire sauce*

Melt the butter in a heavy-based casserole and briskly fry the pork or bacon, stirring continuously, until it starts to colour all over. Add the onions, carrots and garlic and continue to fry until they are all lightly coloured. Add the beans, wine, water, peppercorns, parsley and bay leaves. If you are using belly of pork, you can also add a little salt; if bacon, it would be wiser not to salt until the dish is cooked. Cover the pot tightly and simmer gently for about 1 hour or until the beans are cooked without being mushy. Alternatively, it can be cooked in a low oven (150°C/300°F/Gas Mark 2) for 1–1 ½ hours. If possible, leave the pot for a day after it is cooked, then reheat it and season it to taste with Worcestershire sauce and a little salt if needed. Serve it with a good green salad.

If the dish is to be frozen, it should be done after the cooking is finished; final seasoning should be left until it is defrosted.

Defrost at room temperature or in a microwave. Reheat in a moderate oven (180°C/350°F/Gas Mark 4) or microwave, adjust seasoning as above and serve.

# Pork Fillet with Artichokes

*Serves 6*                                    *3 months*

This is best made with Jerusalem artichokes when they are in season. If they are not available, substitute water chestnuts or artichoke hearts.

*750 g/1½ lb pork fillet, trimmed and slit open along the middle*
*salt and pepper*
*450 g/1 lb Jerusalem artichokes (or water chestnuts or artichoke hearts), trimmed, peeled and sliced*
*100 g/4 oz walnuts*
*25 g/1 oz butter or low fat margarine*
*2 cloves garlic, finely chopped or crushed*
*2 medium onions, finely chopped*
*1 cooking apple, peeled and fairly thinly sliced*
*300 ml/½ pint dry white wine*
*300 ml/½ pint light chicken or veal stock, or water*
*juice of 2 oranges*

Open out the pork fillet, sprinkle it with salt and pepper and lay slices of artichoke and walnuts down the middle. You should have some walnuts left over; toss these in a little butter and set them aside. You may find it easier to cut the fillet completely in two so as to get the filling well distributed. Tie it into a neat sausage.

Melt the fat in a heavy-based pan and fry the pork roll briskly until it is lightly browned on each side. Reduce the heat and add the garlic and onions. Continue to cook until they soften without turning colour, then add the rest of the artichokes, the apple and the liquids. Cover the pan and simmer for 50–60 minutes or until the pork is quite tender; alternatively cook it in a moderate oven (180°C/350°F/Gas Mark 4). Remove the pork from the casserole, cut the strings and slice the sausage neatly. Lay the slices on a warmed serving dish. Adjust the seasoning to taste and spoon the vegetables and sauce over the pork. Decorate with the remains of the walnuts and serve with brown rice and a green vegetable or salad.

If the dish is to be frozen, allow it to cool completely once it is cooked, then freeze the pork in a well-sealed container in its juices *before* slicing.

Defrost at room temperature or in a microwave and reheat in its juices. Slice the pork, finish and serve as above.

# Soy Pork with Beanshoots

*Serves 6*                                    *2–3 months*

Beanshoots freeze suprisingly well. Although they look rather thin and weedy when defrosted, they manage to retain their crispness. Nuts, however, go a bit soggy so, if possible, it is better to add them at the defrosting stage.

> *750 g/1½ lb fillet of pork, sliced quite thinly*
> *50 g/2 oz butter*
> *350 g/12 oz onions, peeled and thinly sliced*
> *600 ml/1 pint orange juice, fresh (chilled) or frozen*
>   *but not canned*
> *450 g/1 lb beanshoots*
> *75 g/3 oz dry roast peanuts*
> *salt, black pepper and soy sauce*

Melt the butter in a heavy-based pan and lightly fry the sliced pork with the onions until both are just turning colour. Add the orange juice, cover and simmer gently for 20 minutes or until the pork is almost cooked. Add the beanshoots, stir together, re-cover and cook for a further 5 minutes. If the dish is to be eaten immediately, add the peanuts, then season to taste with salt, black pepper and soy sauce.

If it is to be frozen, season it *lightly* with salt, pepper and soy sauce, cool and freeze.

Defrost at room temperature or in a microwave. Reheat gently, add the peanuts and adjust seasoning to taste. Serve with brown rice and a salad.

# Pork Fillet with Soured Cream and Mustard

*Serves 6*                                    *4–6 months*

This is a lovely dish as the richness of the pork and cream is given an edge by the apple and the mustard; it is very good with fresh noodles and a green vegetable.

> *750 g/1½ lb pork fillet, cut into strips*
> *50 g/2 oz butter*
> *100 g/4 oz onions, finely sliced*
> *225 g/8 oz button mushrooms, finely sliced*
> *1 medium cooking apple, peeled and coarsley grated*
> *2 tablespoons seasoned flour*
> *1 tablespoon good French mustard*
> *300 ml/½ pint veal or chicken stock*
> *150 ml/¼ pint soured cream*
> *salt and pepper*
> *a handful of finely chopped parsley*

Melt half the butter in a pan and gently fry the onions until they start to soften. Add the mushrooms and the grated apple, cover the dish and cook it gently for 5 minutes. Remove the vegetables with a slotted spoon and set aside. Melt the remaining butter in the pan. Toss the pork in the seasoned flour and fry it quickly in the butter until it is lightly coloured all over.

Return the vegetable mixture to the pan. Mix the mustard with the stock, add it to the pan, cover and simmer for 30 minutes or until the pork is cooked. Add the soured cream and season to taste with salt and pepper. As you serve it, sprinkle over the chopped parsley.

If the dish is to be frozen, it is better to freeze it as soon as it has finished cooking and cooled, and to add the cream, seasoning and parsley when it is defrosted.

Defrost at room temperature or in a microwave. Reheat gently, then add the cream and seasoning and serve as above.

# Ham and Chicory in a Creamy Sauce

*Serves 6*                                    *1–2 months*

I always associate this recipe with Belgium, although whether it is because chicory is so often know as Belgian chicory, or because I used to have to eat it when staying with my aunt as a child, I do not know. I do know that the acidity of the chicory which I hated as a child I now find an excellent foil to the rich creamy sauce.

> *12 thin slices good quality ham*
> *6 good heads chicory, trimmed and cut in half*
>   *lengthways*
> *40 g/1½ oz butter*
> *100 g/4 oz leeks, finely sliced*
> *40 g/1½ oz flour*
> *240 ml/8 fl oz milk*

*Bacon, Apple and Sausagemeat Flan* (see page 84)

*240 ml/8 fl oz chicken or veal stock*
*120 ml/4 fl oz dry white wine*
*150 g/5 oz herbed cream cheese*
*salt and pepper*
*a handful of chopped mustard and cress or watercress*

Blanch the chicory in boiling water for a couple of minutes, then drain it as well as possible. Roll each chicory half in a slice of ham and arrange them on a flan dish or serving dish; if it is to be frozen, the dish should be lined with foil. Cover the dish and heat it through in a low oven (150°C/300°F/Gas Mark 2) or a microwave.

Meanwhile, melt the butter in a pan and gently cook the leeks until they are soft. Add the flour, cook for a minute or two, then gradually add the milk, stock and wine. Cook and stir until the sauce thickens, then add the cream cheese. Cook for another couple of minutes and season to taste.

Take out the ham and chicory and drain off any excess water that may have leaked from the chicory. Pour over the sauce, sprinkle with the cress and serve at once with rice or fresh noodles and a green vegetable.

If the dish is to be frozen, do not reheat the ham and chicory rolls. Underseason the sauce slightly as the salt in the ham and the cheese will be emphasized by freezing. Pour the sauce over the rolls and do not decorate. Open freeze the dish and, when frozen, remove from the serving dish and put in a well-sealed bag for storage.

To defrost, peel off the foil and drop the frozen ham and sauce back into the serving dish. Defrost at room temperature or in a microwave and reheat, covered, for 20–30 minutes in a moderate oven (180°C/350°F/Gas Mark 4) or for 5–8 minutes in a microwave. Decorate and serve as above.

# Bacon, Apple and Sausagemeat Flan

*Serves 6*        *6 months*

This flan freezes extremely well and is useful for picnics, snacks or lunches as you can portion it before freezing and only dig out what you need. It also defrosts very quickly.

> *225 g/8 oz bacon, roughly chopped*
> *1 medium onion, roughly chopped, plus 1 small onion, sliced in rings*
> *100 g/4 oz sausagemeat*
> *1 small cooking apple or large, tart eating apple*
> *25 g/1 oz rolled or porridge oats*
> *salt and pepper*
> *a large pinch of dried or fresh thyme*
> *150 g/6 oz plain or wholemeal shortcrust pastry (see page 161)*
> *25 g/1 oz melted butter*

Fry the bacon with the chopped onion in a pan for 5 minutes or until the bacon is beginning to soften and colour slightly. Work in the sausagemeat and continue to cook for a further 5 minutes. Add half the apple, chopped fairly small, with the oats and seasoning and thyme.

Line a 20-cm/8-inch flan case with the pastry and spoon the sausage mixture into the middle, then spread it out evenly. Slice the rest of the apple and lay it over the flan together with the onion rings. Brush them all well with the melted butter. Bake the flan in a moderately hot oven (190°C/375°F/Gas Mark 5) for 40–45 minutes. If the apple and onion look like burning, paint them with a little more butter and cover the flan with a piece of foil or greaseproof paper. Serve the flan warm or cold.

To freeze, cool completely and pack, either whole or portioned, in well-sealed containers or carefully layered in heavy-gauge bags. If you do pack the flans in bags, take care they do not get too knocked around in the freezer.

Defrost at room temperature or from frozen in a moderate oven (180°C/350°F/Gas Mark 4). Serve warm or cold. Even if it is to be served cold, it is better to crisp the flan up for 15 minutes in a moderately hot oven (190°C/350°F/Gas Mark 5); do not use a microwave as it will go soggy.

# Barbecued Spareribs

*Serves 6*        *6 months*

Well-marinated spareribs freeze extremely well – you can even cheat by reheating them on a barbecue and pretending you have cooked them entirely that way!

> *1.5 kg/3 lb pork spareribs*
> *8 tablespoons tomato ketchup*
> *3 tablespoons clear honey*
> *4 tablespoons soy sauce*
> *5 tablespoons wine vinegar*
> *2 teaspoons tomato purée*
> *1 teaspoon salt*
> *450 ml/¾ pint chicken or veal stock*

Put the ribs in a roasting pan, mix all the remaining ingredients together and pour them over the ribs, making sure that they are well covered. Leave them to marinate for anything from 2–24 hours. Roast the ribs in the marinade in a hot oven (200°C/400°F/Gas Mark 6) for 15 minutes. Remove the ribs to a rack and continue to roast in a slightly cooler oven (180°C/350°F/Gas Mark 4) for a further 30 minutes or until they are brown and crisp. Meanwhile, boil the marinade briskly until it is reduced to a thick sauce. Arrange the ribs on a serving dish accompanied by the sauce.

To freeze, cool the ribs completely, then pack and freeze in heavy-gauge, well-sealed bags with the sauce frozen separately.

Defrost the ribs at room temperature or from frozen in a hot oven. Recrisp in a moderately hot oven (190°C/375°F/Gas Mark 5) or on a barbecue before serving as above.

# Gammon or Ham Marinated with Ginger

*Serves 4*        *1–2 months*

This looks an alarmingly lengthy recipe, but although it stretches over 24 hours, there is, in fact, not much to do. Take care not to oversalt or to leave it in the freezer too long, as gammon can get extremely salty amazingly quickly.

1 kg/2 lb piece of gammon or ham, any cut
2 cloves garlic, crushed or finely chopped
25 g/1 oz fresh root ginger, peeled and finely chopped
1 teaspoon rosemary leaves, chopped
6 bruised juniper berries
1 tablespoon clear honey
2 tablespoons lemon juice
150 ml/¼ pint dry sherry
salt and pepper
25 g/1 oz butter
225 g/8 oz button mushrooms, sliced
300 ml/½ pint water
2 teaspoons cornflour
90 ml/3 fl oz white wine
1 tablespoon redcurrant jelly

Soak the gammon or ham in water for 2–3 hours to remove any excess saltiness. Mix the crushed garlic, ginger, rosemary, juniper berries, honey, lemon juice, sherry and a little seasoning (no salt if the dish is to be frozen) together in a bowl just big enough to hold the gammon – you may need to heat them slightly in a microwave or saucepan to get the honey to mix with everything else. Put in the gammon, make sure it is well covered in the marinade, cover and leave for 12–24 hours.

Melt the butter in a heavy-based saucepan just big enough to hold the gammon and lightly fry the sliced mushrooms. Remove the gammon from the marinade and set aside for a moment. Add the marinade to the mushrooms along with the water, bring to the boil and simmer for 5 minutes. Put in the gammon and again get it as covered as possible in the juices. Bring the pot to the boil and simmer gently for 1 hour, or 30 minutes per 450 g/ 1 lb of meat.

If the dish is to be served at once, remove the gammon from the pot and keep it warm. Mix the cornflour with the white wine and add it to the juices in the pot along with the redcurrant jelly. Cook everything gently together until the sauce thickens and the jelly melts. Adjust the seasoning to taste. Slice the gammon onto a warmed serving dish and spoon over the sauce.

If the dish is to be frozen, cool the gammon completely in the juices, then freeze it in a well-sealed container, leaving room for expansion.

Defrost at room temperature or in a microwave and reheat the gammon, in its juices, in a pot on the hob, in an oven or in a microwave. Remove the gammon from the pot and finish as above.

# Spiced Ham Salad

*Serves 6*                                    *1–2 months*

Although you cannot freeze the original hard-boiled egg garnish in this Cordon Bleu salad, you can freeze both the ham in its sauce and the rice – and if you are really pushed for time you can abandon the egg in favour of some more watercress!

450 g/1 lb cooked ham, thickly sliced
½ teaspoon paprika
a pinch of salt and a good shake of freshly ground
    black pepper
2 drops Tabasco
2 tablespoons red wine vinegar
3 tablespoons tomato ketchup
5 tablespoons olive or good vegetable oil
2 tablespoons mango chutney
350 g/12 oz brown rice
3 hard-boiled eggs
a large bunch of watercress

Remove any extra fat from the ham and cut it into matchsticks. Mix the paprika with the salt and pepper (use very little, if any, salt if the salad is to be frozen as the ham always gets saltier in the freezer). Add the Tabasco, vinegar, ketchup and oil and whisk them together until the dressing is fairly thick. Chop any large lumps in the chutney and mix it into the sauce. Spoon in the ham and make sure it well coated with the sauce. Meanwhile, cook the rice in plenty of fast-boiling water for 9–15 minutes, depending on what type it is – taste frequently to make sure it does not get overcooked. Drain and cool.

If the salad is to be served immediately, arrange the rice on a dish and spoon the ham and dressing over it or in a 'pond' on the top. Decorate the salad with sliced hard-boiled egg and watercress.

If it is to be frozen, freeze the ham in the sauce and the rice in separate containers.

Defrost the ham at room temperature and whisk the sauce which will have separated in the freezer. Defrost the rice at room temperature or in a microwave and serve as above.

# Ham and Apple Pie

*Serves 4*                                              *2 months*

A verson of this pie is known as a 'Fidget pie' in Devon – although I have never discovered why! It freezes well, but like all ham dishes should not be left in the freezer too long or it will go very salty.

*450 g/1 lb cooked ham, diced*
*25 g/1 oz butter*
*225 g/8 oz onions, roughly chopped*
*225 g/8 oz parsnips or young turnips (scrubbed if parsnips, peeled if turnips), sliced*
*225 g/8 oz cooking apples, peeled and sliced*
*salt and pepper*
*1 teaspoon dark brown sugar*
*300 ml /½ pint cider or white wine and water mixed*
*225 g/8 oz wholemeal shortcrust pastry (see page 161)*
*1 egg, beaten*

Melt the butter in a pan and fry the onions and parsnips or turnips until they are lightly coloured but not burnt. Put a layer of this mixture in the bottom of a 20-cm/8-inch pie dish (lined with foil if it is to be frozen) and cover it with half the ham, then cover the ham with the apple. Sprinkle with freshly ground black pepper, but no salt unless the ham is very mild, and the sugar. Cover the apple with the rest of the ham and then the vegetables. Pour in the cider or wine and water mixture. Roll out the pastry and cover the pie, using the scraps to decorate. Brush with beaten egg and bake in a moderately hot oven (190°C/375°F/Gas Mark 5) for 25–30 minutes or until the pastry is golden and cooked. Remove from the oven and serve at once.

The pie is better frozen uncooked and then cooked on defrosting. Open freeze, then pack in a well-sealed bag.

Defrost at room temperature and cook as above.

# Creole Jambalaya

*Serves 4*                                              *2 months*

Although New Orleans is always associated with seafood, one version of the famous Creole Jambalaya uses no fish at all – and is therefore much kinder to English pockets! It freezes well, but should not be left frozen too long.

*175 g/6 oz spiced smoked sausage or good pork sausage, diced*
*175 g/6 oz cooked ham, diced*
*2 tablespoons lard or bacon fat*
*2 medium green peppers, deseeded and chopped or roughly sliced*
*6 large spring onions, cleaned and chopped*
*2 large onions, peeled and sliced*
*350 g/12 oz brown rice*
*2 × 400 g/14 oz cans tomatoes*
*2 tablespoons tomato paste*
*salt and pepper*

Melt the lard or bacon fat in a large heavy-based pan and lightly fry the peppers and onions, both spring and ordinary, until they begin to brown and crisp up at the edges. Meanwhile, cook the rice in plenty of fast-boiling water for about 10 minutes or until it is just cooked; drain it thoroughly.

Lightly fry the smoked sausage in its own fat, then add to the pan of vegetables with the rice and ham.

Add the tomatoes, roughly chopped, with their juice and the tomato paste. Stir the mixture well and cook it gently for 30–45 minutes, by which time all the extra juice should be absorbed. Season with salt and pepper (you may not need much salt if the ham and sausage are salty) and serve warm.

To freeze, cool completely and pack in a well-sealed container.

Defrost at room temperature or in a microwave and serve warm or cold.

# An 'English' Curry

*Serves 6*                                              *3 months*

Now that good Indian food can be easily obtained all over the West we have learnt that there is no such thing as 'English' curry. However, in the days of our ignorance many of us brewed up an excellent concoction with the remains of the joint and liberal dips into the curry powder and the chutney pot, which it seems a shame to lose. My 'curry' can be based on beef, veal, lamb, pork or. chicken and lends itself to unscheduled additions of almost any kind!

*Kidneys Casseroled with Tomato and Red Pepper (see page 90)*

350 g/12 oz beef, veal, lamb, pork or chicken, cooked
3 tablespoons vegetable oil
2 onions, roughly chopped
2 carrots, scrubbed and diced
25 g/1 oz ginger root, peeled and finely chopped
1 teaspoon oregano
1 teaspoon turmeric
½ teaspoon ground cinnamon
½ teaspoon ginger
2–4 tablespoons curry powder
6 runner beans, chopped, or ½ cauliflower, broken
   into florets
½ aubergine, diced
450 ml/¾ pint water or 240 ml/8 fl oz water and
   240 ml/8 fl oz red wine
salt and pepper
25 g/1 oz raisins or currants
1–2 tablespoons chutney (mango or other)
½ cooking or 1 tart eating apple, peeled and diced
25 g/1 oz whole blanched almonds

Heat the oil in a heavy-based pan and briskly fry the onions, carrots and ginger until they start to turn colour. Add the herbs and spices and stir well. Cook for a couple of minutes, then add the beans or cauliflower, the aubergine and the meat. Cook everything together for 5 minutes, then add the water or water and wine mixed. Season lightly with salt and pepper, cover and simmer for 25–30 minutes. Add the raisins or currants and the chutney and cook for another couple of minutes. Add the apple and almonds, cook for a further minute or two to slightly soften the apple, adjust the seasoning to taste and serve with lots of steamed rice and a salad.

To freeze, cool completely before adding the apple and almonds and freeze in a well-sealed container.

Defrost at room temperature or in a microwave. Reheat in a pan or microwave and finish as above.

# Calves' Liver or Lambs' Kidneys with Apple and Cream

*Serves 4*                              *2–3 months*

Do be careful to buy the right liver or kidneys for this dish. Lambs' and pigs' livers and pigs' kidneys are excellent for pies and pâtés but are too strong tasting for this relatively delicate sauce.

> *225 g/8 oz calves' liver or lambs' kidneys, trimmed and sliced*
> *25 g/1 oz butter*
> *1 medium onion, peeled and very finely chopped*
> *2 tablespoons seasoned flour*
> *100 g/4 oz button mushrooms, wiped and halved if large*
> *1 medium cooking apple, peeled, cored and finely chopped*
> *90 ml/3 fl oz medium white wine*
> *120 ml/4 fl oz water*
> *90 ml/3 fl oz double cream*
> *juice of ½–1 lemon*
> *salt and pepper*

Melt the butter in a large pan and gently cook the onion until it begins to soften. Coat the liver or kidneys in the seasoned flour. Add the meat to the onions along with the mushrooms and any flour that is left over. Cook them all gently together for a few minutes, then add the apple, wine and water. Cover the dish and cook slowly for 15 minutes or until the liver or kidneys are just cooked. If the dish is to be frozen, it should be done at this point. If it is to be eaten at once, add the cream and the lemon juice and seasoning to taste. Serve the dish at once with plenty of fresh noodles or brown rice.

If the liver or kidneys are to be frozen, cool them once they have finished cooking, then pack and freeze them, in the sauce, in a well-sealed container.

Defrost at room temperature (a microwave might overcook the meat) and reheat very gently in the sauce in a pan or a microwave. Add the cream and finish the dish as above.

# Tongue and Ginger Pancakes

*Serves 6*                              *3 months*

This is a poor European's version of that wonderful Chinese duck dish where you roll pieces of crispy duck in a pancake and dip it in a spicy soy sauce. The three elements should be frozen separately and amalgamated on defrosting.

> *12 reasonably large pancakes (see page 162)*
> *12 thin slices cooked tongue*
> *40 g/1½ oz butter or sunflower oil*
> *12 spring onions, finely chopped*
> *50–75 g/2–3 oz fresh ginger root, peeled and finely chopped*
> *4 cloves garlic, very finely chopped*
> *2 tablespoons dark brown sugar*
> *1 tablespoon soy sauce*
> *6 tablespoons wine vinegar*
> *300 ml /½ pint white wine*
> *salt and pepper*

Lay out the pancakes (they should be large enough to cover the slices of tongue) and cover each with a slice of tongue. Heat the butter or oil in a heavy-based pan and lightly fry the spring onions, ginger and garlic until they are softening and beginning to colour. Add the sugar, let it melt, then add the soy sauce, vinegar and white wine. Bring the mixture to the boil and simmer for 5 minutes. Season to taste with salt and pepper.

Spread some sauce evenly over the slices of tongue; do not worry if there is quite a lot left. Roll up the pancakes fairly loosely, put them in a dish and heat them through carefully in a microwave for 4 minutes or covered in a moderate oven (180°C/350°F/Gas Mark 4) for 20 minutes. Reheat the rest of the sauce and spoon it over the pancakes just before serving. They are delicious with some stir-fried Chinese cabbage or beanshoots.

If the dish is to be frozen, layer the pancakes with some plastic cling film or greaseproof paper and pack in well-sealed bags. Preferably (unless you cook and press your own tongue) buy the tongue fresh; if you need to freeze it, do so in the piece or in slices in *very* well-sealed bags. Freeze the sauce in small containers.

Defrost at room temperature, then amalgamate and heat as above.

# Sausage, Bacon and Bean Pot

*Serves 2*                         *3 months*

Since the bean pot keeps and freezes well, it is worth making a good batch.

> *2 fat or 4 thin pork sausages, halved or quartered*
> *100 g/4 oz dried butter beans, haricot beans, split peas or lentils*
> *a little butter, margarine, dripping or bacon fat*
> *2–3 rashers bacon, roughly chopped*
> *1 large chopped onion, or 1 tablespoon dried onion*
> *2 teaspoons made English mustard*
> *300 ml/½ pint water or water and wine or beer mixed*
> *1 cube chicken stock*
> *1 × 75 g/3 oz can tomatoes*
> *salt and pepper*

If you are using butter or haricot beans, you should either put them to soak overnight in cold water, then throw away the water, or bring them to the boil in unsalted water and cook them until they are just getting soft, then drain them. Split peas or lentils will not need soaking.

Put the fat, sausages and bacon in the bottom of a heavy saucepan – an electric frying pan (multi-cooker) would do well, or even a slow cooker. Let them fry gently, stirring now and then, over a low heat until they are nicely browned. Add the onion, the beans or peas, the mustard mixed with the water (or water and wine or beer), the chicken stock cube and the tomatoes with their juice. Mix well and bring to the boil. Simmer very gently for 45–60 minutes or until the beans are cooked and most of the liquid is absorbed. Season to taste with salt and pepper.

To freeze, cool completely and freeze in a well–sealed container.

Defrost at room temperature or in a microwave and reheat in a moderate oven (180°C/350°F/Gas Mark 4) for 30–45 minutes or in a microwave for about 8 minutes.

# Lasagne

*Serves 6–8*                     *9 months*

Precooked complete pasta dishes are worth freezing as they are slow to prepare; where the pasta is merely combined with a sauce there is no point in trying to freeze it. Use the precooked lasagne if you can get it, as it saves having to cook the sheets of pasta. Serve it as a main course or as a starter.

> *Bolognese sauce for 6 (see page 156)*
> *100 g/4 oz precooked green lasagne sheets*
> *25 g/1 oz butter*
> *25 g/1 oz flour*
> *300 ml/½ pint milk*
> *150 ml/¼ pint white wine*
> *60 ml/2 fl oz double cream*
> *50 g/2 oz grated Ricotta or other crumbly white cheese*
> *1 egg plus 1 egg yolk*
> *salt and pepper*

Layer the Bolognese meat mixture with the pasta in an ovenproof dish (lined with foil if it is to be frozen) until both are used up, ideally starting and finishing with a meat layer.

Meanwhile, melt the butter in a pan, add the flour, cook for a few minutes, stirring continuously, then gradually add the milk, white wine and cream. Cook gently until the sauce thickens. Add the cheese and continue to cook until it is melted. Remove the pan from the heat, stir in the eggs and season to taste with salt and pepper. Pour the sauce over the lasagne and bake it in a moderate oven (180°C/350°F/Gas Mark 4) for 30 minutes or until it is heated right through and the top is lightly browned. Serve at once.

To freeze, cool the dish completely, then open freeze. Remove the lasagne from the dish and pack in well-sealed bags.

Defrost partially, remove the foil lining and drop back into its original dish. Continue to defrost the lasagne in a microwave or at room temperature and reheat in a moderate oven (180°C/350°F/Gas Mark 4) for 20–30 minutes, or in a microwave.

# Sausage and Aubergine Casserole

*Serves 6*                                    *6 months*

This is a tasty and filling casserole which I found in America; it freezes excellently.

*450 g/1 lb good quality sausagemeat*
*2 medium aubergines, thickly sliced lengthways*
*6–8 tablespoons olive or sunflower oil*
*15 g/½ oz butter or low fat margarine*
*½ bunch spring onions, wiped and chopped*
*225 g/8 oz mushrooms, roughly chopped*
*1 tablespoon wholegrain or French mustard*
*150 ml/¼ pint red wine*
*1 tablespoon Worcestershire sauce*
*salt and pepper*
*225–350 g/8–12 oz tomatoes, sliced*
*50 g/2 oz grated, well-flavoured Cheddar cheese*
*50 g/2 oz brown breadcrumbs*

Heat the oil in a heavy-based pan and fry the aubergines until they are lightly browned on each side. In a separate pan, melt the butter and briskly fry the sausagemeat until it begins to colour. Add the chopped spring onions and mushrooms and cook together for a couple of minutes. Add the mustard, wine and Worcestershire sauce and a *little* salt and pepper

Lay half the aubergines in the bottom of an ovenproof dish (lined with foil if you intend to freeze it), cover them with the sausage mixture, then with a second layer of the aubergines. Cover the aubergines with the sliced tomatoes. Mix together the cheese and breadcrumbs and sprinkle them over the top of the tomatoes. Bake the casserole in a moderate oven (180°C/350°F/Gas Mark 4) for 30 minutes or until the top is well browned. Serve at once.

To freeze, cool the casserole completely and open freeze. Once frozen, remove from its dish and pack in a well–sealed bag.

To defrost, remove the foil and drop the casserole back into its dish. Defrost at room temperature or in a microwave and reheat.

# Spicy Sausage Cakes or Balls

*Serves 6*                                    *6 months*

If you want to make sausage and mash or cocktail sausages a bit more interesting, you can spice them up. This combination is based on a seventeenth-century recipe, but feel free to experiment with other herbs or spices. The sausages can also be served with a dip – a herby mustard mayonnaise is good. If you decide to make this into cocktail sausages you will have enough for 20 people.

*450 kg/1 lb good quality pork sausagemeat or finely minced pork*
*1 onion, very finely chopped*
*1 teaspoon each ground ginger, black pepper, coriander and nutmeg*
*2 teaspoons each dried (or 3 teaspoons fresh chopped) thyme, savory and parsley or chervil*
*2–3 tablespoons wholemeal or wholewheat flour*
*25–50 g/1–2 oz butter or low fat margarine*

Mix the onion, herbs and spices *very* thoroughly into the minced meat. Form the mixture into small balls, sausages or cakes and roll in the flour. Fry them gently in the butter until they are cooked through and lightly browned all over for about 3–8 minutes, depending on size. Serve at once, hot or cold, with or without a dip.

To freeze, cool them completely, then freeze in well-sealed bags.

Defrost at room temperature, in a microwave or from frozen in a moderate oven (180°C/350°F/Gas Mark 4). They are better if recrisped in the oven before being served.

# Kidneys Casseroled with Tomato and Red Pepper

*Serves 6*                                    *2 months*

This is a nice, bright dish. You can add a little soured cream on defrosting if you want to 'posh it up' a bit.

*12 lambs' kidneys, halved with their middles removed*
*25 g/1 oz butter or low fat margarine*
*100 g/4 oz onions, finely sliced*

1 medium red pepper, deseeded and chopped
3 large tomatoes, skinned, deseeded and roughly
    chopped
150 ml/¼ pint dry white wine
salt and pepper
150 ml/¼ pint soured cream (optional)

Melt the fat in a flat pan and gently cook the onions and pepper until they are nearly soft. Add the halved kidneys and continue to cook gently for about 5 minutes – the kidneys should still be pink in the middle. Add the tomatoes and wine, bring to the boil and simmer for a further 5–10 minutes. Season to taste and add the soured cream if you wish to use it.

To freeze, cool the dish completely before adding the cream and freeze in well-sealed containers.

Defrost at room temperature or, with care, in a microwave and reheat gently. Adjust the seasoning and add the cream if you want to use it.

# Moussaka

*Serves 6*                          *6 months*

Like all traditional dishes, there are many different versions of moussaka using either lamb or beef; I am not sure whether my version classes as 'classic' or merely mine! If the dish is to be frozen, a light béchamel sauce is safer than the more authentic egg-based sauce. If you can get it, goat's milk gives a rather nice, sour, Greek flavour.

1 kg/2 lb finely chopped lamb or beef, cooked or
    uncooked
6–8 tablespoons olive or good vegetable oil
350 g/12 oz onions, reasonably finely chopped
3 cloves garlic, finely chopped
1 teaspoon ground cumin
2 sprigs fresh rosemary, chopped, or 1 teaspoon dried
salt and pepper
2 tablespoons tomato purée
350 g/12 oz chopped fresh tomatoes with 150 ml/
    ¼ pint white wine, or 1 can (400 g/14 oz) Italian
    tomatoes, chopped, with their juice
2 tablespoons raisins (optional)
1 kg/2 lb aubergines, wiped and sliced in rounds
    1 cm/½ inch thick
25 g/1 oz butter
25 g/1 oz flour

450 ml/¾ pint milk (see above)
100 g/4 oz fetta or crumbly white English cheese
    (Wensleydale/Caerphilly/White Cheshire)
2 tablespoons soured cream

Heat 2 tablespoons of the oil in a large pan and briskly fry the onions and garlic until both are lightly coloured. Add the chopped meat (this can be chopped in a food processor but do not pulverize it) and continue to cook for a minute or so if it is cooked, or for 4–5 minutes if it is raw. Add the herbs, seasoning, tomato purée and the tomatoes and the white wine, or the canned tomatoes with their juice. Also add the raisins if you are using them. Bring the mixture to the boil, cover and simmer for about 15 minutes.

Meanwhile, using a little of the remaining oil at a time, fry the aubergine slices in a large and heavy pan until they are well browned but not burnt on both sides. Set them aside. Melt the butter in a third pan, stir in the flour, cook for a minute or two, then gradually add the milk and continue to stir and cook until the sauce thickens. Add the cheese and cook until it melts, then add the soured cream and season to taste.

To amalgamate, lay half the aubergine slices in the bottom of a pie or casserole dish (if it is to be frozen, you may wish to line it with foil). Adjust the seasoning of the meat mixture to taste, then spoon it over the aubergines with all its juice. Lay the remaining aubergines over the meat and pour the sauce over the whole thing.

If it is to be eaten at once, put the casserole, uncovered, into a moderate oven (180°C/350°F/Gas Mark 4) for about 30 minutes to allow all the ingredients to heat through again and the top to brown. Serve it bubbling from the oven with a really crisp green salad and crusty brown bread.

If it is to be frozen, allow the dish to cool completely after pouring over the sauce, then open freeze. Once frozen, it can be removed from the dish and packed in a well-sealed bag.

Defrost at room temperature or in a microwave (having first removed the foil and turned the moussaka back into its dish), then reheat in a moderate oven (180°C/350°F/Gas Mark 4) for about 45 minutes from cold, or in a microwave. If you use a microwave, you may want to brown the top of the dish lightly under the grill. Serve as above.

# A 'Battered' Meat Loaf

*Serves 6*                                        *4–6 months*

This is the most delicious way of using up the remains of a joint – based, surprisingly enough, on a sixteenth-century recipe. The 'battered' element is the cheesy batter with which it is coated.

   *350 g/12 oz cold meat (beef, lamb, ham, pork, etc.)*
   *1 egg yolk*
   *50 g/2 oz flour*
   *100 ml/3½ fl oz beer (real ale if possible but any beer will do)*
   *175 g/6 oz grated well-flavoured cheese (Cheddar is ideal)*
   *1 onion, roughly chopped*
   *15 g/½ oz butter*
   *1 tart eating apple or ½ cooking apple, peeled and roughly chopped*
   *50 g/2 oz brown breadcrumbs*
   *1 tablespoon wholegrain mustard*
   *1 teaspoon allspice*
   *2 eggs*
   *2 tablespoons plain yoghurt*
   *salt and pepper*

Beat the egg yolk, flour and beer in a food processor or mixer to make a batter and set aside. Meanwhile, chop the meat reasonably finely in a processor or mincer and mix it with 100 g/4 oz of the cheese. Fry the onion in the butter until it is lightly browned and add to the mixture along with the apple, breadcrumbs, mustard and allspice. Mix the eggs with the yoghurt and mix well into the meat; season fairly liberally.

Form the mixture into a loaf shape on a baking tray or an ovenproof serving dish; if it is to be frozen, it would be wise to line the dish with foil. Beat half the remaining cheese into the batter and spoon half of this over the loaf. Bake it in a moderately hot oven (190°C/375°F/Gas Mark 5) for 15 minutes. Remove from the oven, spoon over the rest of the batter, sprinkle the remaining cheese on top and return to the oven for another 15 minutes or until the top is nicely browned. Meanwhile, the extra batter will have dripped down the side and made a crunchy layer around the loaf. Serve either hot or cold.

To freeze, cool entirely, open freeze, then remove from the dish and pack for storage.

Defrost at room temperature or in a microwave. The loaf can be eaten as soon as it is defrosted but the batter topping will not be crisp. Even if you want to eat it cold, it is better to reheat it in a moderately hot oven (190°C/375°F/Gas Mark 5) for 10–15 minutes just to crisp the batter, then allow it to cool and serve with a green salad.

# Spicy Pork Kebabs

*Serves 6*                                        *6 months*

   *450 g/1 lb pork fillet*
   *2 small onions, finely chopped*
   *2 dried red chillies, finely chopped, or 2 tablespoons chilli paste*
   *2 tablespoons Worcestershire sauce*
   *2 tablespoons tomato paste*
   *1 tablespoon honey*
   *2 tablespoons red wine vinegar*
   *4 tablespoons vegetable oil*
   *3 tablespoons medium sherry*
   *2 large handfuls parsley, finely chopped*
   *½ teaspoon salt*
   *plenty of black pepper*
   *100 g/4 oz mushrooms*
   *1 green pepper, cut into large squares*
   *3 tomatoes, quartered*

Cut the pork into reasonable-sized chunks. Mix all the other ingredients apart from the mushrooms, pepper and tomatoes in a bowl, add the pork and leave to marinate for 2–24 hours.

When you are ready to cook the kebabs, take the pork out of the marinade and thread it alternately with pieces of mushroom, pepper and tomato onto kebab sticks. Cook either under a hot grill or on a charcoal barbecue, basting periodically with the remains of the marinade, for 5–7 minutes or until the pork is cooked. Whereas with lamb or beef you need to get the outside crisp but need not worry about the middle being too cooked, with pork you must be sure the meat is cooked through. Serve with lots of brown rice.

If you wish to freeze the kebabs, it is best to do so in their marinade.

Defrost at room temperature or in a microwave.

NOTE: This recipe would also work very well with beef or lamb.

# Sweetbreads with Cream and Anchovies

*Serves 6*                                   *3 months*

The combination of anchovies and orange juice in this recipe dates from the eighteenth century and gives an added dimension to the sweetbreads without killing their own delicate flavour.

> 750 g /1½ lb calves' or lambs' sweetbreads, cleaned
>   and prepared
> 50 g/2 oz butter
> 4 anchovies, finely chopped
> 6–8 spring onions, finely chopped
> 1 heaped tablespoon flour
> 300 ml/½ pint veal or chicken stock
> 120 ml/4 fl oz dry white wine
> juice of 2 oranges
> 1 small sprig fresh rosemary, or ½ teaspoon dried
>   rosemary leaves, chopped
> 150–180 ml/5–6 fl oz double cream
> a little salt and pepper

If you have time, soak the sweetbreads in acidulated water for 30–45 minutes; take them out and dry them thoroughly with kitchen paper towel.

Melt the butter in a large, heavy pan and gently fry the anchovies and spring onions until the latter are beginning to soften. Add the sweetbreads and fry them gently on both sides for a couple of minutes. Add the flour, stir for a minute or two, then add the stock, wine, orange juice and sprig of rosemary. Cover the pan and simmer gently for 15 minutes.

Remove the rosemary sprig and add most of the cream with a little seasoning – the anchovies may already have given the sauce quite enough flavour. Taste and add more cream if you think the sauce is too thick – or too strong! Serve at once with rice or noodles and a green vegetable or salad.

If the dish is to be frozen, cool the sweetbreads completely once they are cooked and before you add the cream. Freeze in a well-sealed container.

Defrost at room temperature or in a microwave and reheat gently in a pan. Add the cream and finish the dish as above.

# Macaroni Pie

*Serves 6*                                   *3–4 months*

This pie can be made with fresh or dried pasta and has lots of flavour; it really only needs a salad with it to make a complete meal.

> 350 g/12 oz macaroni
> 2 tablespoons olive or vegetable oil
> 350 g/12 oz onions, roughly chopped
> 3 large cloves garlic, finely chopped or crushed
> 3 dried red chillies, finely chopped
> 175 g/6 oz rashers bacon, roughly chopped
> 75 g/3 oz mushrooms, sliced
> 225 g/8 oz good garlic sausage, chorizo or good
>   quality salami
> 2 tablespoons tomato purée
> 1 × 400 g/14 oz can tomatoes
> 360 ml/12 fl oz dry white wine
> salt and pepper
> 50–75 g/2–3 oz grated Parmesan or mature Cheddar
>   cheese

Cook the macaroni in plenty of fast-boiling water for 3–4 minutes if fresh; 9–11 minutes if dried – in both cases the pasta should be 'al dente' not mushy. Drain.

Meanwhile, heat the oil in a heavy-based pan and fry the onions, garlic, chillies and bacon until they start to colour. Add the mushrooms and sausage or salami and cook gently for 4–5 minutes. Add the tomato purée, the tomatoes with their juice, and then the wine. Mix them well together, add the drained macaroni and season to taste. Turn the mixture into a pie dish (if it is to be frozen it should be lined with foil) and sprinkle the top with the cheese. Bake for 20 minutes in a moderate oven (180°C/350°F/Gas Mark 4) to amalgamate the flavours and brown the cheese. Serve at once with a good salad.

If the pie is to be frozen, cool completely then open freeze. Remove from the dish and pack for storage.

To defrost, remove the foil and drop the pie back into the dish. Defrost at room temperature or in a microwave and reheat for about 25 minutes in a moderate oven (180°C/350°F/Gas Mark 4) before serving as above.

# VEGETABLES AND VEGETARIAN DISHES

## Chick Peas with Chillies and Green Peppers

*Serves 6*                    *4–6 months*

This is an excellent vegetarian recipe which can double as a lunch dish or a vegetable for those who still like a little meat with their vegetables.

 350 g/12 oz chick peas
 3 fresh green chillies, or 6 small dried red ones
 4 tablespoons olive or vegetable oil
 3 medium onions, peeled and roughly chopped
 3 cloves garlic, finely chopped or crushed
 2 large green and 1 large red pepper, cored, deseeded and roughly chopped
 3 large tomatoes, peeled and roughly chopped
 juice of 2 lemons
 salt and pepper

Soak the chick peas overnight. Drain them and put them in a saucepan with approximately 1.2 litres/2 pints cold water. Bring to the boil and simmer for 40 minutes or until the peas are tender but not mushy. Drain them and set them on one side.

If the chillies are fresh, core, seed and chop them roughly; if they are dried, slice them very finely. In either case, take care not to rub your face with your hands until you have washed the burning chilli oils off. Heat the oil in a heavy-based pan, add the onions, garlic, chillies and peppers and fry them gently for 5 minutes without burning.

Add the chick peas, tomatoes, lemon juice and seasoning. Cover and simmer for 20 minutes. Adjust the seasoning to taste and serve either hot or cold.

Freeze, when cooled, in a well-sealed container.

Defrost at room temperature or in a microwave. Serve warm or cold.

## Braised Red Cabbage Salad

*Serves 6*               *2–3 months*

*750 g/1½ lb red cabbage, thinly sliced*
*approx 2 tablespoons olive oil*
*1 medium cooking apple, peeled and cubed*
*45 ml/1½ fl oz red wine vinegar*
*120 ml/4 fl oz beef or veal stock*
*salt and pepper*

Sweat the cabbage in the oil in a large flat pan for about 10 minutes. Add the apple, vinegar and stock, cover and continue to sweat for a further 10 minutes or until the cabbage is cooked but still crunchy. Season to taste with salt and pepper. The cabbage can be served hot or left to cool and used cold.

To freeze, cool completely and pack in well-sealed containers.

Defrost at room temperature or in a microwave.

NOTE: See Francatelli's Braised Beef à la Polonaise (page 66).

*Chick Peas with Chillies and Green Peppers, Vine Leaves Stuffed with Potgourri Milanese (see page 96) and Spiced Aubergine Salad (see page 97)*

# Macaroni Cheese with Tomatoes

*Serves 4*          *6 months*

Macaroni cheese is such an old favourite that it is worth keeping a stock in the freezer for cold winter nights when you can't be bothered to cook anything else! The addition of tomatoes stops it being too 'claggy'.

> 450 g/1 lb macaroni, wholewheat if possible
> 25 g/1 oz butter
> 4–6 rashers bacon, derinded and roughly chopped
> 2 onions, roughly chopped
> 1 tablespoon flour
> 600 ml/1 pint milk
> 150 ml/¼ pint dry white wine
> 175 g/6 oz well-flavoured cheese (Parmesan, Cheddar, etc.), grated
> 4–6 tomatoes, skinned or not, as you prefer, and roughly chopped
> salt and pepper

Cook the macaroni in plenty of fast-boiling water for 3–4 minutes if it is fresh; 10–12 minutes if it is dried. Taste it to make sure it is still *'al dente'*, then drain it throughly.

Meanwhile, melt the butter in a pan and gently cook the bacon and onions until they are beginning to colour. Add the flour, stir for a couple of minutes, then gradually add the milk and the wine. Cook gently until the sauce thickens, then add the cheese and tomatoes. Cook until the cheese melts and the tomatoes are warmed through, and season to taste. Stir in the macaroni, continue to cook until the macaroni is well heated, then turn into a warmed ovenproof serving dish and put it under a hot grill for a few minutes to brown the top before serving.

If it is to be frozen, turn the macaroni into a well–sealed container rather than an ovenproof dish and freeze.

Defrost at room temperature or in a microwave, reheat in a microwave or in a moderate oven (180°C/350°F/Gas Mark 4), covered, then brown under the grill before serving.

# Vine Leaves Stuffed with Potgourri Milanese

*Serves 6*          *3 months*

If you want to turn this into a vegetarian dish, the bacon rashers can be replaced with 75 g/3 oz salted peanuts and the chicken stock with vegetable stock or wine and water.

> 30–36 vine leaves
> 175 g/6 oz potgourri or cracked wheat
> 40 g/1½ oz butter or low fat margarine
> 175 g/6 oz onions, chopped
> 75 g/3 oz rashers bacon, roughly chopped
> 175 g/6 oz mushrooms (preferably open and not button), finely chopped
> approx 60 ml/2 fl oz dry white wine
> salt and freshly ground black pepper
> approx 300 ml/½ pint chicken stock or mixed water and dry white wine

Soften and swell the potgourri or cracked wheat according to the instructions on the packet – this involves adding the specified amount of boiling water.

Meanwhile, melt the butter or low fat margarine in a pan and fry the onions and bacon until both are softened and lightly browned. Add the mushrooms and cook for a further couple of minutes. Add the potgourri or cracked wheat and the wine, cook together for a couple of minutes, then season to taste with salt and freshly ground black pepper.

Spread out the vines leaves, fill each with a tablespoonful of the mixture, then fold them into small parcels and place them in an ovenproof dish or casserole. Pour over the chicken stock or water and wine, cover and cook in a moderate oven (180°C/350°F/Gas Mark 4) for 30 minutes. Serve either hot or cold.

To freeze, pack in well-sealed containers, just covered with stock.

Defrost at room temperature or in a microwave and reheat, drained of stock and covered, in a moderate oven (180°C/350°F/Gas Mark 4) or in a microwave.

# A Wholemeal Dumpling

*Serves 4*                                                    *6 months*

Dumplings are a sadly neglected alternative to potatoes or Yorkshire pudding with the Sunday joint and little dumplings are delicious in a soup or stew. The dumplings should be frozen in their wrappings or they are liable to fall apart!

> 100 g/4 oz wholemeal flour
> 50 g/2 oz fresh brown breadcrumbs
> 50 g/2 oz beef suet (fresh is nice, but 'packet' is quite acceptable)
> 50 g/2 oz butter
> 40 g/1½ oz raisins (optional)
> grated rind of 1 small lemon
> sea salt and freshly ground black pepper
> 240 ml/8 fl oz milk
> approx 1.2 litres/2 pints stock

Crumble the flour, breadcrumbs, suet and butter as though you were making pastry. Add the raisins, if you are using them, and lemon rind, season with salt and pepper and add the milk. Mix the whole lot together well – it will make a fairly 'wet' mixture. Put the dumpling mixture in the middle of a well-floured cloth – a piece of muslin or a new dishcloth will do fine – and tie it securely into a ball. Alternatively, make 4 individual dumplings and tie each separately. Submerge the dumpling in the stock (or in a soup or stockpot if you happen to have one) and simmer it gently for 30–45 minutes, depending on whether you have individual dumplings or just one dumpling. Remove the dumpling, drain it and untie it carefully. Serve it with the joint and lots of good gravy.

You can also make the dumplings in teaspoon sizes and float them on top of a casserole or stew pot. In this case they will not need to be wrapped, but should be simmered gently on top of the casserole for 15–20 minutes.

The dumplings can be frozen before they are cooked, either in one container or in their muslin bags. Mini dumplings can be open frozen and then packed in well-sealed bags.

Defrost as slowly as possible to prevent disintegration and cook as above.

# Spiced Aubergine Salad

*Serves 6*                                                *2–3 months*

The ginger, chilli and soy sauce make this a very Oriental-tasting salad. If you do not want to serve it as a salad, cut the aubergine pieces a little smaller, impale them on cocktails sticks and serve the pieces, with the sauce spooned over, as a cocktail snack.

> 1 large aubergine
> 1½ tablespoons soy sauce
> 2 tablespoons red wine vinegar
> 1 tablespoon sugar
> a pinch of salt
> 1 teaspoon sesame oil (if available)
> ½ tablespoon groundnut oil (if available), or 1 tablespoon vegetable oil
> ½ tablespoon finely chopped garlic
> 2 tablespoons fresh ginger, peeled and finely chopped
> ½ fresh green chilli, seeds removed and finely chopped
> ½ green pepper, seeds removed and finely chopped
> 15 g/½ oz sesame seeds, lightly toasted

Wash the aubergine and trim off the stem. If the salad is to be frozen, peel the aubergine as the skin can become tough in the freezer; if it is to be eaten at once, you needn't bother. Cut into whatever size you need to get it into your steamer. Steam it for 10–15 minutes or until the flesh is soft. Cool the flesh slightly and then dice it into aproximately 2.5-cm/1 inch squares.

While the aubergine is cooking, combine the soy sauce, vinegar, sugar, salt and sesame oil and set aside. Heat the groundnut or vegetable oil in a heavy pan and fry the garlic, ginger, chilli and green pepper very quickly, stirring constantly – take care not to burn them. Add the soy and vinegar mixture, bring to the boil, cool slightly and then pour it over the aubergine pieces.

Cool completely, then pack in containers to freeze.

Defrost at room temperature or in a microwave. Serve sprinkled with sesame seeds.

*Vegetarian Stuffed Peppers*

# Celeriac and Spinach Bake

*Serves 4–6*                                              *3 months*

This is a rich and delicious vegetable or a vegetarian main course for four.

> *1 kg/2 lb cleaned and peeled celeriac, diced*
> *60–90 ml/2–3 fl oz double cream*
> *25–50 g/1–2 oz butter*
> *salt, pepper and nutmeg*
> *750 g/1½ lb fresh spinach, washed*
> *40 g/1½ oz browned, flaked almonds*

Cook the celeriac in a steamer or a microwave until the pieces are cooked without being mushy. Purée them in a food processor, liquidizer or *mouli légumes* and add cream, butter, salt, pepper and nutmeg to taste. Meanwhile, cook the spinach (in the water that clings to its leaves) on the hob or in a microwave until it is just cooked. Drain it very thoroughly, squeezing as much water as possible from it with a spoon.

Spoon half the celeriac purée into the bottom of an ovenproof cassserole, then lay the spinach over the top. Sprinkle half the almonds over the spinach, and cover them with the rest of the celeriac. Dot the top with butter and sprinkle with the rest of the almonds. Cook for 20 minutes in a moderate oven (180°C/350°F /Gas Mark 4) to reheat the vegetables and just brown the top.

If it is to be frozen, line the dish with foil and do not reheat in the oven after the layering has been completed. Open freeze, then remove from the dish to store well packed in a polythene bag.

Defrost at room temperature or in a microwave and reheat as above.

# Vegetarian Stuffed Peppers

*Serves 6*                                              *4–6 months*

If you like your peppers crisp rather than soft, even when stuffed, it is better to make and freeze the stuffing on its own (ideally leaving out the peanuts as well) and fill the peppers just before serving them. However, if you want the whole thing done in advance, it works perfectly well.

*6 green or red peppers, halved and deseeded*
*25 g/1 oz butter*
*2 tablespoons vegetable oil*
*175 g/6 oz onions or leeks, finely chopped.*
*175 g/6 oz carrots, scrubbed and diced small*
*3 cloves garlic, finely chopped or crushed*
*175 g/6 oz mushrooms (open if possible; otherwise button), halved or quartered*
*225 g/8 oz red or brown lentils*
*3 tomatoes, roughly chopped.*
*450 ml/¾ pint water or water and white or red wine mixed*
*a generous handful of parsley, roughly chopped*
*175 g/6 oz dry roast peanuts*
*salt, pepper and soy sauce*

Melt the butter and oil in a pan and briskly fry the onions or leeks, carrots and garlic until they start to colour. Add the mushrooms and cook for a couple more minutes, then add the lentils, tomatoes and liquid. Cover the pot and simmer for about 35 minutes or until the lentils are soft without being mushy. Add the parsley and peanuts, stir and cook for a minute or two, then season to taste with salt, pepper and soy sauce, but remember that both the peanuts and the soy sauce are salty and that freezing emphasizes saltiness, so go lightly with the salt pot. Pile the mixture into the pepper shells and put them into a hot oven (200°C/400°F/Gas Mark 6) for 5–10 minutes just to warm through the pepper shells. Alternatively, they can be served cold, in which case allow the filling to cool, then fill the shells and serve.

If the dish is to be frozen, it is better to freeze the filling separately, without the peanuts, and to season only lightly.

Defrost at room temperature or in a microwave, warm the mixture through if you wish, add the peanuts and adjust the seasoning to taste. Fill the pepper shells as above.

*Celeriac and Spinach Bake*

# Vegetarian Pancakes

*Serves 4*          *6 months*

   *8 medium-sized pancakes (see page 162)*
   *1 tablespoon good vegetable oil*
   *1 large onion, peeled and chopped*
   *1–2 cloves garlic, finely chopped or crushed*
   *1 green or red pepper, deseeded and chopped*
   *½ green chilli, deseeded and finely chopped*
    *(optional)*
   *75 g/3 oz fennel or celery, finely chopped*
   *75 g/3 oz mushrooms, chopped*
   *3 tomatoes, cored and roughly chopped*
   *450 g/1 lb courgettes, wiped*
   *salt and pepper*
   *approx 1 tablespoon mushroom ketchup*
   *25 g/1 oz butter*
   *½ tablespoon flour*
   *approx 300 ml/½ pint chicken or vegetable stock*
   *50 g/2 oz grated cheese – Parmesan or Gruyère for*
    *preference (optional)*

Heat the oil in a large pan and fry the onion, garlic, pepper, chilli and fennel or celery until they are beginning to soften and are lightly coloured. Add the mushrooms, then the tomatoes and 100 g/4 oz of the courgettes, chopped fairly small. Cover the pan and simmer for 5–10 minutes or until the vegetables are *just* cooked, not soggy. Season to taste with salt, pepper and mushroom ketchup (you could use Worcestershire sauce as an alternative).

Meanwhile, cook the remaining courgettes, sliced, in the butter until they are soft. Remove them, with a slotted spoon, into a food processor or liquidizer and purée them. Add the flour to the butter in the pan and cook together for a minute or two. Add the puréed courgettes, then a little of the stock. Cook until the sauce thickens and add a little more stock if it is too thick. If you wish to use the cheese and the pancakes are to be eaten at once, add it at this point and cook until it melts. Season to taste with salt and pepper. If the pancakes and sauce are to be frozen, do not add the cheese or season the sauce until they are defrosted. Fill the pancakes with the vegetable mixture and reheat if necessary, in a covered serving dish, in a moderate oven (180°C/350°F/ Gas Mark 4) or in a microwave. Pour the sauce over the top just before serving.

If the pancakes are to be frozen, fill them with the vegetable mixture and pack them in foil parcels or containers. Freeze the sauce separately.

Defrost the pancakes and sauce at room temperature or in a microwave and reheat, covered, in a moderate oven (180°C/350°F/Gas Mark 4) or a microwave. Heat the sauce separately, add the cheese if you wish and adjust the seasoning to taste. Serve as above.

# Potato or Swede and Apple Purée

*Serves 6*          *6 months*

'Heaven and earth' is what the Germans call this particularly delicious mixture – I think that the 'heaven' is meant to be the apple and the 'earth' the more plebian vegetable.

   *1.25 kg/2½ lb potatoes or swedes, peeled and diced*
   *25–50 g/1–2 oz butter*
   *350 g/12 oz sharp cooking apples (preferably*
    *Bramleys), peeled and sliced*
   *salt, pepper, nutmeg and possibly a little sugar*
   *a little double cream (optional)*

Boil or steam the potatoes or swedes until cooked, then mash them, using a ricer or masher, with the butter until you have a smooth purée. Meanwhile, cook the apples in 2.5 cm/1 inch of water until they, too, are mushy. Drain them, mash with a fork if they are not sufficiently puréed and stir them into the potato or swede. Mix the two well together, then season to taste with salt, pepper and nutmeg. You may, wish to add a little sugar, although I prefer to keep the tartness of the apples. You may, alternatively, prefer to add some cream to take the edge off very sharp apples, although be careful that the purée does not become too sloppy. If it does, reduce it slightly by simmering it very gently on a low heat. Serve the purée to accompany any roast or casseroled meats.

To freeze, cool completely and freeze in well-sealed containers.

Defrost at room temperature or in a microwave and reheat in an oven or microwave to serve.

# A Hot or Cold Bean Pot

*Serves 6*                                              *6 months*

Now that beans are accepted as being delicious as well as nutritious and cheap, it is worth cashing in on them! The following mixture can be used hot as a vegetable, or dressed and used cold as a salad. Since the beans are slow to cook, it might be worth doing a large pot and freezing part of it. You will need to decide which beans (kidney, etc.) will need soaking first and which (lentil family) can be cooked from dry – it normally tells you on the packet. The herbs you select should include some mint, but not too much or it will overpower everything else.

> 350–450 g/¾–1 lb mixed dried beans
> 2 tablespoons olive or good vegetable oil
> 1 large onion, finely chopped
> 2–3 cloves garlic, finely chopped or crushed
> 2 tomatoes, chopped fairly small (optional)
> a handful of fresh parsley, chopped
> a handful of chopped fresh herbs, or 1–2 teaspoons
>    dried mixed herbs
> approx 12 peppercorns
> 600 ml–1.2 litres/1–2 pints well-flavoured beef,
>    chicken or vegetable stock (see page 152)
> salt

Check the beans and soak any that need presoaking overnight. Alternatively, put them in a deep pot covered with water (but no salt), bring them slowly to the boil and simmer them gently until they just start to soften. Drain them and set them aside. Rinse any other beans in cold water to remove any dust.

Heat the oil in a heavy-based pan and gently cook the onion and garlic until they are soft but not brown. Add the tomatoes if you are using them (in fact they almost totally disintegrate in the bean pot and just leave a vestige of their flavour but you may still prefer to leave them out) and cook for a further couple of minutes. Add the herbs and peppercorns and then the beans. Stir well together, then add enough stock to cover the beans generously. Bring the pot to the boil and simmer it gently for about 1 hour or until the beans are cooked – cooking times for different beans vary quite widely so you will need to keep an eye on them. If the pot dries up, add more stock, but only enough to get totally absorbed during the course of the cooking. When the beans are nearly done, taste and add salt to taste – not too much if the pot is to be frozen.

If the pot is to be served hot, it is ready as soon as the beans are cooked, although the flavours will develop if you leave it in the fridge for a day or so. If it is to be used as a salad, cool the pot partially, then dress with more olive or vegetable oil and some lemon juice – you should not need any further seasoning. Allow to cool completely but do not chill before serving.

If the pot is to be frozen, allow it to cool completely, then freeze in well-sealed containers.

Defrost at room temperature, dress or reheat and use as above.

# Parsnips with Mustard and Honey

*Serves 6*                                              *4–6 months*

The mustard in this recipe adds bite to what otherwise might be a rather sweet vegetable.

> 1 kg/2 lb parsnips, scrubbed and finely sliced
> 3 tablespoons wholegrain mustard
> 3 tablespoons honey
> 240 ml/8 fl oz orange juice
> 240 ml/8 fl oz chicken stock or water and white wine
>    mixed
> salt and pepper

Mix the mustard thoroughly with the honey, then gradually stir in the orange juice and stock. Season lightly. Put the parsnips in an ovenproof dish or casserole and pour over the mixture, making sure the parsnips all get well coated in it. Cover the dish and and cook in a moderate oven (180°C/350°F/Gas Mark 4) for 40–45 minutes or until the parsnips are cooked without being mushy. Remove the lid and cook for a further 10 minutes to brown the top.

If the dish is to be frozen, it should be removed and cooled once the parsnips are cooked. They can then be transferred into a container to freeze.

Defrost at room temperature or in a microwave. Spoon into an ovenproof serving dish and reheat uncovered so as to brown the top.

## Rice with Apricots

*Serves 6*           *3 months*

Rice freezes well and it is useful to keep something slightly exotic in the rice line in the freezer in case of emergencies. It goes particularly well with duck or game birds.

*350 g/12 oz unhusked brown rice*
*25 g/1 oz butter or low fat margarine*
*100 g/4 oz onions, very finely chopped*
*2–3 sticks celery, very finely chopped*
*1.2 litres/2 pints water*
*100 g/4 oz presoftened dried apricots, chopped fairly*
  *small*
*juice of 1–2 oranges*
*a handful of parsley, chopped*
*salt and pepper*

Melt the fat in a large pan and gently cook the onions and celery until they begin to soften. Add the rice and stir together for a couple of minutes, then add the water. Cook fairly briskly for 15–20 minutes by which time the rice should be cooked and the water absorbed; if necessary, add a little more water during the cooking. Add the chopped apricots (if they are rather dry, add them halfway through the cooking process to soften them up), the orange juice, parsley and seasoning to taste. Serve at once.

If the rice is to be frozen, it is better (although not essential) to add the apricots, parsley and seasoning once it is defrosted as they can lose texture and flavour in the freezer. To freeze, cool the rice completely and pack in well-sealed containers or bags.

Defrost at room temperature and reheat in a steamer or microwave, or very well covered in a moderately cool oven (160°C/325°F/Gas Mark 3).

## Pepperonata

*Serves 6*           *2–3 months*

This is a simple but rich and very Italian dish; a little goes a long way. You can serve it either as a starter with lots of fresh bread or as a side salad.

*Rice with Apricots, Celery with Green Beans (see page 105),
Pepperonata and Avocado and Mint Ice Cream (see page 9)*

750 g/1½ lb peppers (red and green, red and yellow,
  or just red)
225 g/8 oz onions, roughly chopped
4 large cloves garlic, finely chopped
4 tablespoons good olive oil
salt and freshly ground black pepper

Gently cook the onions and garlic in the oil in a
heavy–based open pan until they are softened.
Add the peppers, stir well and continue to cook
gently for 30 minutes, stirring now and then.
Season lightly with salt and pepper and continue
to cook until the peppers are quite soft; this can
take over an hour. Adjust the seasoning to taste
and allow to cool before serving.

Freeze in its juices in a well–sealed container.

Defrost at room temperature or in a microwave.

# Cheese Stuffed Peppers with Tomato Sauce

*Serves 6*                                                    *6 months*

These are rich – but good!

6 small or 3 large green peppers
1 tablespoon cornflour
salt and pepper
1 tablespoon olive or corn oil
225 g/8 oz well–flavoured cheese
1.2 litres/2 pints tomato sauce, unpuréed (see
  page 154)

Halve the peppers lengthways and remove the
seeds and ribs. Dust them lightly with the
cornflour, salt and pepper. Brush a dish with the
oil and lay the pepper halves in it. Fill each half
with the cheese, crumbled or sliced. Spoon over
the tomato sauce.

Cover the dish and bake for 35 minutes in a moderate oven (180°C/350°F/Gas Mark 4) or in a microwave for about 10 minutes. Serve at once with a little more black pepper freshly grated over the top.

Freeze the peppers in a foil dish or rigid container before baking them.

Defrost at room temperature or in a microwave and bake as above.

# Tomato Casserole with Basil

*Serves 6*                                    *6 months*

This is a good dish to make when tomatoes are cheap – and freeze for when they are not!

> 6 large tomatoes (if beef tomatoes, 3 or 4 will
>   probably be enough)
> 75 g/3 oz butter
> 3 large onions, peeled and sliced in rings
> salt and pepper
> 1 teaspoon dark brown sugar
> 2 tablespoons fresh chopped basil, or 2 teaspoons
>   dried
> 75–100 g/3–4 oz brown breadcrumbs

Melt 50 g/2 oz of the butter in a pan and cook the onions gently until they are soft and lightly coloured. Meanwhile, peel the tomatoes. If you leave the skins on, they can become tough in cooking and in the freezer. However, some people would rather put up with the toughness so as to retain the flavour of the skin – it is up to you. Grease the bottom of a pie dish or soufflé dish with a little of the remaining butter (if the dish is to be frozen, you may want to line it with foil) and lay half the onions in the bottom of the dish. Slice the tomatoes and lay half of them over the onions. Season well with salt, pepper, half the sugar and half the basil. Cover this with a second layer of onions, a second layer of tomatoes, the remainder of the basil and sugar and some more seasoning. Sprinkle the breadcrumbs over the top in an even layer and dot with the rest of the butter. Bake in a moderate oven (180°C/350°F/Gas Mark 4) for 30 minutes. Serve at once.

To freeze, cook as above, cool entirely, open freeze and then turn out of the dish. Pack in a well-sealed bag.

To defrost put back into its dish and defrost at room temperature or in a microwave. Reheat in a moderate oven (180°C/350°F/Gas Mark 4) or in a microwave, although if you use a microwave you may have to toast the breadcrumb topping under a grill to crisp it up.

# Tomato Rice Cakes

*Serves 4*                                    *6 months*

These can be used either as a vegetable or as a dish on their own – they are a great way of using up cooked rice and are good hot or cold!

> 225 g/8 oz brown rice, cooked
> 15 g/½ oz butter
> 1 medium onion, finely chopped
> 50 g/2 oz lean bacon or ham, finely chopped
> 2 large tomatoes, roughly chopped, or 200 g/7 oz can
>   Italian tomatoes, drained
> 1 teaspoon dried basil
> 1 teaspoon dark brown sugar
> 8–10 black olives, roughly chopped
> 60 ml/2 fl oz dry white wine
> 2 egg yolks
> 25 g/1 oz brown breadcrumbs
> salt and pepper
> butter or oil for frying
> a little chopped parsley

Melt the butter in a large pan and fry the onion and bacon until they are just turning colour. Add the tomatoes, cook for a couple of minutes, then add the rice, basil, sugar, olives and wine. Cook everything together well for a few minutes. Remove from the heat and add the egg yolks and breadcrumbs. Amalgamate thoroughly, then season to taste. Either form the rice into smallish cakes, like fish cakes, and fry them gently on both sides in butter or oil – about 4 minutes each side – or pile the whole mixture into a dish and sprinkle it with a little chopped parsley to serve.

Freeze the rice cakes, before cooking, in well-sealed bags, interleaved with greaseproof paper. If you do not want to make the mixture into cakes, freeze it in a well-sealed container.

Defrost at room temperature or in a microwave and reheat in a moderate oven (180°C/350°F/Gas Mark 4), covered, or fry the cakes in a little butter.

# Cauliflower Cheese

*Serves 4*                                    *2–3 months*

This is an old favourite with adults as well as children – the almonds can be left out if you want to keep the cost down.

> *1 large cauliflower, broken into reasonable-sized*
> *   florets*
> *2 medium onions, peeled and roughly chopped*
> *4 rashers bacon, diced*
> *25 g/1 oz butter*
> *40 g/1½ oz flour*
> *450 ml/¾ pint milk*
> *75 g/3 oz whole almonds*
> *175 g/6 oz strong cheese (Cheddar is ideal), grated*
> *salt and pepper*

Steam the cauliflower florets and the onions, or cook them in the microwave until they are just cooked but not soggy; set them aside but keep them warm. Reserve the water.

Meanwhile, lightly fry the bacon in the butter, then add the flour. Mix well and cook for a minute or two. Gradually add the milk and a little of the cauliflower cooking water to make a light white sauce. Add the almonds and most of the cheese. Cook for a minute or two and then season to taste – if the bacon was salty you may not need much. Arrange the cauliflower and onion in a warmed serving dish (lined with foil if it is to be frozen), pour over the sauce and sprinkle over the remaining cheese. Brown under a hot grill for 5–6 minutes, grate over a little black pepper and serve at once.

To freeze, line the dish with foil and do not brown the top. Cool the dish entirely, freeze it, then remove the cauliflower in the foil from the dish. Pack tightly in a polythene bag and return to the freezer.

To defrost, peel the foil off the cauliflower when it is still frozen and drop it back into the original dish. Defrost at room temperature. Reheat, covered, in a moderate oven (180°C/350°F/Gas Mark 4) or a microwave, then brown the top under the grill before serving.

# Celery with Green Beans

*Serves 6*                                    *6 months*

Here are a couple of useful ways to serve celery when it is cheap.

> *2 small heads celery, washed, strings removed and*
> *   roughly chopped*
> *40 g/1½ oz butter or low fat margarine*
> *225 g/8 oz green beans, roughly chopped*
> *240 ml/8 fl oz white wine*
> *salt and pepper*

Melt the fat in a pan and gently cook the celery for 5 minutes. Add the beans and the wine with a little seasoning, cover and simmer for 10–15 minutes or until the vegetables are soft without being mushy. Adjust the seasoning to taste and serve at once.

To freeze, cool completely and pack in well-sealed containers.

Defrost at room temperature or in a microwave and reheat gently in a pan or microwave.

# Celery with Spring Onions

*Serves 6*                                    *6 months*

> *2 heads celery, cleaned, strings removed and roughly*
> *   chopped*
> *50 g/2 oz butter or low fat margarine*
> *3 bunches spring onions, cleaned and chopped small*
> *3 handfuls parsley, chopped*
> *salt and pepper*

Melt the fat in a pan and add the celery and onions. Cover the pan and sweat the vegetables for 20–25 minutes or until the celery is soft but not mushy. Add the parsley and season to taste. Serve at once.

To freeze, cool completely and pack in well-sealed containers.

Defrost at room temperature or in a microwave and reheat gently in a pan or microwave.

# Stewed Cucumbers

*Serves 6*                                      *3 months*

Cooked cucumber keeps its 'crunch' in the freezer surprisingly well and is better cooked and frozen rather than being frozen and then cooked.

*750 g/1½ lb cucumber (unpeeled), sliced into thick matchsticks*
*50 g/2 oz butter or low fat margarine*
*9 large spring onions, chopped fairly small*
*150 ml/¼ pint white wine*
*150 ml/¼ pint chicken stock or water*
*salt and pepper*

Melt the butter or margarine in a pan and lightly cook the spring onions for a couple of minutes. Add the cucumber matchsticks and cook for a further few minutes until they are beginning to soften. Add the liquid and some seasoning and simmer gently for 5 minutes (2 minutes in a microwave). Adjust seasoning to taste and serve.

If this is to be frozen, cool completely and freeze in a well-sealed container in the juices.

Defrost at room temperature or in a microwave and reheat to serve.

# Jerusalem Artichoke and Brussels Sprout Purée

*Serves 6*                                      *2–3 months*

This recipe started life as a way to rescue overcooked Brussels sprouts but the result was so delicious and froze so well that it has now become one of my party pieces.

*750 g/1½ lb Jerusalem artichokes, scrubbed and trimmed*
*750 g/1½ lb Brussels sprouts, trimmed*
*25 g/1 oz butter*
*salt, pepper and nutmeg (the last two freshly ground if possible)*

Steam or microwave the artichokes and the sprouts until tender – you can halve or quarter them to speed up the process. Purée both vegetables in a processor or liquidizer, then add the butter. Season to taste with the salt, pepper and nutmeg. Spoon into a dish and reheat.

If freezing, spoon into a container and allow to cool completely before packing and freezing.

Defrost at room temperature or in a microwave. Reheat, adjust seasoning to taste and serve.

# Mr Janssen's Temptation

*Serves 6*                                      *2–3 months*

This is a traditional Swedish dish which conceals juicy anchovies beneath relatively boring-looking potatoes. Mr Janssen was said never to be able to resist it! The 'temptation' can be served on its own as a supper dish or with plain meat as a vegetable.

*1.5 kg/3 lb potatoes, peeled and very thinly sliced*
*40 g/1½ oz butter*
*350 g/12 oz pickled anchovies, or 750 g/1½ lb jar Matjes herrings (see below)*
*3 onions, peeled and thinly sliced*
*270 ml/9 fl oz double cream*
*approx 60 ml/2 fl oz juice from the can or jar (see below)*
*black pepper*

Use half the butter to grease the inside of a pie dish (lined with foil if it is to be frozen). Lay half the potatoes in a layer in the bottom. Cover them with the anchovy or herring fillets, roughly chopped, then the sliced onions. Mix half the cream with the juice from the fish and pour it over the onions. Top with the rest of the potatoes. Cover the dish and bake in a moderate oven (180°C/350°F/Gas Mark 4) for 30 minutes. Take off the lid, pour over the rest of the cream and dot the top with the rest of the butter. Bake the dish, uncovered, for a further 30 minutes.

If it is to be frozen, cool it completely, then freeze. Once frozen, remove from the dish and pack.

Defrost at room temperature or in a microwave. Reheat, uncovered, in a microwave for about 8 minutes or in a moderate oven (180°C/350°F/Gas Mark 4) for about 30 minutes and sprinkle with freshly ground black pepper before serving.

NOTE: You will find pickled anchovies in some delicatessens and in most Scandinavian food shops. If you choose to use Matjes herrings, be careful as the juice can be rather sweet, so add with caution.

*Rhubarb Soup* (see page 9), *Stewed Cucumbers and Celery and Water Chestnut Casserole* (see page 108)

*Stewed Radishes with Baby Corn*

# Stewed Radishes with Baby Corn

*Serves 6*                         *6 months*

This is a pretty vegetable to serve and freezes well if you are not always able to lay hands on either ingredient.

> *350 g/12 oz radishes, trimmed*
> *350 g/12 oz baby corn, halved or sliced, depending on size*
> *300 ml/½ pint chicken stock*
> *salt and pepper*

Trim the vegetables and put them in a pan with the chicken stock and a little seasoning. Bring to the boil and simmer for 10 minutes or cook in a microwave for about 3 minutes. Serve at once.

If freezing, allow to cool completely and freeze in a well-sealed container.

Defrost at room temperature or in a microwave and reheat in their juice to serve.

# Artichoke Heart, Date and Almond Pie

*Serves 6*                      *4–6 months*

This recipe is based on a seventeenth-century English dish, despite its almost Middle Eastern flavours.

> *750 g/1½ lb artichoke hearts (fresh, frozen or canned), well drained*
> *50 g/2 oz dates, stoned and roughly chopped (see below)*
> *75 g/3 oz whole blanched almonds*
> *½ teaspoon ground mace*
> *salt and pepper*
> *1 egg, beaten*
> *90 ml/3 fl oz medium sweet sherry*
> *grated rind and juice of 1 large orange*

### Pastry
> *225 g/8 oz wholemeal flour*
> *150 g/5 oz butter or low fat margarine*

To make the pastry, cut the fat and rub into the flour, then mix to a stiff dough with a little cold water. Roll out two-thirds of the pastry, line a 15-cm/6-inch flan case, then bake it blind – about 20 minutes in a moderately hot oven (190°C/375°F/ Gas Mark 5). If the pie is to be frozen, line the dish with foil so the pie can be removed from the dish.

Mix together the artichoke hearts, dates and almonds and pile them into the flan case. Sprinkle over the mace and some salt and pepper. Top the pie with the rest of the pastry, making a vent hole in the middle and brush well with the beaten egg. Return to the oven for a further 20 minutes. Mix together the sherry and orange rind and juice to make a thin sauce. Remove the pie from the oven, pour the juices carefully through the vent hole and return to the oven for 5 minutes before serving. The pie can be eaten hot or cold.

If the pie is to be frozen, remove it from the oven once the lid is cooked without adding the sherry and orange. Cool completely, then freeze.

Defrost at room temperature or in a microwave. Reheat in a moderate oven (180°C/350°F/Gas Mark 4) and 5 minutes before it is ready add the sherry and orange rind and juice as above.

NOTE: If possible, get fresh dates as they are better; if not, preserved dates will do quite well.

*Preparing Artichoke Heart, Date and Almond Pie*

# Rice, Chilli and Bamboo Shoot Casserole

*Serves 4–6*                    *6 months*

This is excellent as a dish on its own or as a vegetable. You can substitute water chestnuts for the bamboo shoots if you prefer.

*350 g/12 oz unhusked brown rice*
*2 tablespoons olive or sunflower oil*
*6–8 large spring onions, trimmed and chopped*
*40 g/1½ oz fresh green chillies, deseeded and finely sliced*
*900 ml/1½ pints mixed white wine and water, vegetable stock or chicken stock*
*450 g/1 lb bamboo shoots, drained*
*300 ml/½ pint soured cream*
*salt and pepper*
*225 g/8 oz grated well-flavoured cheese*

Heat the oil and gently fry the onions and chillies until they are soft. Add the rice, cook for a couple of minutes, then add the liquid. Bring to the boil and simmer for about 20 minutes or until the rice is cooked and most of the liquid absorbed. Add the bamboo shoots and soured cream and season to taste. Spoon half the mixture into the bottom of a casserole (lined with foil if you wish to freeze the dish), sprinkle over half of the cheese, then cover that with the rest of the rice mixture. Sprinkle the remainder of the cheese over the top and cook in a moderate oven (180°/350°F/Gas Mark 4) for 25 minutes or until the cheese is melted and lightly browned. Alternatively, heat the casserole in a microwave, then brown the top under the grill.

To freeze, allow the mixture to cool completely, then open freeze. Remove from the dish and pack in a well-sealed container.

Defrost at room temperature or in a microwave. Return to its dish and reheat as above.

# Parsnips Molly Parkin

*Serves 6*                    *6 months*

I have had this recipe for years although I absolutely cannot remember where it came from. If the dish is to be eaten fresh, without being frozen, the liquid can be reduced slightly.

*1 kg/2 lb parsnips, scrubbed, topped and tailed and thinly sliced*
*approx 5 tablespoons vegetable oil*
*75 g/3 oz butter or low fat margarine*
*750 g/1½ lb tomatoes, peeled and thickly sliced*
*salt and pepper*
*3 level tablespoons soft brown sugar*
*175 g/6 oz grated Cheddar or other strong-flavoured hard cheese*
*450 ml/¾ pint double cream*
*4 heaped tablespoons fresh brown or white breadcrumbs*

Heat the oil in a heavy pan and briskly fry the parsnips on both sides until they are light brown. Meanwhile, grease a medium-sized (1.2-litre/2-pint) casserole dish with half the butter or margarine. If the parsnips are to be frozen, line the dish with foil and grease the foil not the dish. Layer the parsnips and tomatoes alternately, sprinkling each layer with salt and pepper, sugar, cheese and cream, and ending with a layer of parsnips topped with cream and cheese. Sprinkle the breadcrumbs over the top and bake in a moderately hot oven (190°C/375°F/Gas Mark 3) for 40 minutes.

Cool completely and freeze. Remove from the dish and pack as usual.

Defrost at room temparature or in a microwave. Reheat, uncovered, in a microwave or a conventional oven – the crumb topping will stay crispier in the latter.

# Cooked Cabbage and Plum Salad

*Serves 6*                    *2–3 months*

This salad is based on an Old English combination salad which substituted raisins or sultanas when plums were not available. It can be eaten either hot or cold, although the flavour is really too distinct for it to be used with anything except a plain meat. It freezes remarkably well and is a good way of using up an excess of plums – or courgettes. For the herbs, use a mixture of tansy, mint, marjoram, lemon balm, etc.

*2 onions, peeled and roughly chopped*
*1 carrot, diced*

½ swede or 1 turnip or parsnip, scrubbed and diced
2 tart eating or small cooking apples, peeled and
  diced
225 g/8 oz plums or other similar soft fruit, or
  50 g/2 oz raisins or sultanas
a handful of fresh chopped herbs, or 1 tablespoon
  mixed dried herbs
25 g/1 oz butter
1 tablespoon honey
50 g/2 oz white cabbage, finely sliced
100 g/4 oz marrow or courgettes, diced
salt and pepper

Put the onions, carrot, swede or alternative, fruits and herbs into a large pan with the butter and honey. Sauté lightly for a couple of minutes, then cover and cook gently until the vegetables are beginning to soften. Add the cabbage and marrow or courgettes and continue to cook for a further 10 minutes. Season to taste with salt and pepper, turn into a dish and serve hot or cold.

If it is to be frozen, season only lightly and pack in a plastic container.

Defrost at room temperature or in a microwave. Adjust seasoning before serving.

# Spinach, Cream Cheese and Artichoke Bake

*Serves 4–6*                                    *6 months*

This can be served as a rich but excellent vegetable with plain meat, or on its own as a starter or vegetarian main course.

1.5 kg/3 lb fresh spinach, blanched and well drained
25 g/1 oz butter
350 g/12 oz curd cheese
salt, pepper and nutmeg
350 g/12 oz artichoke hearts, halved and drained
150 ml/¼ pint white wine
150 ml/¼ pint water
a small packet of plain potato crisps, crushed
50 g/2 oz grated Parmesan cheese

Rub a 20-cm/8-inch pie dish with half the butter. (If the dish is to be frozen, the pie dish can be lined with foil rubbed with butter, so that the dish can be rescued from the freezer.) Spread half the spinach over the bottom and cover it with half the curd cheese. Sprinkle this with salt, pepper and nutmeg. Spread the halved artichoke hearts over the cheese, then cover them with the rest of the curd cheese. Season this layer again with salt, pepper and nutmeg and then lay over the rest of the spinach. Add the liquid. Mix the crisps with the Parmesan cheese and sprinkle over the spinach. Bake in a moderate oven (180°C/350°F/ Gas Mark 4) for 25 minutes and serve at once.

Open freeze, then remove from the dish and pack in a well-sealed bag.

Defrost at room temperature or in a microwave and reheat in a moderate oven (180°C/350°F/Gas Mark 4) or a microwave; if you use a microwave, you may want to crisp the top under the grill.

# Broccoli, Rice and Water Chestnut Casserole

*Serves 4–6*                                    *6 months*

If you want to use this as a vegetable rather than a vegetarian dish, it will go well with any plain meat.

225 g/8 oz fresh broccoli, the stems chopped and the
  florets kept whole and blanched, or 225 g/8 oz
  frozen broccoli, chopped
25 g/1 oz butter
175 g/6 oz onions, finely chopped
175 g/6 oz brown rice, cooked but still crunchy
175 g/6 oz water chestnuts, cooked, drained and
  sliced
2 teaspoons wholegrain mustard
150 ml/¼ pint soured cream
300 ml/½ pint white wine
salt and pepper
50 g/2 oz pumpkin seeds

Melt the butter in a pan and gently cook the onions until they soften. Add the rice and the water chestnuts. Mix the mustard with the cream, stir in the wine and mix into the vegetables. Season to taste with salt and pepper, then gently fold in the broccoli and the pumpkin seeds. Reheat gently and turn into a warm serving dish.

To freeze, cool the mixture completely, then pack in a well-sealed container.

Defrost at room temperature or in a microwave and reheat, covered, in a moderate oven (180°C/ 350°F/Gas Mark 4) or in a microwave.

# DESSERTS

## Seventeenth-century Apple Cake

*Serves 6*                                            *3–6 months*

This recipe is based on a seventeenth-century recipe for a 'pupton' or terrine of apples. It is a great way to use up windfalls after a storm as it freezes very well.

*1.25 kg/2½ lb cooking or sharp eating apples*
*50 g/2 oz sugar*
*1 level teaspoon ground cinnamon*
*60 ml/2 fl oz water*
*75 g/3 oz brown breadcrumbs*
*3 egg yolks*
*40 g/1½ oz melted butter*
*150 ml/¼ pint lightly whipped cream*

Peel and chop 1 kg/2 lb of the apples and stew them gently with the sugar, cinnamon and water until they are pulped. Remove from the heat, strain off any extra juice and mix in the breadcrumbs and egg yolks. Brush the inside of a 15-cm/6-inch soufflé dish with a little of the melted butter and stir the remains into the mixture. If the dessert is to be frozen, line the dish with foil and grease the foil with the butter. Spoon in half of the apple mixture. Peel and slice the remaining apples and lay them over the mixture, cover them with the remaining mixture. Cover the dish and bake it in moderately cool oven (160°C/325°F/Gas Mark 3) for about 30

*Seventeenth-century Apple Cake, Upside-down Gingerbread (see page 116) and Orange and Almond Tart (see page 125)*

minutes or until the mixture is set. Remove it from the oven and cool. To serve, unmould onto a serving dish and top with the whipped cream. This dish can be served warm or cold.

Freeze in the dish, then remove and pack in a polythene bag.

To defrost, peel off the foil and put the apple cake on a serving dish. Defrost at room temperature or in a microwave. Serve as above.

# Walnut Tart

Serves 6                                    4–6 months

Lovers of pecan pie will recognize this as a close relative – some might even claim, ancestor. It is very rich so a little goes a long way.

### Pastry
125 g/5 oz plain white or wholemeal flour
1 tablespoon icing sugar
75 g/3 oz butter or low fat margarine

### Filling
100 g/4 oz soft brown sugar
100 g/4 oz butter
3 eggs
6 large tablespoons golden syrup
grated rind and juice of 1 large lemon
175 g/6 oz broken walnuts
150 ml/¼ pint lightly whipped cream

Mix the flour with the icing sugar, cut and rub in the butter and mix to a firm dough with a little cold water. Roll out the pastry, line a 20–25-cm/ 8–9-inch flan dish and bake it blind.

Meanwhile, cream the sugar and butter in a mixer, then gradually add the eggs. Warm the syrup slightly and mix it well in together with the lemon rind and juice. Finally, fold in the broken walnuts and spoon the mixture into the pie shell. Bake for about 45 minutes in a moderately cool oven (160°C/325°F/Gas Mark 3) until the filling is set. Serve warm or cold with the lightly whipped cream.

To freeze, cool completely, then freeze in its dish. Once frozen you should be able to lift the pie out of the container and put it in a bag for storage.

Defrost at room temperature or in a microwave, preferably dropping the flan back into the original dish while it is still frozen. Reheat gently in a moderate oven (180°C/350°F/Gas Mark 4) if you wish to serve it hot.

# Upside-down Gingerbread

*Serves 6*                                    *2–3 months*

This is a dark, sticky, log fire pudding – it is divine any way, but especially with piles of whipped cream! Take advantage of cheap pears and freeze some spare puddings.

> *100 g/4 oz plain flour*
> *½ teaspoon bicarbonate of soda*
> *½ teaspoon ground nutmeg*
> *1 teaspoon ground ginger*
> *2 teaspoons ground cinnamon*
> *a pinch of ground cloves*
> *1 egg*
> *100 g/4 oz soft brown sugar*
> *3 tablespoons black treacle*
> *120 ml/4 fl oz sour milk*
> *50 g/2 oz melted butter*

> **Topping**
> *50 g/2 oz butter*
> *100 g/4 oz soft brown sugar*
> *4 small pears, halved, cored and peeled*
> *25 g/1 oz walnut halves (optional)*

To make the topping, melt the butter and brown sugar together and spread it over the bottom of an 18–20-cm/7–8-inch ovenproof dish. If the pudding is to be frozen, line the dish with foil so that you can get it out. Arrange the pear halves, cut sides facing upwards, on top of the sugar and butter base and intersperse with the walnut halves.

Sift the flour with the bicarbonate and the spices, then mix in the egg, sugar, treacle, milk and melted butter and beat it until the mixture is smooth. Carefully pour it over the fruit, taking care not to dislodge your pattern, and bake in a moderate oven (180°C/350°F/Gas Mark 4) for about 45 minutes or until it resists your finger when you press it. Take it out of the oven and loosen the edges with a knife.If it is to be eaten immediately, turn it out onto a warmed dish and serve with whipped cream.

If it is to be frozen, allow it to cool completely and then freeze it; once frozen it can be removed from the dish and packed in a polythene bag.

To defrost, peel off the foil casing and drop the pudding back into the dish in which it was made. Defrost at room temperature or in a microwave. Reheat and serve as above.

# Apple Pie with Orange

*Serves 6*                                    *3–6 months*

Plate pies do not tend to freeze well if they are too juicy. To avoid a soggy and generally revolting pastry bottom, the base should be baked blind first and the liquid in the filling only added just before serving.

> *approx 1.5 kg/3 lb cooking apples or sharp eating*
> *   apples, peeled and sliced*
> *40–50 g/1½–2 oz sugar*
> *150 ml/¼ pint double cream*

> **Pastry**
> *75 g/3 oz butter*
> *160 g/6 oz plain flour*
> *grated rind and juice of 2 small oranges*

Make the pastry by rubbing the butter into the flour, then add the orange rind and enough orange juice to make a firm dough. Roll out two-thirds of it and line an 18–20-cm/7–8-inch flan case; bake it blind. When the case is cooked, pile in the apples – you need to make them stand quite high as they shrink so much in the cooking. Sprinkle on the sugar – how much you use will depend on whether you are using eaters or cookers and on how sweet you like your apples; remember though that you can always add more, but once it is in you cannot get it out. Cover the pie with the remaining pastry and decorate, leaving a hole in the middle to pour in the juice. Bake it for a further 30 minutes in a moderate oven (180°C/350°F/ Gas Mark 4).

If the pie is to be eaten immediately, 5 minutes before it is done, take it out of the oven. Mix the cream with the remaining orange juice and pour as much as will easily go in through the hole in the top of the pie. Return the pie to the oven for 5 minutes before serving to heat the juice and serve the remains of the cream and orange juice with it.

If the pie is to be frozen, take it out of the oven, cool it and freeze it without adding the juices. It can be frozen in the dish, then removed and put in a bag.

Defrost at room temperature but not in a microwave as the pastry will go soggy. Reheat in a moderate oven (180°C/ 350°F/ Gas Mark 4 ) for 15–20 minutes, then take the pie out and add the cream and orange juice as above.

# Summer Pudding

*Serves 6*                                              *6–8 months*

Summer pudding, for those who are addicted to it, is the elixir of the gods; those who do not like it usually cannot stand the stuff so they can be left out of the reckoning. However, the fruit season is so short that enthusiasts should either obtain and freeze the fruit raw or else go to town and brew summer puddings, as they would Christmas puddings, to cover themselves for years to come. The most successful combination of fruit is redcurrants, blackcurrants and raspberries, but you can also use blackberries, loganberries, bilberries and strawberries, although neither of the latter really have sufficient acidity to make a good pudding.

> *1.5 kg/3 lb mixed red summer fruits, including*
>   *redcurrants*
> *approx 2 tablespoons sugar*
> *150 ml/¼ pint water*
> *approx 8 slices good quality, unsliced brown or white*
>   *bread*
> *150 ml/¼ pint lightly whipped cream*

Trim the fruits and cook with the sugar and water for about 10 minutes until they are soft without being totally mushy. Taste and add more sugar if too tart. Drain off most of the juice and reserve.

Trim the crusts from the bread. Take a medium sized pudding basin and line it with the bread, soaking each slice thoroughly in the fruit juices before using it. (If the pudding is to be frozen, line the bowl with plastic cling film.) Overlap the slices so that they make a firm and solid wall. End with one slice in the bottom of the bowl. Pile in the cooked fruits, smooth off the top and fold the upstanding edges of the bread 'walls' over the fruit. Put a final 'lid' of soaked bread on the top. Find a plate or saucer that will fit over the pudding inside the bowl, put it on top and weight it down with a couple of cans or weights. Put the bowl on a plate in the fridge (it nearly always leaks!) and chill for at least 24 hours.

To serve, remove the weights and plate, loosen the sides of the pudding with a knife and invert it onto a serving dish. Provided it has been well weighted, it should hold together with no trouble. Serve it in wedges, like a steamed pudding, with the cream and the extra juice.

Open freeze the pudding in the bowl, then remove it from the bowl and pack for storage.

To defrost, peel off the plastic cling film and drop the pudding back into the bowl to defrost at room temperature or in a microwave. Turn out and serve as above.

# Baked Apples

*6 months*

Baked apples freeze so well that I thought it was worth suggesting a few possible fillings. Allow 1 large cooking apple per person.

Core each apple carefully and run the tip of a sharp knife horizontally around the middle of the apple to prevent the skin splitting. Put the apples in a dish and fill the cavities with the filling of your choice (see below). Pour 1 cm/½ inch of water or whatever liquid you are using into the dish and bake the apples, uncovered, in a moderate oven (180°C/350°F/Gas Mark 4) for 25–45 minutes, depending on the size of the apples.

To freeze, transfer the apples to a well-sealed container and freeze.

Defrost at room temperature and reheat in a moderate oven (180°C/350°F/Gas Mark 4) or in a microwave (if you do not mind the skin being soggy) to serve.

**Fillings**
1  Demerara sugar and butter with a little water.
2  Raisins, walnuts, dark brown sugar and a little cider or cider mixed with water.
3  Demerara sugar and whole cloves with a little water.
4  Lightly fried pieces of bacon with some presoftened, chopped prunes and a little cider.
5  Honey, raisins and whole almonds with a little water.
6  Mincemeat with some dates or dried apricots and a little water.
7  Celery, finely chopped, walnuts and brown sugar with a little water.
8  Demerara sugar with a little cinnamon and chopped lemon rind and water.

# Chocolate and Pear Meringue Pie

*Serves 6*                    *3–4 months*

The combination of chocolate and pear is almost as popular as that of chocolate and orange – but this is an unusual way of doing it! In an ideal world, you would prebake and freeze the flan case, then fill it with pears and top it with meringue when you defrost it. However, the completed dessert works very well, although it should be eaten on the day it is defrosted.

2–3 ripe pears, peeled and quartered
2 egg whites
100 g/4 oz caster sugar
15 g/½ oz cocoa powder

**Pastry**
100 g/4 oz plain flour
25 g/1 oz cocoa powder
75 g/3 oz butter or low fat margarine

To make the pastry, mix together the flour and cocoa powder, cut and rub in the fat and mix it to a firm dough with a little cold water. Roll out the pastry and line a 20-cm/8-inch flan case, reserving any bits of pastry left over. Bake the flan case blind but take care not to overcook it as its colour is too dark to be able to see when it is burning – 20 minutes in a moderately hot oven 190°C/375°F/ Gas Mark 5) should be quite enough.

Arrange the pear quarters in the bottom of the flan case. Whisk the egg whites until they are dry and form peaks, then whisk in the sugar and continue to whisk until the meringue is shiny. Fold in the cocoa powder and spoon the mixture over the pears, taking care to cover them all well. Bake in a moderately hot oven (190°C/375°F/Gas Mark 5) for 30 minutes. Serve warm or cold.

To freeze, cool the flan completely, then freeze it in its dish. Once it is frozen, you should be able to get it out of the dish to be packed in a bag for storage.

*Summer Pudding* (see page 117)

*Chocolate and Pear Meringue Pie*

Defrost at room temperature or in a microwave, preferably dropping it back into the serving dish before it defrosts. Reheat gently in a moderate oven (180°C/350°F/Gas Mark 4) if you wish to serve it warm.

# Texas Osgood Pie

*Serves 8*                      *3 months*

This is not unlike a pecan pie but with a crunchy top.

*1 × 20-cm/8-inch flan case, baked blind*
*175 g/6 oz vanilla sugar*
*100 g/4 oz softened butter*
*¼ teaspoon cinnamon*
*¼ teaspoon ground cloves*
*1 teaspoon vinegar*
*4 eggs, separated*
*225 g/8 oz chopped pecans or walnuts*
*225 g/8 oz raisins*

Cream the sugar with the butter until they are light and fluffy, then add the cinnamon, cloves, vinegar and the egg yolks. Stir in the nuts and raisins. Whisk the egg whites until they are really stiff, as for meringues. Fold the egg whites into the mixture, pile into the flan case and flatten out. Bake in a moderately cool oven (160°C/325°F/Gas Mark 3) for 35–45 minutes – the top should end up as a crispy meringue layer with the gooey nut mixture below. Serve warm with whipped cream.

To freeze, cool completely, then open freeze. Remove from the dish and pack in a well-sealed bag.

Reheat from frozen in a moderately cool oven (160°C/325°F/Gas Mark 3) for 20–30 minutes.

# Crêpes Suzettes

*Serves 6*                                              *3 months*

This glamorous dessert is really very easy to make and its two components freeze excellently.

### Crêpes
*3 egg yolks*
*5 tablespoons melted butter*
*1 tablespoon sugar*
*350 g/12 oz sifted plain flour*
*180 ml/6 fl oz milk*
*180 ml/6 fl oz water*
*3 tablespoon orange-based liqueur (Cointreau, Grand Marnier, etc.) or brandy or rum*
*a little extra butter*

### Suzette Butter
*4 large lumps sugar*
*2 oranges*
*75 g/3 oz sugar*
*225 g/8 oz softened, unsalted butter*
*150 ml/¼ pint strained fresh orange juice*
*60 ml/2 fl oz orange liqueur (see above)*

### To Serve
*90 ml/3 fl oz orange liqueur (see above)*
*90 ml/3 fl oz brandy*

To make the crêpes, if you have a food processor or liquidizer, place all the crêpe ingredients in it and blend at top speed for a couple of minutes. If you have an electric mixer, put the eggs and butter in the bowl and mix at a medium speed, then gradually add the sugar, flour and liquids until they are all amalgamated into a smooth cream. If you have made the batter in a mixer, set it aside for ½–2 hours before making the crêpes. Heat a small frying pan over a high heat, grease it lightly with unsalted butter and make the batter into 18–24 very thin crêpes. Stack them, layered with greaseproof paper or plastic cling film, and pack them in polythene bags for freezing.

To make the butter, rub the sugar lumps over the oranges until the sides of the lumps have absorbed all the oil from the orange skins. Remove the peel from the oranges with a vegetable peeler or very sharp knife, making sure that you do not get any pith. Mash the sugar lumps on a chopping board with the point of a heavy knife, then add the orange peel and the sugar and chop them all together until they are very finely minced. Scrape the mixture into a mixing bowl. Add the softened butter and beat until the mixture is light and fluffy – use an electric mixer if possible. Add the orange juice and orange liqueur drop by drop – it must be done slowly or the butter will not absorb the liquid. Scrape the butter into a container and freeze.

To serve, defrost the crêpes at room temperature. Put some butter in a reasonably large chafing dish or heavy-based frying pan and heat slowly until it is bubbling. Dip both sides of each crêpe in the butter, fold in half and then in half again to make a wedge and stack at the side of the pan until they are all well soaked and warmed. Pour over the orange liqueur and stir into the sauce. Warm the brandy in a ladle or pan, then pour it gently over the crêpes and set alight immediately, before it has time to amalgamate with the rest of the sauce. If you are nervous that it will not catch, cheat by lighting the brandy while it is still in the ladle and pour it over as it is flaming.

# Chocolate and Orange Curd Tart

*Serves 6*                                              *3–4 months*

For those who are hooked on the combination of orange and chocolate, this is an unusual way to get a fix of your favourite flavours; the dark pastry case with the bright orange filling also looks rather dramatic.

*100 g/4 oz plain flour*
*25 g/1 oz cocoa powder*
*75 g/3 oz butter or low fat margarine*

### Filling
*50 g/2 oz butter*
*25 g/1 oz sugar*
*3 eggs*
*grated rind and juice of 2 large oranges and 1 lemon*

Mix together the flour and cocoa powder, cut the fat and rub in. Mix it to a firm dough with a little cold water. Roll out the pastry and line a 20-cm/ 8-inch flan case, reserving any bits of pastry left over. Bake the flan case blind but take care not to overcook it as its colour is too dark to be able to see when it is burning – 20 minutes in a moderately hot oven (190°C/375°F/Gas Mark 5) should be quite enough.

Meanwhile, melt the butter in the top of a double saucepan or boiler, or very gently in a heavy-based pan. Add the sugar, then beat in the eggs followed by the rind and juice of the oranges and lemon. Cook the mixture over a low heat, stirring continually, until the curd thickens. This can also be done in a microwave. Spoon the mixture into the flan case. Roll out the remaining bits of pastry very thinly and cut into lattice strips with which you can decorate the top of the flan. Bake in a moderately cool oven (160°C/325°F/Gas Mark 3) for 20 minutes. Serve either warm or cold.

To freeze, cool the flan completely, then freeze it in its dish. Once it is frozen, you should be able to get it out of the dish to be packed in a bag for storage.

Defrost at room temperature or in a microwave, preferably dropping it back into the serving dish before it defrosts. Reheat gently in a moderate oven (180°C/350°F/Gas Mark 4) if you wish to serve it warm.

## Steamed Ginger Pudding

*Serves 6*                                              *6 months*

This is a good old-fashioned pudding which freezes excellently and can be cooked or reheated in a microwave in a couple of minutes.

> *225 g/8 oz wholemeal brown breadcrumbs*
> *50 g/2 oz wholemeal flour*
> *1 teaspoon ground ginger*
> *grated rind of 1 lemon*
> *50 g/2 oz stem ginger, chopped*
> *1 tablespoon stem ginger syrup*
> *4 tablespoons golden syrup*
> *90 ml/3 fl oz double cream*
> *2 eggs*
> *approx 15 g/½ oz butter*

Mix the breadcrumbs, flour, ground ginger, lemon rind and stem ginger together. Warm the syrups slightly and mix them with the cream, then add the eggs and mix the liquids into the dry ingredients. Grease a 900-ml/1½-pint pudding

basin thoroughly with the butter and spoon in the mixture. Cover the bowl with greaseproof paper, secure it and lower it into a steamer. Steam for 1–1½ hours. Alternatively, cover the pudding with plastic cling film, pierce a hole in it and microwave it on full power for 2½–3 minutes, but do take care not to overcook it or it will become as tough as leather. Unmould the pudding onto a warmed serving dish and serve at once with cream or custard.

To freeze, cool completely in the bowl, then turn it out and pack in a well-sealed bag.

Drop back into its bowl to defrost at room temperature. Reheat by steaming or microwaving and serve as above.

## Lemon Cheesecake

*Serves 6*                                              *6–9 months*

This is a very simple, traditional cheesecake which could have been designed especially for the freezer.

> *1 × 20-cm/8-inch round sponge cake, cut in half*
>   *horizontally*
> *10 g/¼ oz gelatine*
> *juice and grated rind of 2 lemons*
> *225 g/8 oz curd cheese*
> *75  100 g/3–4 oz caster sugar*
> *210 ml/7 fl oz double cream*
> *2 eggs, separated*
> *50 g/2 oz sultanas*

Lay half the sponge on the bottom of a loose-bottomed cake tin. Save the other half for another cheesecake as the whole cake is too thick. Melt the gelatine in the lemon juice and cool. Mix the lemon rind, curd cheese, sugar, cream, egg yolks and gelatine well together. Whisk the egg whites until they hold their shape in soft peaks, then fold the whites into the cheese mixture along with the sultanas. Spoon the mixture over the sponge cake and chill for at least 4 hours. Unmould, from the cake tin onto a serving dish.

Open freeze in the cake tin. Once it is frozen, turn it out and pack in a bag for storage.

Remove from the bag onto a serving dish and defrost at room temperature or in a microwave.

# Strawberry Mousse

*Serves 6*                    *2 months*

This is an excellent way of preserving a glut of June strawberries for a couple of months. I prefer the mousse 'bitty' as I think the flavour is better preserved in the 'bits'. If you would rather have a smooth purée, continue to mash or process until you have one.

> 450 g/1 lb strawberries
> 25 g/1 oz sugar
> 15 g/½ oz gelatine
> juice of 1 lemon
> 120 ml/4 fl oz double cream
> 2 egg whites

Mash the strawberries lightly with a fork or in a food processor but do not purée them; there should still be distinct pieces of strawberry. Mix in the sugar. Melt the gelatine in the lemon juice, cool it partially and carefully mix it into the strawberry purée. Whisk the cream until it just holds its shape, then fold it into the strawberry purée. Chill the mixture until it is beginning to set, then whisk the egg whites until they hold in soft peaks and fold them into the strawberry mixture. Spoon it into glass dishes or a soufflé dish and chill it until set. Decorate the mousse with more strawberries or other berries and serve with small sweet biscuits.

The mousse freezes very well. If it is to be frozen, line the mousse dish with plastic cling film so that it can be turned out when frozen.

To defrost, remove from the freezer, unwrap the plastic cling film and drop the mousse into the dish while it is still frozen. Leave it to defrost in the fridge for 12–15 hours. Decorate with frozen redcurrants, raspberries or loganberries; frozen strawberries will go mushy and weep all over the mousse.

*Blackcurrant and Pear Cobbler (see page 124)*

# Rhubarb and Plum Crumble

*Serves 6*                    *6 months*

This is a real nursery pudding, and therefore terribly 'moreish'! If you cannot get fresh plums or they are hideously expensive, use bottled, frozen or canned.

> 1 kg/2 lb rhubarb
> 1 kg/2 lb plums
> 150–300 ml/¼–½ pint water
> 2–3 tablespoons sugar
>
> ***Topping***
> 100 g/4 oz wholemeal flour
> 50 g/2 oz sugar
> 50 g/2 oz butter

Stew the rhubarb and the plums in the water and sugar – you will need to add sugar to taste according to the sweetness of the fruit and more or less water depending on how much juice you want over. (If you cannot get fresh plums, bottled or frozen will do well.) When the fruit is cooked, drain off most of the juice and save it to serve with the crumble. Put the fruit in a pie dish.

Crumble the flour with the sugar and butter as for pastry. When it is finely crumbed, spread it evenly on the top of the fruit and bake in a moderate oven (180°C/350°F/Gas Mark 4) for 30–40 minutes or until the crumble is lightly browned. Serve hot with cream and the fruit juices which should be warmed.

*Strawberry Mousse and Lemon Cheesecake* (see page 121)

To freeze, cool completely and then open freeze. Turn out of the dish and pack in a well-sealed bag.

To defrost, turn the crumble back into its dish and reheat from frozen in a moderately cool oven (160°C/325°F/Gas Mark 3) for about 30 minutes.

NOTE: The pie dish should be lined with foil if the crumble is to be frozen.

# Blackcurrant or Raspberry and Pear Cobbler

*Serves 4*                                          *6 months*

You can use frozen blackcurrants or raspberries to make this pudding in mid winter when pears are in season and hot, filling puddings go down a bundle.

> *225 g/8 oz blackcurrants or raspberries, fresh or*
>   *frozen*
> *½ teaspoon cinnamon*
> *¼ teaspoon nutmeg*
> *1 level teaspoon cornflour*
> *150 ml/¼ pint water*
> *100 g/4 oz sugar*
> *2 large pears, peeled and sliced*
> *150 g/6 oz wholemeal flour*
> *1 teaspoon baking powder*
> *40 g/1½ oz melted butter*
> *1 egg*
> *150 ml/¼ pint soured cream*

Mix the spices and cornflour, then gradually add the water to make a smooth paste. Put the blackcurrants or raspberries and 50 g/2 oz sugar in a pan, add the liquid paste, bring gradually to the boil and simmer for 3 minutes. Put the peeled and sliced pears in a 20-cm/8-inch pie dish and pour over the blackcurrant or raspberry mixture.

Meanwhile mix the flour, the rest of the sugar and the baking powder in a bowl. Add the melted butter (slightly cooled), egg and soured cream and mix them thoroughly together. Drop spoonfuls of the mixture on top of the fruit until it is almost all covered. Bake in a moderately hot oven (190°C/375°F/Gas Mark 5) for 30 minutes or until a skewer comes out of the crust clean. Serve hot with cream.

To freeze, cool completely, cover and freeze. You can line the dish with foil before making the dessert as it can be difficult to prise it out of the dish once frozen.

Defrost at room temperature, then reheat in a moderate oven (180°C/350°F/Gas Mark 4) or a microwave – although the crust will not remain so crisp in a microwave.

# Chocolate Meringue Gâteau

*Serves 8*                                          *3 months*

The meringue case can be frozen with or without its filling – in either case it makes a very luscious, fattening and delicious dessert.

> *4 eggs*
> *¼ teaspoon cinnamon*
> *225 g/8 oz sugar*
> *175 g/6 oz good quality plain chocolate*
> *2 tablespoons Grand Marnier, Cointreau or Tia*
>   *Maria*
> *240 ml/8 fl oz double cream*
> *chocolate curls, toasted flaked almonds or chopped*
>   *hazelnuts to decorate*
> *300 ml/½ pint pouring cream (optional)*

Separate the eggs and whisk the whites until stiff and spiky, then add the cinnamon and sugar and continue whisking until the meringue is very stiff and shiny – you must not underbeat it. When it is ready, spoon it into a flan dish, spread the mixture out and mound the edges so as to leave a well in the middle for the chocolate filling. Bake the meringue for 1–2 hours at 150°C/300°F/Gas Mark 2 or until cooked through.

Melt the chocolate in a double saucepan or boiler or a microwave. Cool slightly, then beat in the egg yolks and liqueur. Whisk the double cream until it holds its shape, then fold it into the chocolate mixture. Spoon the chocolate into the centre of the meringue case and decorate the top with chocolate curls, toasted flaked almonds or toasted chopped hazelnuts.

If the gâteau is to be frozen complete, do not decorate it until it is defrosted and ready to serve. Alternatively, freeze only the meringue case and fill it with the mousse before serving.

Defrost at room temperature, *not* in a microwave.

# Rum and Macaroon Mould

*Serves 4–6*                                    *6 months*

This dessert can be made in a caramel-lined ring or fancy mould and served either with whipped, rum-flavoured, sweetened cream or with a coffee-flavoured *crème pâtissière*. Don't worry if the mixture separates in cooking into a sponge and a set cream; it will taste just as good and will look as though you intended it!

> 50 g/2 oz plus 1 tablespoon sugar
> 225 g/8 oz macaroons, crushed
> 60 ml/2 fl oz dark rum
> 180 ml/6 fl oz milk brought to the boil with 50 g/2 oz sugar
> 4 eggs, separated

Melt 50 g/2 oz of sugar in a pan and caramelize it carefully. Line the mould with the melted caramel and allow it to cool. Beat the macaroons with the rum, then gradually add the sweetened milk and egg yolks and beat thoroughly. Whisk the egg whites until they form soft peaks, add the tablespoon of sugar and beat until stiff. Fold the whites into the macaroon mixture; make sure they are well amalgamated but don't worry if the resulting mixture is very runny. Pour it into the mould, place the mould in a *bain-marie* and bake it for about 40 minutes in a moderately cool oven (160°C/325°F/Gas Mark 3). It should be set and show a faint line of shrinkage around the edge. Remove from the oven and cool completely.

To serve, dip the mould into a little hot water and unmould onto a serving dish. Heat the mould to melt any remaining caramel and pour it over the dessert. Fill the middle or surround the mould with rum-flavoured, sweetened cream or coffee-flavoured *crème pâtissière*.

To freeze, cool the mould completely, then pack in a well-sealed container.

Defrost at room temperature, then unmould, or unmould from frozen, and serve as above.

# Orange and Almond Tart

*Serves 6*                                    *4–6 months*

As with all things almondy, this tart is rich – but yummy! It is not dissimilar in texture to a bakewell tart and, like a bakewell tart, can be found in various guises in English cookery books from the sixteenth century onwards. As with almost all tarts, it pays to bake the flan case blind first.

> 2 large oranges
> 150 g/5 oz soft butter
> 100 g/4 oz soft brown sugar
> 75 g/3 oz nibbed almonds
> 3 eggs plus 2 egg yolks
>
> **Pastry**
> 75 g/3 oz plain flour
> 25 g/1 oz ground almonds
> 1 teaspoon caster sugar
> 75 g/3 oz butter

To make the pastry, mix the flour with the ground almonds and the caster sugar, cut the butter and rub in, then mix to a firm dough with a little cold water. Roll out the pastry and line a 20-cm/8-inch flan case, reserving any spare pastry. Bake the flan case blind – about 20 minutes in a moderately hot oven (190°C/375°F/Gas Mark 5).

Meanwhile, pare the rind from the oranges and squeeze out the juice. Put the orange rind with the juice in a small pan and simmer until the rind is tender. Purée the rind with the juice in a liquidizer or food processor. Beat the butter until it is really soft. Gradually add the brown sugar, then the almonds and eggs and, finally, the orange purée. Spoon the mixture into the flan case and use the pastry trimmings to make a latticework decoration over the top. Reduce the heat of the oven to moderately cool (160°C/325°F/Gas Mark 3) and bake the tart for 35 minutes or until the filling is set and the latticework cooked. Serve either warm or cold. Some people like to serve whipped cream with it, others feel that it disguises the flavour.

To freeze, cool completely, then open freeze. Once frozen, the flan should come out of the dish to be packed for storage.

Drop back into its dish to defrost at room temperature or in a microwave. It can be eaten as soon as it is defrosted, but the pastry is crisper if the flan is reheated for around 20 minutes in a moderate oven (180°C/350°F/Gas Mark 4).

*Chocolate Brandy Gâteau (see page 128)*

# Fruit and Nut Chocolates

*Makes about 20*                                    *3 months*

These are extremely quick and easy to make (if you are really pushed for time, you do not even need to coat them in chocolate) and they can be varied according to your own taste and the contents of your store cupboard. They will keep for several weeks in the fridge but for longer storage would be better in the freezer.

*50 g/2 oz presoftened prunes or dried apricots*
*50 g/2 oz sultanas or raisins*
*25 g/1 oz dried apple, fig or date*
*25 g/1 oz flaked or nibbed almonds*
*25 g/1 oz hazelnuts or walnuts*
*approx 1 tablespooon sugar*
*juice of ½–1 lemon*
*1–2 tablespoons brandy (optional)*
*175–225 g/6–8 oz good dark chocolate*

Chop the fruits and nuts with the sugar and lemon juice in a food processor or liquidizer until fairly small. Add the brandy if you wish to be festive and mix well. Taste the mixture and add a little more sugar or lemon juice if necessary. Melt approximately 50 g/2 oz of the chocolate and mix it into the fruit and nuts; allow the mixture to cool completely.

Melt the remaining chocolate in a double saucepan or boiler. Roll the fruit mixture into small balls then, with tongs or two forks, roll half the balls in the melted chocolate and put them on greased foil to cool completely; leave the other half plain to give a nice contrast. (If the chocolate gets too solid to work easily, add a little boiling water to thin it down.) Once the balls are cold, they can be removed from the foil onto dishes or into boxes as presents.

Open freeze on a tray, then pack in well-sealed bags or containers.

Defrost at room temperature, *not* in a microwave.

# Chocolate Cheesecake

*Serves 8*          *3 months*

This is amazingly rich, so use it for dinner parties – and you will have some left for the next day!

*225 g/8 oz packet dark chocolate biscuits*
*75 g/3 oz butter or low fat margarine, melted*
*350 g/12 oz cream cheese, softened*
*50 g/2 oz sugar*
*225 g/8 oz good quality dark chocolate, melted and cooled, plus 50 g/2 oz plain chocolate, chilled*
*3 eggs*
*1 tablespoon Kirsch*
*2 tablespoons double cream*
*300 ml/½ pint thick soured cream*

Mash the biscuits in a processor or in a bowl with a rolling pin, pour in the melted butter and mix thoroughly. Press the mixture into the bottom of a 20-cm/8-inch flan case or dish; if the cake is to be frozen, line the dish with foil.

Beat the cream cheese thoroughly with the sugar and melted chocolate, then add the eggs, one at a time, the Kirsch and, finally, the double cream. Pour the mixture into the flan case and bake in a low oven (150°C/300°F/Gas Mark 3) for 30 minutes. Cool the cake and, when it is totally cold, spread the top with the soured cream. Decorate with the remainder of the chocolate grated into curls.

If you are going to open freeze the cheesecake, freeze it before topping it with soured cream. Once it is frozen, remove it from the dish and pack it in a well-sealed bag.

Defrost at room temperature, remove the foil when it is sufficiently defrosted and return it to the dish. Once it is defrosted, top and decorate it as above.

# Rich Chocolate Mousse

*Serves 6*          *3 months*

This may appear to be overstating the case, as an un-rich chocolate mousse does not exist! However, this one is richer than most and should only be served in small portions.

*225 g/8 oz good quality dark chocolate*
*1 teaspoon instant coffee dissolved in 60 ml/2 fl oz boiling water*
*2 tablespoons brandy or rum*
*15 g/½ oz butter*
*3 eggs, separated*
*60 ml/2 fl oz double cream, lightly whipped*
*toasted chopped hazelnuts or almonds to decorate*

Dissolve the chocolate with the coffee in a bowl over hot water, in a double saucepan or boiler, or in a microwave – take care not to overcook the chocolate. Stir in the brandy or rum and then add the butter in small pieces, alternately with the egg yolks. Cool partially, then stir in the cream. Whisk the egg whites into soft peaks and fold them into the mixture, making sure that it is well amalgamated. Pour into a soufflé dish or individual pots (lined with plastic cling film if they are to be frozen) and chill until set. Decorate with the nuts and serve.

Freeze the mousses after they are set and before they are decorated. They can be turned out of their dishes once frozen and packed in well-sealed bags.

*Fruit and Nut Chocolates*

To defrost, remove the plastic cling film and drop the mousses back into their dishes. Defrost at room temperature or in the fridge (not in a microwave or you will melt them) and decorate.

# Italian Baked Cheesecake

*Serves 6*                            *4–6 months*

This cheesecake is based on the most delicious Torta di Ricotta in Anna del Conte's Italian cookery book. Because of the difficulty of getting fresh Ricotta, I have included more accessible ingredients.

*225 g/8 oz curd cheese*
*50 g/2 oz caster sugar*
*50 g/2 oz ground almonds*
*3 eggs, separated*
*4 oranges*
*½ teaspoon nutmeg*
*15 g/½ oz rice or potato flour*
*75 g/3 oz sugar*
*3 tablespoons Grand Marnier*

Beat the cheese thoroughly with the caster sugar. Add the ground almonds and the egg yolks, beating between each yolk, followed by the grated rind and juice of 1 orange and the nutmeg. Whisk the egg whites and fold them into the mixture alternately with the rice or potato flour. Line a 20-cm/8-inch loose-bottomed or springclip-sided tin with buttered greaseproof paper, pour in the mixture and bake it in a preheated, moderate oven (180°C/350°F/Gas Mark 4) for about 40 minutes or until it is set. Take out the cheesecake and cool it completely before turning out onto a serving dish.

Meanwhile, peel the remaining oranges *very* thinly and cut the peel into thin slivers. Blanch them for a couple of minutes in a little boiling water. Melt the sugar in 4 tablespoons of water. When it is boiling, add the juice from the oranges and bring back to the boil. Add the strips of rind and simmer over a gentle heat for about 10 minutes or until the rind is soft. Add the Grand Marnier and serve as a sauce with the cheesecake.

Freeze the cheesecake and sauce separately.

Defrost at room temperature or in a microwave and serve as above.

# Chocolate Brandy Gâteau

*Serves 8*                            *2–3 months*

This is a very rich chocolate cake which *could* be served for tea but probably works better with lots of whipped cream as a dessert. It is better to freeze the cake without its filling or topping and to finish it off when it is defrosted.

*50 g/2 oz presoftened prunes, very finely chopped*
*3 tablespoons brandy*
*175 g/6 oz good quality dark chocolate*
*5 eggs, separated*
*150 g/5 oz caster sugar*
*25 g/1 oz sifted flour*
*approx 100 g/4 oz fresh or preserved damsons, black*
  *cherries, raspberries or loganberries*

### Topping
*2 tablespoons cocoa powder*
*2 tablespoons sugar*
*4 tablespoons water*
*50 g/2 oz butter*
*150–300 ml/¼–½ pint double cream*

Soak the prunes in the brandy for up to 12 hours. Melt the chocolate in the top of a saucepan or double boiler, draw off the heat and gradually add the prunes and brandy, stirring all the time. Meanwhile, beat the egg yolks with the sugar until they are white and fluffy. Mix them well into the chocolate and prunes. Whisk the egg whites to soft peaks and carefully fold the whites and the sifted flour into the chocolate mixture.

Spoon into two 18–20-cm/7–8-inch sandwich tins lined with greased greaseproof paper to make sure you can get the cakes out intact. Bake them in a moderate oven (180°C/350°F/Gas Mark 4) for about 45 minutes or until a skewer comes out clean. Turn the cakes out and cool on a rack. When the cakes are quite cold, put one cake on a serving dish and cover it with the fruit. Cover it with the second cake.

For the topping, carefully melt the cocoa with the sugar and the water in a pan, then add the butter and simmer the mixture for a couple of minutes. Take it off the heat and allow it to get almost cold but still just runny. Spoon it carefully over the top of the cake allowing it to run down the sides. Lightly whisk the cream and either use it to decorate the top of the gâteau or, if you prefer the luscious dark look, serve the cream separately.

Freeze the cakes, tightly wrapped in a polythene bag. If the gâteau is to be frozen complete, open freeze it on a serving dish. Once it is frozen you will be able to prise it off with a spatula or knife and pack it.

Defrost the cakes at room temperature or, carefully, in a microwave, and decorate.

Remove the completed gâteau from its wrapping and place on a serving dish to defrost. Do not try to defrost the completed gâteau in a microwave.

NOTE: This is not a normal sponge cake, so don't be surprised if it turns out thin and gooey.

# Chocolate and Orange Mousse

*Serves 6*                                  *3 months*

Chocolate and orange has always been a very popular combination. Although I prefer my chocolate naked, even I had to admit that this was a pretty good mixture!

> *175 g/6 oz good quality dark chocolate*
> *grated rind and juice of 2 oranges*
> *1 tablespoon hot water*
> *1 tablespoon Grand Marnier or Cointreau*
> *15 g/½ oz cocoa*
> *scant 5 g/¼ oz gelatine*
> *2 whole eggs plus 2 egg yolks*
> *50 g/2 oz caster sugar*
> *90 ml/3 fl oz double cream*
> *grated orange rind, toasted flaked almonds or extra*
>    *cream to decorate*

Break up the chocolate in a bowl over hot water or in a double saucepan or boiler. Add the orange rind and water and stir until the chocolate is melted and creamy. Add the liqueur and remove from the heat. Meanwhile, mix the cocoa and gelatine in a small bowl with the orange juice. Melt the gelatine by heating the bowl over hot water.

Mix the eggs with the sugar in yet another bowl or double saucepan or boiler and whisk them over hot water until they are light, fluffy and thick. Carefully add the chocolate and gelatine mixtures to the egg, folding all well together until

thoroughly amalgamated. Set aside in a fridge until the mixture is just beginning to set. Meanwhile, whisk the cream until it just holds its shape. Once the chocolate mixture is ready, fold in the cream and pour into a serving dish or individual glasses or sundae dishes – these can be lined with plastic cling film if the mousse is to be frozen. Chill thoroughly before decorating.

Freeze the mousse in the dish or dishes once it is set but before it is decorated. The mousses can be removed from the dishes once frozen and packed in well-sealed bags.

To defrost, take out of the freezer, remove the plastic cling film if it was used and drop the mousses back into their original containers. Defrost at room temperature or in a fridge, *do not try to defrost in a microwave* as you will just melt the mousse. Decorate and serve as above.

# ICE CREAMS AND SORBETS

## Basic Yoghurt Ice Cream

*Serves 6*                                    *3 months*

This can be eaten on its own (sprinkled with liqueur if you want to jazz it up) or used as a basis for almost any flavouring – it works particularly well with fresh soft fruit purées. It is not as rich as the custard-based ice creams but tastes as good and, if whisked really thoroughly, will almost double in quantity, making it relatively economical.

   *180 ml/6 fl oz double cream*
   *180 ml/6 fl oz plain yoghurt*
   *100 g/4 oz sugar*

Mix the ingredients together well and put them in the freezer until they are just beginning to freeze. Remove them and whisk until they almost double in size – this may take 5 minutes or more. Return the mixture to the freezer in a well-sealed container and use as required.

## Stem Ginger Ice Cream

*Serves 6*                                    *3 months*

Even for lukewarm ginger addicts this is a delicious ice cream as the almonds and the brandy temper the sweetness of the stem ginger; for addicts it is heaven.

**From left to right:** *Stem Ginger Ice Cream, Yoghurt Ice Cream with raspberry and nectarine toppings, Pineapple Mint Sherbet (see page 132) and Berry and Watermelon Ice Cream Sorbet*

*300 ml/½ pint double cream*
*50 g/2 oz stem ginger, finely sliced*
*50 g/2 oz toasted, nibbed almonds*
*3 tablespoons brandy*
*approx 2 tablespoons ginger syrup, or 2 tablespoons*
  *caster sugar*
*1 egg white*
*a pinch of salt*

Whisk the cream until it begins to hold its shape.
Fold in the ginger, the nuts and the brandy and
then the syrup to taste. If the ginger taste is too
strong, substitute 2 tablespoons caster sugar for
the syrup. Whisk the egg white with the salt into
soft peaks and fold into the ice cream.

Pile into glasses, a dish or a freezer container and
freeze.

Serve topped with more toasted nibbed almonds
or some sliced ginger.

# Berry and Watermelon
# Ice Cream Sorbet

*Serves 8–10*                            *2 months*

This was one of those recipes which happened
because I found half a watermelon sitting in the
fridge and did not want it to go to waste. The
result is a refreshing and rather delicate cross
between an ice cream and a sorbet.

*approx 225 g/8 oz raspberries, loganberries,*
  *redcurrants or blackcurrants*
*300 ml/½ pint plain yoghurt*
*300 ml/½ pint double cream, very lightly whipped*
*juice of 1 lemon*
*½ small or ¼ large watermelon*
*approx 5 tablespoons caster sugar*

Clean the berries or currants and mash them
lightly – you do not want a purée, so if you use a
processor or liquidizer, do so with discretion. Mix
the fruit with the yoghurt, cream and lemon juice.
Remove the seeds from the watermelon and
purée the flesh, then add the purée to the fruit
and cream mixture. Mix them well together, and
sweeten to taste with the sugar; how much you
need will depend on which fruit you have used

and how sweet you like your ice cream, but remember that freezing dulls the sweetness, so do not undersweeten.

If you have an ice cream maker, pour the mixture into it to freeze. If not, put the mixture in a metal or ceramic bowl in the freezer until it is just beginning to freeze. Take it out and whisk it in an electric mixer for 3–5 minutes until it is quite thick. Pour it into a container and freeze fully.

Serve by itself or with some berries or currants scattered over the top.

# Pineapple Mint Sherbet

*Serves 6*                                    *2–3 months*

This recipe comes from the southern states of America and for anyone who is into mint juleps it is a must!

*300 g/10 oz fresh pineapple, crushed*
*150 g/5 oz sugar*
*150 ml/¼ pint water*
*3 large sprigs mint, finely chopped, or 2 tablespoons*
  *dried*
*juice of 1 small lemon*
*juice of 1 small orange*
*1 small ripe banana, mashed*
*1 egg white*
*a few sprigs of fresh mint to decorate*

Melt the sugar in the water, bring it to the boil and allow it to boil for about 3 minutes. Take it off the heat, add the chopped mint leaves and leave the mixture to steep for about an hour. If you have to use dried mint, simmer the herb in the syrup for 5 minutes and then leave to steep. Add the lemon and orange juice, the pineapple and the banana and mix all very thoroughly together. Beat the egg white until it stands in soft peaks and fold it into the mixture.

If you have an ice cream maker, pour it in and freeze. If you do not, pour it into a metal or ceramic bowl and put it in the freezer. After about 30 minutes it will just have started to freeze, so take it out and stir well. Continue to stir at 20–30 minute intervals until it is quite frozen. The stirring is to prevent large ice crystals forming as it freezes. Pack in a covered container to store.

Serve in glasses, each topped with a sprig of mint.

# Banana Ice Cream

*Serves 6*                                    *1 month*

This recipe was given to me by a bachelor friend who uses it, very successfully, to 'chat up' girls. Maybe it is the brandy that does the trick!

*4 ripe bananas*
*300 ml/½ pint double cream*
*50 g/2 oz browned, nibbed almonds*
*50 g/2 oz demerara or soft brown sugar*
*4 tablespoons brandy*

Mash the bananas roughly with a fork – I like to keep a certain amount of texture and find they go too gluey if mashed in a processor. Whisk the cream until it holds its shape, then mix it into the bananas together with the almonds, sugar and brandy. If you want to use it at once, spoon the mixture into glasses or a dish and freeze for a couple of hours. Otherwise, spoon it straight into a container to freeze. Because of the dense texture of the bananas and the cream it is scarcely necessary to use an ice cream maker.

# Tia Maria Ice Box Cake

*Serves 6*                                    *3 months*

This a cross between an ice cream and a cake – it tastes richer if partially defrosted, so serve it whichever way you think your meal merits!

*a small sponge cake*
*100 g/4 oz soft butter*
*65 g/2½ oz icing sugar*
*2 eggs*
*2 tablespoons cocoa*
*1 tablespoon instant coffee, melted in as little water*
  *as possible*
*4 tablespoons Tia Maria*
*150 ml/¼ pint double cream*
*toasted sesame seeds to decorate*

Slice the cake into thin strips and put a layer in the bottom of a cake tin. Meanwhile, cream the butter with the sugar and beat in the eggs one at a time. Mix the cocoa, coffee and Tia Maria together and add to the mixture. Pour half the mixture over the cake. Cover with another layer of cake and then the remains of the mixture. Freeze it for 24 hours.

To serve, unmould and cover the top with whipped cream and toasted sesame seeds. It is best if taken out of the freezer about an hour before you want to eat it, decorated and left in the fridge.

# Christmas Ice Cream

*Serves 8*                                    *2 months*

This is for those who are fed up with Christmas pudding but, you are warned, it is very rich.

> *150 ml/¼ pint double cream*
> *150 ml/¼ pint plain yoghurt*
> *2–3 tablespoons caster sugar*
> *25 g/1 oz each mixed peel, chopped glacé cherries,*
>   *raisins, nibbed almonds and chopped crystallized or*
>   *stem ginger (optional)*
> *a pinch each of ground cloves, cinnamon and nutmeg*
> *2–3 tablespoons brandy*

Mix the cream, yoghurt and 2 tablespoons of the sugar together in a metal or ceramic bowl and put it in the freezer until it is just starting to freeze. Take it out and whisk it, preferably in an electric mixer, until it almost doubles in size. Fold in the fruits, spices and 2 tablespoons of the brandy. Taste and add more sugar or brandy according to your own preference. Spoon into glasses, a dish or a pudding bowl and freeze. The ice cream should not be rock hard when you serve it, so take it out of the freezer 15–20 minutes ahead of time – depending on the heat of your kitchen.

# Frozen Coffee Dessert

*Serves 6*                                    *3 months*

If you are feeling energetic, you can make your own ice cream for this; if not, use a good quality bought ice cream and it will still taste delicious. The longer the ice cream remains in the freezer, the soggier the macaroons will get, so if you want crunchy macaroons, use it within 2 or 3 days.

> *4–5 large or 10–12 small macaroons*
> *90–120 ml/3–4 fl oz brandy or rum*
> *600–900 ml/1–1½ pints coffee or mocha ice cream*
> *150 ml/¼ pint double cream, whipped (optional)*

Line a soufflé dish with plastic cling film, then lay out the macaroons, head down, until the bottom is totally covered. Dribble the brandy or rum over them. If you are using bought ice cream, soften it until it is spoonable, then spoon it in a thick layer over the macaroons and put the dish in the freezer to harden up. If you are making your own ice cream, use the yoghurt ice cream recipe on page 130. Add 120–150 ml/4–5 fl oz strong instant coffee and approximately 2 tablespoons grated dark chocolate – you may want to increase or decrease these amounts depending on how strong you like your coffee flavour. Spoon the mixture over the macaroons as above and freeze.

Once the ice cream is frozen, you can remove it from the dish by the plastic cling film and refreeze it in a well-sealed bag.

To serve, turn it onto a plate with the macaroons facing upwards. You can decorate it with a little whipped cream, although I find it unnecessary.

# Grapefruit and Gin or Vodka Sorbet

*Serves 6*                                    *3 months*

This is a deliciously refreshing (and alcoholic) sorbet if you can keep it frozen long enough to serve it. Because of the high proportion of alcohol, its freezing temperature is very low and it melts on the slightest provocation. If it should do so, pour it into glasses and serve it as a post-prandial cocktail!

> *1 × 400 g/14 oz can grapefruit segments*
> *90–120 ml/3–4 fl oz gin (or vodka if you prefer)*
> *1–2 tablespoons caster sugar*

Purée the grapefruit segments and juice in a liquidizer or food processor. Add the gin or vodka and sugar to taste. You can also increase the quantity of alcohol, but the more alcohol you put in, the less chance you have of persuading it to freeze. Turn it into an ice cream maker if you have one and freeze. If not, put it in a metal or ceramic bowl in the freezer until it is starts to freeze, then take it out and stir it every 15–20 minutes while it is freezing to prevent large ice crystals forming.

Serve in glasses.

*Frozen Coffee Dessert* (see page 133)

# Amaretto Ice Cream Bombe

*Serves 6*                                   *3 months*

This is pretty delicious as it is, but if you really
want to be dashing you could dribble some extra
Amaretto or ginger wine over the top when you
serve it.

> *180 ml/6 fl oz double cream*
> *180 ml/6 fl oz plain yoghurt*
> *100 g/4 oz caster sugar*
> *3 tablespoons Amaretto*
> *juice of ½ orange*
> *juice of ½ lemon*
> *100–175 g/4–6 oz ginger biscuits*

Mix together the cream, yoghurt and sugar in a
bowl and put it in the freezer until it is just
beginning to freeze. Take it out and whip until
the mixture increases considerably in bulk – you
can go on until it almost doubles, but not many
people have that much patience! Add the
Amaretto and fruit juices and whisk again to get

them well amalgamated. (You may need a little
more or less juice depending on the size of the
fruits.)

If you want the filling very crunchy, freeze the ice
cream at this point; if you do not mind the filling
slightly less crunchy but would like the job
finished, pour half the mixture into a bowl, break
up the biscuits and lay them on top in a thick
layer. Top with the rest of the ice cream and
freeze. If you want to get your bowl back, the
bombe can be prised out once it is frozen and
packed in a well-sealed bag.

Alternatively, pack the ice cream in a container
for storage. Several hours before you want to use
it, remove it from the freezer and allow to soften.
Spoon half of the mixture into the bottom of the
bowl and make the bombe as above. Return to the
freezer for a couple of hours and unmould to
serve.

*Christmas Ice Cream* (see page 133)

# BREADS, CAKES AND BISCUITS

## Brown or White Yeast Bread

*1–2 months*

This is a basic yeast bread which can be used for all purposes. It also has the advantage that it only needs one rising. The wholemeal version will be slightly heavier due to the heavier nature of the flour. I find that fresh yeast is much more reliable than the dried variety which does not have as long a shelf life as it claims. Since you have no idea how long it was in the shop, you always risk dead yeast and unrisen bread.

> *½ teaspoon dark brown or granulated sugar,*
> *  depending on which colour bread you are making*
> *½ tablespoon fresh yeast*
> *300 ml/½ pint warm water (about blood heat –*
> *  43°C/110°F)*
> *450 g/1 lb wholemeal or strong white flour*
> *a pinch of salt*
> *1 teaspoon black treacle (for brown bread only)*

Mix the sugar with the yeast and add half the water. Put the mixture in a warm place until it froths – this will take 10–20 minutes. Put the flour and salt in a bowl. Mix the treacle (if you are using it) with the rest of the water. Make a well in the flour and pour in the yeast mixture plus the extra water or treacle and water. Mix well by hand and knead the dough for a couple of minutes. Turn the dough into a greased 20-cm/8-inch loaf tin, cover with a cloth and leave in a warm, not hot, place (do not try to rush it by putting it in an oven as you will kill the yeast – unless you leave the door *open*) for 30–60 minutes to rise. It should almost double in size, but will do so faster or slower according to the ambient temperature.

Bake for 10 minutes in a hot oven (200°C/400°F/ Gas Mark 6), then reduce the temperature to moderate (180°C/350°F/Gas Mark 4) and bake for a further 30–40 minutes or until the loaf sounds hollow when the bottom is rapped with the knuckles. It is is a good idea to take it out of the tin for the last 10–15 minutes to crisp the bottom and sides. Cool on a rack.

When completely cold, freeze in a well-sealed bag.

Defrost at room temperature or in a microwave, although a microwave can make the crust go soggy.

## Wholemeal Bran Loaf

*Makes enough for 2 loaves*　　　　　　*1 month*

This is a close-textured, quite moist bread and therefore freezes better than some of the more open–textured breads. It is also full of roughage!

> *25 g/1 oz fresh yeast, or 15 g/½ oz dried yeast*
> *1 teaspoon brown sugar, black treacle or honey*
> *800 ml/26 fl oz warm water (blood heat)*
> *1 teaspoon salt*
> *75 g/3 oz fresh, unprocessed bran*
> *1 kg/2 lb wholemeal flour (preferably stone ground)*

Mix the yeast and sugar, treacle or honey together in a small bowl, add 90 ml/3 fl oz of the warm water, stir well and leave for 10 minutes to froth up. Add the salt and bran to the flour, then, when it has frothed, add the yeasty water plus the rest of the warm water and mix well using first a spoon and then your hands until the dough feels elastic. It should be slippery but not 'wet'. Divide the dough in two and either shape it into round loaves or put it into warmed and greased loaf tins. Cover it with a damp cloth and put it in a warm place to rise. If you have an airing cupboard, that is fine; otherwise use the oven turned to the lowest possible setting and with the door left open. (If the dough is heated above 50°C/110°F, the yeast will be killed and the bread will never rise.) Leave it for 30–45 minutes until the dough has risen by half its size. If the dough rises too much, the bread will be crumbly and hard to cut.

Meanwhile, heat the oven to hot (200°C/400°F/Gas Mark 6). Put the risen loaves in near the top and reduce the heat to moderately hot (190°C/375°F/

Gas Mark 5) after 15 minutes. Bake for a further 15–20 minutes (35 minutes altogether) until the loaves are golden brown all over and hollow when you tap their bottoms. It is a good idea to remove them from the tins, or turn them over if they are not in tins, for the last 10 minutes to brown the bottoms. Cool thoroughly on a rack.

To freeze, wrap tightly in a polythene bag.

Defrost at room temperature or in a microwave.

# Almond Shortbread

*Makes about 15 pieces*                    *6 months*

Like all biscuits, shortbread freezes excellently and defrosts in no time. You can make it either in triangles or in fingers – the latter are less likely to break in the freezer.

> 100 g/4 oz soft butter
> 50 g/2 oz caster sugar
> 50 g/2 oz rice flour or semolina
> 100 g/4 oz plain flour
> 25 g/1 oz nibbed or flaked almonds
> a little extra sugar

Beat the butter until very soft, then beat in the sugar. Add the two flours and the almonds and mix them in as lightly as possible with a wooden spoon; do not beat the mixture further or it can become tough. As soon as everything is fairly well amalgamated, press out the mixture with your fingers in the bottom of a round or square cake tin; it should be 1–2 cm/½–¾ inch thick. Cook the shortbread in a moderately hot oven (190°C/375°F/Gas Mark 5) for about 10 minutes. Take it out and cut into whatever shapes you want the biscuits. Sprinkle it with a little extra sugar and return to the oven for a further 5 minutes. The biscuits should end up lightly browned. Remove from the oven and cool before removing from the tin.

To freeze, pack in well-sealed containers or stacked neatly in bags once they are quite cold.

Defrost at room temperature or in a microwave, although they defrost so quickly it is scarcely worth the risk of burning them in the microwave.

# Brown Baps

*Makes 8–12 baps*                    *1 month*

These make excellent outsides for really filling sandwiches – as well as good dinner rolls. They freeze well, although they should be freshened up in an oven or microwave after freezing. Remember that all frozen breads become stale quicker than fresh ones, so use them the same day as they are defrosted.

> 25 g/1 oz fresh yeast
> 1 teaspoon sugar
> 150 ml/¼ pint warm milk mixed with 150 ml/
>    ¼ pint warm water
> 50 g/2 oz butter
> 450 g/1 lb wholemeal flour
> 1 teaspoon sea salt
> a little extra milk

Mix the yeast with the sugar and add about 90 ml/3 fl oz of the liquid. Set aside in a warm place until it froths – this will take about 10 minutes. Meanwhile, rub the butter into the flour along with the salt. Once the yeast has frothed, make a well in the centre of the flour and pour in the yeast together with the rest of the liquid. Mix it to a slack dough, cover the bowl with a damp cloth and leave it in a warm place to rise. It should almost double in size in 1–2 hours depending on the heat of the kitchen. Take the dough out and knead it lightly on a floured board. Divide the dough into 8 or 12 bits, depending on how large you want your baps, knead each lightly, then flatten into a round or an oval. Place on a floured baking tin and leave to rise again. Brush with a little milk and bake in a hot oven (200°C/400°F/Gas Mark 6) for 15–20 minutes or until they are lightly browned and sound hollow if you tap them. Cool on a rack.

When completely cold, freeze in well-sealed bags.

Defrost at room temperature or in an oven or microwave and use at once.

# Brown Soda Bread

*1–2 months*

Soda bread is an Irish speciality and devotees maintain that it never tastes the same outside the Emerald Isle as it is impossible to get the same quality of flour. However, even 'inferior' English flour makes a delicious, coarse brown bread which freezes well.

*575 g/1¼ lb coarse brown flour*
*125 g/5 oz strong white flour*
*1 heaped teaspoon salt*
*1 tablespoon bicarbonate of soda*
*600–900 ml/1–1½ pints buttermilk*

Mix the dry ingredients thoroughly together. Make a well in the middle and lightly mix in enough buttermilk to make a soft dough. Shape the loaf into a round cob shape on a floured baking tin and cut a cross in the top. Bake it in a moderately hot oven (190°C/375°F/Gas Mark 5) for 35–45 minutes or until the bottom sounds hollow when you tap it. It is a good idea to turn the loaf upside down for the last 10 minutes to make sure the bottom gets crisp. Cool on a rack. It is said that bread should be left for 24 hours before it is cut, but I have yet to meet a person who can resist the smell of it when warm!

If it is to be frozen, allow the loaf to get completely cold, then pack in a well-sealed bag.

Defrost at room temperature or in a microwave – although a microwave tends to make the crust less crisp.

# Guernsey Apple Cake

*6 months*

This makes a very moist, spicy, quite solid cake – not unlike a parkin – which because of its moistness freezes excellently. Addicts of really coarse brown bread will go dotty about it!

*225 g/8 oz cooking apple, peeled and diced*
*juice of ½ lemon*
*225 g/8 oz plain wholemeal flour*
*100 g/4 oz soft butter*
*175 g/6 oz demerara sugar*
*2 large eggs*
*1 teaspoon ground nutmeg*
*1 teaspoon ground cinnamon*

Toss the apple well in the lemon juice, then add the flour. Mix them well together, cover and leave for 1–12 hours.

Cream the butter, then add the sugar. Mix in the eggs, one by one, making sure they are well amalgamated. Add the spices to the flour and apple mixture and mix thoroughly into the creamed butter, sugar and eggs. Grease a loose-bottomed 20-cm/8-inch cake tin and spoon in the cake mixture. Smooth it out with a spoon or spatula and bake in a moderately cool oven (160°C/325°F/Gas Mark 3) for 1 hour. Take out of the oven and allow to cool in the tin. Once cool, remove from the tin onto a rack and allow to get completely cold.

Freeze in a well-sealed bag.

Defrost at room temperature or in a microwave if in a hurry.

*Almond Shortbread* (see page 137)

*Wholemeal Bran Loaf* (see page 136), *Brown Soda Bread and Almond Bread* (see page 140)

# Almond Bread

*3 months*

This is a rather expensive, but positively delicious, nut bread which, like all sweet breads, freezes excellently.

*100 g/4 oz ground almonds*
*50 g/2 oz wholemeal flour*
*1 teaspoon baking powder*
*50 g/2 oz dark brown sugar*
*25 g/1 oz melted butter*
*2 eggs, separated*
*grated rind and juice of 1 small lemon*

Mix the almonds, flour, baking powder and brown sugar in a bowl. Melt the butter and add it along with the egg yolks. Beat the mixture well, then add the lemon rind and juice. Whisk the egg whites until they hold their shape in soft peaks and mix them into the bread. Pour the mixture into a 15-cm/6-inch well-greased loaf tin. Bake in a moderately hot oven (190°C/375°F/Gas Mark 5) for 25 minutes or until the loaf has risen slightly and a skewer comes out clean.

Cool on a wire rack. The bread can be eaten alone or with butter.

When completely cold, freeze in a well-sealed bag.

Defrost at room temperature or in a microwave and serve as above.

# Banana Bread

*2–3 months*

Not only is this a divine way of using up ancient, blackened and unappealing bananas, but it also freezes well and will put up with being returned to the freezer once, or even twice.

*125 g/5 oz butter*
*125 g/5 oz sugar*
*275 g/10 oz plain flour*
*1 teaspoon bicarbonate of soda*
*2 eggs*
*2 very ripe bananas*
*2–3 tablespoons sour milk*

Cream the butter with the sugar until they are pale and fluffy. Sift the flour with the bicarbonate and add it alternately with the eggs. Mash the bananas and add them to the mixture with the sour milk. Spoon the mixture into a loaf tin and bake in a moderate oven (180°C/350°F/Gas Mark 4) for 1–1½ hours or until a skewer comes out clean. Cool on a rack and serve sliced and buttered.

To freeze, wrap tightly in a polythene bag.

Defrost at room temperature or in a microwave.

# Treacle Parkins

*2 months*

A parkin is a Yorkshire cross between a wholemeal loaf and gingerbread; it is usually eaten as cake, although you can butter it. The original of this recipe specified that the parkins were to be eaten on November 5th, but did not say why! Maybe because the taste is quite fiery?

*225 g/8 oz medium oatmeal*
*225 g/8 oz wholemeal flour*
*40 g/1½ oz lard*
*40 g/1½ oz butter*
*2 heaped teaspoons ground ginger*
*60 g/2½ oz dark brown sugar*
*275 g/10 oz black treacle or molasses*
*1 teaspoon bicarbonate of soda*
*30 ml/1 fl oz milk*

Mix together the oatmeal and flour, then rub in the lard and butter as though for pastry. Add the ginger and sugar and mix in well. Heat the treacle and mix the bicarbonate of soda with the milk. Add both liquids to the dry ingredients and mix well. Press the mixture into a baking tray so it is about 1 cm/½ inch thick and cut into biscuit shapes (as for shortbread). Alternatively, cut into shapes with a biscuit cutter and lay on a tray. Bake in a low oven (150°C/300°F/Gas Mark 2) for 30–40 minutes. Cool on a rack.

To freeze, pack in plastic boxes to prevent breakages. Alternatively, stack neatly before packing in bags.

Defrost at room temperature (about 30 minutes if spread out) or in a microwave, although care should be taken that they do not burn.

# Flapjacks

*Makes about 20*          *9 months*

This recipe was devised specially for someone who could not eat any wheat products. Maple syrup will give a slightly different flavour to the flapjacks.

*100 g/4 oz low fat margarine or butter*
*50 g/2 oz dark Barbados sugar*
*50 g/2 oz golden or maple syrup*
*225 g/8 oz porridge oats*
*50 g/2 oz pine kernels, sunflower seeds or any other small or chopped nut or seed of your choice*

Dissolve the fat, sugar and syrup in a pan or microwave; do not let them boil or the flapjacks will go tacky rather than crisp. Stir in the oats, nuts or seeds and mix them all well together. With your fingers press out the mixture in a *thin* layer in the bottom of a metal or pyrex flan dish. Cook the biscuits for 30 minutes in a moderate oven (180°C/350°F/Gas Mark 4) or for 3½–4 minutes in a microwave on full power. As soon as they are cooked, cut into sections and cool slightly. Remove them from the tin and allow to cool on a rack.

To freeze, cool completely, then pack them in a well-sealed container or stack in a well-sealed bag.

Defrost at room temperature or with care in a microwave, although they defrost so quickly it is scarcely worth risking burning them in the microwave.

# A Simnel Cake for Easter

*Serves 8–10*          *3 months*

The traditional way to make a simnel cake is to bake the almond paste or marzipan in a layer in the middle. However, since not everyone likes marzipan it may be better to bake it as an ordinary cake and merely fill and ice it with the marzipan so it can be easily discarded. Using wholemeal flour gives the cake quite a nutty texture; if you would prefer a smoother texture, substitute plain white flour.

*175 g/6 oz sultanas*
*50 g/2 oz mixed peel*
*300 ml/½ pint cider*
*225 g/8 oz wholemeal flour*
*1 teaspoon bicarbonate of soda*
*100 g/4 oz dark brown sugar*
*1 teaspoon cream of tartar*
*50 g/2 oz very soft butter*
*raspberry or apricot jam*

**Almond Paste**
*225 g/8 oz icing sugar or icing and caster sugar mixed*
*225 g/8 oz ground almonds*
*1 egg white*
*juice of 1 lemon*

If you have time, soak the sultanas and peel in the cider for an hour or so before making the cake. Mix all the dry ingredients together (an electric mixer is good for this) and then add the softened butter, the fruit and peel and, gradually, the cider. Spoon into a greased 18–20-cm/7–8-inch cake tin (either with a loose bottom or lined with greased greaseproof paper to avoid problems getting it out). Bake the cake in a moderate oven (180°C/350°F/Gas Mark 4) for about 1 hour or until a skewer comes out clean. Take it out of the tin and cool it on a rack.

(NOTE: If you want to make the cake in the traditional way, you will need to make the almond paste (below) before making the cake. Spoon half the cake mixture into the cake tin, then put a layer of marzipan over it and top with the rest of the cake mix. Bake as above.)

To make the almond paste or marzipan, mix together the sugar and almonds and beat in the egg white and enough lemon juice to make a solid paste. Chill. When the cake is quite cold, cut it in half horizontally and spread the lower side with raspberry or apricot jam. Dust a board with icing sugar and roll out half the marzipan in a circle. Lay it in the middle of the cake, spread some more jam over it and place the top half of the cake on it. Spread another thin layer of jam on top of the cake, then roll out the rest of the marzipan and use it to 'ice' the cake. Use any offcuts and bits to roll into little balls which should be placed on top of the cake as decoration.

Wrap tightly in a polythene bag to freeze.

Defrost at room temperature.

*A Simnel Cake for Easter* (see page 141)

# Chocolate Cake

*6 months*

For those who are addicted to raw cake mix this is quite delicious, but it also freezes extremely well either iced (see page 148) or undecorated.

*150 g/6 oz soft butter*
*200 g/7 oz caster sugar*
*1 tablespoon cocoa dissolved in 2 tablespoons hot water*
*3 eggs*
*150 g/6 oz self-raising flour*
*1 tablespoon milk*

Cream the butter and sugar in an electric mixer until they are really light and fluffy, then add the dissolved cocoa. Mix in the eggs one at a time, adding approximately 1 tablespoon of flour with the last egg. Fold in the rest of the flour and stir in the milk. Pour or spoon the mixture into a greased, loose–bottomed 20-cm/8-inch cake tin, or a solid tin lined with greaseproof paper. Bake the cake in a moderate oven (180°C/350°F/Gas Mark 4) for 30 minutes or until a skewer inserted in the middle comes out clean. Remove the cake from the tin and cool on a rack.

The cake can be halved and filled and topped with chocolate butter icing, or whatever other icing you want to use, before being frozen. Alternatively, pack the undecorated cake in a well-sealed bag and decorate when defrosted.

Defrost at room temperature and ice as above.

*Wholemeal Soured Cream 'Coffee Cake'* (see page 148), *Walnut Tart* (see page 115) *and Chocolate Cake*

# Traditional Fruit Cake

*6–12 months*

Both Catercall and I have been through many recipes for Christmas or wedding cakes and we have always come back to the recipe for a Traditonal Christmas Cake to be found in Katie Stewart's *Times Cookery Book*. It does keep well if wrapped in foil and tightly sealed in a polythene bag, but if it is only to appear on rare occasions, moistness is guaranteed by freezing it. This quantity makes a relatively small cake (20-cm/ 8-inch), but it is so rich that small slices go a long way.

> 275 g/10 oz plain flour
> 1 teaspoon mixed spice
> 1 teaspoon salt
> 225 g/8 oz butter
> 225 g/8 oz soft brown sugar
> 4 large eggs
> 1 tablespoon black treacle
> ½ teaspoon vanilla essence
> 100 g/4 oz glacé cherries, washed, dried and halved
> 225 g/8 oz each currants, sultanas and seedless raisins
> 100 g/4 oz chopped candied peel
> 50 g/2 oz blanched chopped almonds or broken walnuts
> 2 tablespoons brandy or milk.

Sieve the flour with the mixed spice and salt and set aside. Cream together the butter and sugar until very soft and light. Lightly mix the eggs, treacle and vanilla essence, then gradually beat them into the creamed mixture a little at a time. Add some of the flour together with the last few additions of egg mixture. Put the cherries with the rest of the fruits, the peel and the nuts into a bowl. Add a couple of spoonfuls of flour to the fruit and mix well. Using a metal spoon, fold in the remaining flour and the creamed mixture together with the brandy or milk.
Spoon the mixture into a greased and lined 20-cm/ 8-inch deep, round cake tin and hollow out the middle slightly. Place it fairly low in a slow oven (150°C/300°F/Gas Mark 2) and bake it for 1½ hours, then lower the temperature to very low (140°C/275°F/Gas Mark 1) and bake for a further 2½ hours. Cool the baked cake in the tin, turn it out and eat immediately or store.

Freeze in a well-sealed bag.

Defrost at room temperature or in a microwave if you are in a rush – it is better at room temperature.
NOTE: If you want to ice and decorate the cake, it is better to do so after it is defrosted. Marzipan and royal icing will freeze, but they tend to go dry, hard and crumbly. If you want to freeze the remains of a Christmas or wedding cake, do so with the icing on, then, when you defrost it, chip off the old icing and replace it with new.

# Oatcakes

*Makes about 40 small or*                              *2 months*
*20 large oatcakes*

Home-made oatcakes are a delicious alternative to bought cheese biscuits, especially with hard cheeses, but, more usefully, small oatcakes make excellent bases for cocktail canapés as they do not go soggy. You can use fine, medium and coarse oatmeal, but exactly what proportion you use will depend on how coarse you like your oatcakes to be. I would not recommend more than 50 g/2 oz of pinhead (coarse) or the biscuits will tend to disintegrate.

> 225 g/8 oz mixed oatmeals
> 100 g/4 oz plain white flour
> ½ teaspoon salt
> 1 teaspoon baking powder
> 40 g/1½ oz butter
> 40 g/1½ oz lard

Mix the oatmeals in a bowl, then sift in the flour, salt and baking powder. Rub in the fats as for pastry and mix to a stiff dough with cold water. Turn the mixture onto a board sprinkled with oatmeal. Knead it lightly, then roll it out quite thinly and cut into circles with biscuit cutters or a glass – I find that rounds have less of a tendency to break than squares or oblongs. Place on a baking tray and cook in a moderate oven (180°C/ 350°F/Gas Mark 4) for 10–15 minutes – take care that they do not burn. Cool the oatcakes on a tray.

Freeze in boxes if possible to prevent breakages; otherwise stack before packing tightly in polythene bags.

Defrost at room temperature; if they are spread out, they only take 5–10 minutes.

# Ginger Biscuits

*Makes about 20 biscuits*                    *2 months*

This is almost like a ginger shortbread – and very more-ish!

> *100 g/4 oz sugar*
> *225 g/8 oz self-raising flour*
> *2 teaspoons ground ginger*
> *a pinch of salt*
> *175 g/6 oz butter*

Mix the sugar, flour, ginger and salt in a bowl, then rub in the butter. Press the mixture out in a baking tin – about 1 cm/½ inch thick. Bake it for 10 minutes in a preheated moderately hot oven (190°C/375°F/Gas Mark 5). Take the tray out, cut the mixture into biscuit shapes as for shortbread and return to the oven for a further 10 minutes or until the biscuits are golden – but take care that they do not burn. Cool on a rack.

Freeze in boxes if possible to prevent breakages; otherwise stack before packing tightly in polythene bags.

Defrost at room temperature (about 30 minutes if spread out) or in a microwave, but take care not to burn.

# Sweet Bannock Biscuits

*Makes about 12 biscuits*                    *3 months*

These very plain biscuits are ideal for someone who does not have a very sweet tooth – they set off a cup of coffee 'a treat'.

> *125 g/5 oz wholemeal flour*
> *75 g/3 oz medium oatmeal*
> *2 teaspoons baking powder*
> *75 g/3 oz dark Barbados sugar*
> *50 g/2 oz butter or low fat margarine*
> *1 egg*
> *3 tablespoons sour milk or buttermilk*

Mix the flour, oatmeal, baking powder and sugar together in a bowl, then rub in the fat. Make a well in the middle of the mixture, add the egg and the milk and mix to a soft dough. Roll the dough out on a lightly floured board – it should be about 1 cm/½ inch thick. Cut out rounds either with a

biscuit cutter or a wine glass, place on a baking sheet and bake in a hot oven (200°C/400°F/Gas Mark 6) for 15–20 minutes. You should look after 15 minutes to make sure they are not burning. Remove the biscuits from the oven and cool on a rack.

If they are to be frozen, they should be packed and frozen only when they are cold.

Defrost at room temperature.

# Simple Sponge Cake

*3 months*

This is a very simple eggless sponge, but is invaluable to have in the freezer for emergencies as it defrosts very quickly. Spread with jam and cream to turn it into a teatime cake; pour some whipped cream over it and scatter some fresh (or even frozen) fruit on top to make a delicious dessert. Stale or broken cakes make excellent bases for trifle. It is worth making a batch at a time; as long as you interleave them with greaseproof paper or plastic cling film, you can pack several in one bag. This quantity will make 2–3 sponges depending on the size of your tins.

> *6 eggs*
> *150 g/6 oz caster sugar*
> *150 g/6 oz plain flour*

Whisk the eggs and sugar together until they are *really* thick and light. Sift the flour into the bowl and fold carefully into the mixture. It is very easy to end up with little lumps of flour. Pour the mixture into loose-bottomed 7–9-inch/18–23 cm cake tins that have been lined with lightly floured greaseproof paper. Bake in a cool oven (160°C/325°F/ Gas Mark 3) for 20–30 minutes or until the cake bounces back when you press it gently. Remove from the oven and cool on racks. The cakes can be used once they are cold.

To freeze, interleave each cake with greaseproof paper or plastic cling film when it is quite cold and freeze in well-sealed bags.

Defrost at room temperature or with care in a microwave and use as above.

*Lemon Brandy Cake, Gooey Gingerbread, Raisin Scones and Brown Baps (see page 137)*

## Raisin Scones

*Makes about 12 scones*                    *1–2 months*

Although a frozen scone will never taste as good as a freshly baked one, you can always toast them so that no one will know the difference!

    450 g/1 lb strong white flour
    1 teaspoon salt
    ¾ teaspoon bicarbonate of soda
    ¾ teaspoon cream of tartar
    50 g/2 oz granulated sugar
    150–175 g/5–6 oz raisins
    50 g/2 oz butter
    1 egg
    150–300 ml/¼–½ pint buttermilk

Sieve the dry ingredients together, add the raisins, then rub in the fat as though for pastry. Mix in the egg and enough of the buttermilk to make a moist dough. Knead the dough lightly on a floured board, then press it out to approximately 2 cm/¾ inch thickness and cut out rounds (with a pastry cutter or a glass) or triangles. Lay the scones on a floured baking tray and cook them in a hot oven (200°C/400°F/Gas Mark 6) for 7–15 minutes, depending on how large you have made them. They should be lightly browned but not burnt. Cool completely on a rack – unless you intend to eat them fresh!

Freeze when quite cold in a well-sealed bag.

Defrost at room temperature or in a microwave, toast and serve with lots of butter.

## Gooey Gingerbread

                                          *6 months*

This sticky gingerbread keeps very well out of the freezer but it is better frozen for long storage.

    100 g/4 oz butter
    100 g/4 oz demerara, dark brown or granulated
      sugar

450 g/1 lb black treacle
3 eggs
225 g/8 oz self-raising flour (you can use white or
    wholemeal for a nuttier texture)
2 teaspoons ground ginger
1½ teaspoons mixed spice
1½ teaspoons ground cinnamon

Melt the butter, sugar and treacle together in a
pan or microwave. Draw away from the heat.
Beat the eggs into the melted mixture followed by
the flour and spices. Pour into a greased loaf tin
or cake tin and bake in a moderately cool oven
(160°C/325°F/Gas Mark 3) for an hour. Take out of
the oven and the tin and cool on a wire rack.
Serve it sliced, either plain or buttered.

To freeze, cool completely and pack in a well-
sealed bag.

Defrost at room temperature or in a microwave
and serve as above.

## Lemon Brandy Cake

Serves 8–10                                    2 months

The combination of lemon and brandy manages
to make this cake both rich and refreshing – if it is
possible for a cake to be refreshing!

grated rind of 2 large lemons
150 ml/¼ pint brandy
3 large eggs
the weight of the eggs in butter, caster sugar and
    plain white flour
175 g/6 oz sultanas
½ teaspoon baking powder

If you have time, infuse the lemon rind in the
brandy for an hour or longer before making the
cake. Cream the butter and sugar until white and
fluffy. Separate the eggs and add the yolks, one at
a time, with a spoonful of flour each time to
prevent the mixture curdling. Beat thoroughly.
Mix in the brandy, lemon rind, sultanas and a
little more flour. Sift together the remaining flour
and baking powder and whisk the egg whites
until they stand in soft peaks. Fold the egg whites

and the flour and baking powder into the mixture, then spoon or pour it into a 20-cm/8-inch cake tin lined with greased greaseproof paper. Bake in a moderate oven (180°C/350°F/Gas Mark 4) for about 1 hour or until a skewer comes out clean. Turn onto a rack and cool. The cake can be eaten as it is, without icing, or it can be lightly iced with a lemon glacé or lemon butter icing.

To freeze, pack tightly in a polythene bag, preferably before it is iced.

Defrost at room temperature or in a microwave with care. If it has not been iced, it can be once it is defrosted.

# Wholemeal Soured Cream 'Coffee Cake'

*6 months*

American recipes for 'coffee cake' (of which this is one) can be misleading as they contain no coffee at all – but are meant to be eaten *with* coffee!

> 100 g/4 oz soft butter
> 150 g/6 oz demerara sugar
> 3 eggs
> a pinch of salt
> a pinch of bicarbonate of soda
> 200 g/7 oz wholemeal flour
> 120 ml/4 fl oz soured cream
> 2 drops vanilla essence
> 75 g/3 oz chopped walnuts or pecans
> 75 g/3 oz dark brown sugar
> 2 teaspoons ground cinnamon

Cream the butter with the demerara sugar. Add the eggs, one at a time, beating well after each addition. Sift the salt and bicarbonate of soda with the flour and gently beat into the mixture alternately with the soured cream and the vanilla essence. Grease a loose-bottomed 20-cm/8-inch cake tin. Spoon half the cake mixture into the bottom and smooth it out. Mix the chopped nuts, dark brown sugar and cinnamon and sprinkle half over the cake mix. Add the rest of the cake batter and sprinkle the remains of the nut mixture over the top. Cook the cake for 1 hour in a moderately cool oven (160°C/325°F/Gas Mark 3). Remove it from the oven and take the cake out of the tin and cool it on a rack.

Freeze it when completely cold in a well-sealed bag.

Defrost at room temperature – a microwave may caramelize the sugar topping.

# Easy Chocolate Butter Icing

> 75 g/3 oz salted butter, softened
> 2–3 tablespoons chocolate spread

Beat the butter until thoroughly soft, then add the chocolate spread, a tablespoon at a time, until it tastes chocolaty enough. Ice the cake as usual (see page 142) and chill in the fridge for 30 minutes to firm up the icing.

# Walnut Cake

*Serves 8–10*                                    *3 months*

This is a splendidly simple cake which freezes well because of its moistness.

> 75 g/3 oz soft brown sugar
> 150 g/6 oz soft butter
> 3 eggs
> 3 heaped tablespoons golden syrup
> 150 g/6 oz self-raising flour
> 75 g/3 oz chopped walnuts

Cream the sugar with the butter in an electric mixer until they are reasonably light and fluffy. Gradually add the eggs and syrup, then fold in the flour and chopped nuts, making sure they are all well mixed. Spoon the mixture into a greased non-stick, loose-bottomed or greaseproof-paper-lined cake tin and bake in a moderate oven (180°C/350°F/Gas Mark 4) for 30 minutes or until a skewer comes out clean. Take out of the tin and cool on a rack.

If you want, you can ice the cake with a white glacé icing and decorate it with halved walnuts, but it scarcely needs it.

Freeze the cake before you ice it, packed tightly in a polythene bag.

Defrost at room temperature or, carefully, in a microwave.

# Chocolate and Sesame Biscuits

*Makes about 15 biscuits*                    *4–6 months*

These are for real chocolate freaks, they are so chocolaty that all but real aficionados will find themselves pulling out after about two.

> *75 g/3 oz soft butter*
> *50 g/2 oz caster sugar*
> *100 g/4 oz wholemeal flour*
> *25 g/1 oz cocoa powder*
> *1 teaspoon baking powder*
> *2 tablespoons toasted sesame seeds*

Beat the butter and sugar together until they are light. Sift together the flour, cocoa and baking powder and mix them in thoroughly together with the sesame seeds. Roll or squash out the mixture with your hands until it is about 1 cm/ ½ inch thick, then cut into rounds either with a cutter or a wine glass. Transfer carefully onto a baking tray and bake in a moderately hot oven (190°C/375°F/Gas Mark 5) for 15 minutes – take care that they do not burn. Remove them from the oven, cool slightly, then transfer them onto a rack to cool completely. If liked, sprinkle with caster sugar before serving.

Freeze the biscuits in boxes to prevent breakage.

Defrost at room temperature or, with care, in a microwave.

# Stollen Bread

*Makes 1 large loaf*                    *2–3 months*

This is a very rich and really delicious sweet, German bread – it is ideal for Christmas, if you have space after lunch, Although the recipe is long, it is not complicated; it just needs a lot of rising time. It is less frustrating to make if you are already embarking on an afternoon's cooking, so you can merely return to the bread between other things. Since the loaf is quite large, it might be wise to cut it in half before freezing. It will also look better if you leave the final decoration until just before you serve it; it will freeze perfectly well, but the cherries tend to get knocked off in the freezer.

> *240 ml/8 fl oz lukewarm milk*
> *100 g/4 oz sugar*
> *1 teaspoon salt*
> *30 g/1¼ oz fresh yeast or 15 g/½ oz dried yeast*
> *100 g/4 oz vegetable shortening (not lard)*
> *2 eggs*
> *625 g/22 oz sifted plain flour*
> *100 g/4 oz roughly chopped blanched almonds*
> *50 g/2 oz chopped citron peel*
> *50 g/2 oz glacé cherries, chopped*
> *1 tablespoon grated lemon rind*
> *25 g/1 oz softened butter, plus 15 g/½ oz melted butter*

> ### Glacé icing
> *100 g/4 oz sifted icing sugar*
> *2 tablespoons warm water or warm water and lemon juice mixed*

Mix together the milk, sugar and salt in a bowl and crumble in the yeast. Stir together until the yeast is dissolved. Soften the shortening, mix it with the eggs and stir it into the yeast mixture. Gradually add the flour, mixing first with a spoon and then with your hands. When the dough begins to leave the sides of the bowl, turn it onto a lightly floured board and knead it by folding the dough over towards you and then pressing it down and away from you with the heel of your hand. Give the dough a quarter turn and repeat the kneading and turning until it is smooth and elastic and does not stick to the board.

Put the dough in a greased bowl, turning once to bring the greased side upwards. Cover with a damp cloth and let it rise in a warm, draught-free spot for about 1½ hours – an airing cupboard or an oven turned to the lowest setting with the door left open. It should nearly double in size. To test, press two fingers into the dough – they will leave indentations when it has risen enough. Punch your fist down into the dough, pull the edges into the centre and turn the dough completely over in the bowl. Let it rise again until it has almost doubled its original size. It should take 35–40 minutes.

After the second rising, turn the dough onto a lightly floured board and flatten it out. Distribute the almonds, peel, cherries (saving a few to decorate the top) and the lemon rind evenly over the dough. Knead them into the dough, then pat it into an oval of about 20×30 cm/8×12 inches.

*Stollen Bread* (see page 149)

Spread the dough with the softened butter and fold it in two lengthways; form it into a crescent, pressing the edges well together so that they do not spring apart. Place the crescent on a lightly greased baking tray, brush the top with the melted butter and let it rise (in a warm place but not in the oven this time) until it is double its original size. Bake the loaf in a moderately hot oven (190°C/375°F/Gas Mark 5) for 35 minutes, then remove it and cool on a rack.

To make the glacé icing, mix the sugar well with the warm water or water and lemon juice mixed to make a runny paste. Dribble this over the loaf, preferably when it is still warm, and decorate with the reserved cherries. Serve sliced and spread lightly with butter – unsalted if possible.

To freeze, pack tightly (preferably before decorating), whole or halved, in polythene bags.

Defrost at room temperature or in a microwave.

*Chocolate and Sesame Biscuits* (see page 149)

# SAUCES AND STOCKS

## Barbecue Sauce or Marinade

*Serves 6*                                            *6 months*

A sunny July brings all the barbecues out into the garden so it is as well to have the freezer stocked with a couple of good barbecue sauces. Although they are quick to make, they are even quicker to defrost!

> *4 tablespoons olive or vegetable oil*
> *2 large cloves garlic, finely chopped*
> *2.5 cm/1 inch ginger root, finely chopped*
> *10 spring onions, finely chopped*
> *2 tablespoons soy sauce*
> *3 tablespoons honey*
> *2 tablespoons vinegar*
> *2 tablespoons tomato purée*
> *600 ml/1 pint well-flavoured stock*
> *salt and pepper*

Heat the oil in a pan and gently cook the garlic, ginger and onions until they are all beginning to soften. Add the soy sauce, honey, vinegar and tomato purée, stir thoroughly, then gradually add the stock. Bring to the boil and simmer fairly fast, uncovered, for 25–30 minutes or until the flavours are thoroughly amalgamated and the sauce has reduced to about 450 ml/¾ pint. Season to taste with salt and pepper.

The sauce can then be used as a marinade for whatever is to be cooked. Submerge the meat, fish or vegetables in it for 1–24 hours. Barbecue as usual, using the sauce/marinade to baste. Finally, amalgamate the sauce with any juices that come out of the meat while it was cooking, reheat and serve with the barbecue.

If the sauce is to be frozen, do not season before freezing. Allow the reduced sauce to get completely cold, then freeze in a well-sealed container, leaving room for expansion.

Defrost at room temperature or in a microwave and use as above.

## Gooseberry or Rhubarb Sauce

*Serves 6*                                            *6–9 months*

Since the season for gooseberries especially is quite short, it is worth making some sauce when they are available and just keeping it for future use. Gooseberry sauce is a traditional French accompaniment to mackerel, but both of these sauces are good with any rich fish or meat as their acidity helps to counteract the richness of the meat. They are also good with root vegetables and can, in times of need, be converted into dessert fools or pie fillings!

> *25 g/1 oz butter*
> *225 g/8 oz fresh gooseberries, topped and tailed, or*
> *  fresh rhubarb, cleaned and chopped*
> *juice of 1 small lemon*
> *150 ml/¼ pint double cream*
> *a little sugar (optional)*
> *a little salt and pepper (optional)*

Melt the butter in a pan, add the gooseberries or rhubarb, cover and stew very slowly until the fruit is quite soft – this usually takes 20–30 minutes. It can also be very successfully done in a microwave. If you like your sauce very smooth, sieve it once it is cooked; if you would rather have the pips and bits, liquidize or process it. If the sauce is to be frozen, it is better to do so before adding the lemon juice and cream. If it is to be used at once, add the lemon juice and the cream – you should not need any sugar unless the fruit was very tart indeed. If it is too thick (it should be the consistency of thick pouring cream), thin it down with a little of the juice from the fish, if it is to be served with fish, or a little stock, milk or water. If you like, you can also season it with a *little* salt and pepper. Serve the sauce hot or cold.

Freeze in a well-sealed container, leaving room for expansion.

Defrost at room temperature or in a microwave and finish as above.

# Chicken Stock

*Makes about 2.5 litres/4 pints*                    *6 months*

If you want to make *really* delicious stock, you can poach a whole chicken in the liquid (which can be used for anything you fancy), but this is obviously extravagant unless you have a specific use for the chicken. You can also add any leftover bits of vegetable you may have in the fridge.

> *the bones, giblets, etc. from a 1.5–2 kg/3–4 lb*
>   *chicken, or some cheap chicken pieces*
> *1 large onion, roughly sliced*
> *1 large carrot, scrubbed and chopped*
> *2 sticks celery, washed and chopped*
> *6–8 mushroom stalks or a couple of whole*
>   *mushrooms*
> *2–3 parsley stalks*
> *2–3 bay leaves*
> *a little salt*
> *6–8 peppercorns*
> *3 litres/5 pints cold water*
> *150–300 ml/¼–½ pint dry white wine (optional)*

Put all the ingredients in a large pot and bring slowly to the boil. Skim off any scum that rises to the surface. Simmer, uncovered, for 45–60 minutes, then strain the stock and discard the bits (except, of course, the whole chicken if you are using one). Allow the stock to cool completely, then remove any fat that has risen to the surface. Use in sauces, soups, etc., or freeze in well-sealed, convenient-sized containers (ice trays are quite useful), leaving room for expansion.

Defrost at room temperature, in a microwave or in a pan on the hob and use as above.

# Brown Stock

*Makes about 2.5 litres/4 pints*                    *6 months*

If you wish, you can include a bit of ham bone in this stock, but not too much as it can be very salty. You can also add a little of any other vegetable you may have in the fridge.

> *2–2.5 kg/2–3 lb beef or veal bones with most*
>   *of the fat trimmed off*
> *2 onions, roughly chopped*
> *2 cloves garlic, chopped*
> *2 carrots, scrubbed and chopped*
> *2 sticks celery, cleaned and chopped*
> *100 g/4 oz mushroom stalks or mushrooms*
> *2 bouquet garni*
> *8–10 peppercorns and a little salt*
> *3 litres/5 pints water*
> *300 ml/½ pint red wine (optional)*

If you have time, put the bones in a baking dish in a moderate oven (180°C/350°F/Gas Mark 4) for 30 minutes to give them colour and to get rid of the rest of the fat, then put them (without the fat) in a large pot with all the rest of the ingredients and bring slowly to the boil, skimming off any scum as it rises. Simmer, uncovered, for 1–1¼ hours. Strain the stock and discard the bits. Allow to become completely cold, then remove any fat that rises to the top.

Use for sauces, soups, etc., or freeze in well-sealed, convenient-sized containers (ice trays are quite useful), leaving room for expansion.

Defrost at room temperature, in a microwave or in a pan on the hob and use as above.

# Fish Stock

*Makes about 1.2 litres/2 pints*                    *2–3 months*

> *approx 225 g/8 oz fish bones and skin (these should*
>   *be from the fish you are to cook in the stock)*
> *4 spring onions or 1 small onion, chopped*
> *2 slices fennel bulb (optional)*
> *1 small carrot, scrubbed and chopped*
> *bouquet garni*
> *a little salt and a few peppercorns*
> *a slice of lemon (optional)*
> *1 litre/1¾ pints water*
> *300 ml/½ pint dry white wine*

Put all the ingredients in a pan and bring slowly to the boil, removing any scum as it rises. Simmer, uncovered, for 20 minutes, then strain the stock and discard the bits.

Use for soups, sauces, etc., or freeze in well-sealed, convenient-sized containers, leaving room for expansion.

Defrost at room temperature, in a microwave or in a pan on a hob and use as above.

# Shellfish Stock

Make as above except that shrimp, prawn shells, etc. should be substituted for the fish bones. If you have fresh shellfish, you can poach the whole fish in the mixture (as with a whole chicken), which will give an even better flavour.

# Button Mushroom and Soured Cream Sauce

*Serves 6*          *3 months*

This is a pale, slightly tangy sauce – good for veal, chicken, noodles and pasta or vegetables. I prefer to leave the mushroom pieces in it; if you would rather have it smooth, you should put it through a liquidizer or processor and, if necessary, strain it afterwards.

> *25 g/1 oz butter*
> *100 g/4 oz onions, very finely chopped*
> *225 g/8 oz button mushrooms, wiped and very thinly sliced*
> *1 2 tablespoons lemon juice (depending on how sharp you like your sauce)*
> *2 teaspoons cornflour*
> *300 ml/½ pint milk*
> *300 ml/½ pint light chicken, veal or vegetable stock*
> *150 ml/¼ pint white wine*
> *salt and pepper*
> *150 ml/¼ pint soured cream*

Melt the butter in a pan and very gently cook the onions until they are quite soft. Add the mushrooms and lemon juice and continue to cook until the mushrooms are also soft. Stir in the cornflour, then gradually add the milk, stock and finally the wine. Bring to the boil and simmer gently for 15 minutes.

If the sauce is to be used at once, draw it off the heat, season it lightly, add the soured cream and adjust the seasoning to taste. Reheat, but do not boil or the cream may separate. Serve.

If the sauce is to be frozen, cool it and freeze it in well-sealed containers, leaving room for expansion.

Defrost at room temperature or in a microwave, reheat and finish as above.

# Bread Sauce

*Serves 10*          *3 months*

Since it is not exactly expensive to make, it is always better to have too much bread sauce than too little – you are certainly not going to want to make more as the turkey is coming out of the oven! It is traditionally made with white bread; wholefood enthusiasts can certainly make it with wholemeal bread but they must expect it to be brown in colour rather than white and to have a much coarser texture. If you do not like the flavour of cloves, substitute 1 teaspoon ground mace or nutmeg.

> *1 large or 2 small onions stuck with 8–10 cloves (see above)*
> *1.2 litres/2 pints fresh milk*
> *225 g/8 oz good quality 1- or 2-day-old white or wholemeal bread, crusts removed and coarsley crumbled*
> *25 g/1 oz butter*
> *salt and pepper*
> *150 ml/¼ pint double cream (optional)*

Put the onion stuck with cloves (or with the spice) in a pan with the milk and bring it slowly to the boil. Add the bread and simmer gently for 20–30 minutes, stirring now and then to make sure it does not stick. Remove the onion and beat the sauce thoroughly with a wooden spoon to make sure it is smooth. Add the butter, seasoning to taste and some or all of the cream if you wish to use it. Put in a warmed sauce boat to serve.

If the sauce is to be frozen, do not season or add the cream but cool it completely, then pack in a well-sealed container, leaving room for expansion.

Defrost at room temperature or in a microwave. Reheat in a microwave or a pan (taking care that it does not burn or stick), and finish as above.

# Tomato Sauce

*Makes 1.2 litres/2 pints*                          *6 months*

Tomato sauce is invaluable for almost anything from spaghetti to a dip for crudités and, since it is very tolerant (it will put up with being frozen and unfrozen several times), it is well worth keeping a stock of it in relatively small pots for quick defrosting and one-off needs.

> *450 g/1 lb onions, finely chopped*
> *3 cloves garlic, finely chopped*
> *1.5 kg/3 lb ripe tomatoes, roughly chopped*
> *2 teaspoons sugar*
> *2 teaspoons dried basil, or 3 teaspoons fresh basil, chopped*
> *salt and pepper*

Put the onions in a heavy pan with the garlic, tomatoes, sugar and basil. Bring slowly to the boil and simmer gently for 30–45 minutes or until the juices are considerably reduced. Season to taste with salt and pepper. The sauce can either be left as it is or liquidized or processed to make a smoother sauce. If the latter is required, it will probably need to be sieved as well. It can be used either hot or cold.

Freeze in well-sealed containers of a convenient size.

Defrost at room temperature or in a microwave and use as required.

# Chilli Tomato Sauce

Make as above but substitute 2–3 dried red chillies, finely chopped, for the basil.

# Espagnole Sauce

*Makes 600 ml/1 pint*                              *6 months*

This is an excellent brown sauce for all occasions. It also makes a good base for slightly more exotic sauces for specific purposes – with orange for game, olives for duck or beef – or anything else you feel like adding to it. You can also add any odds and ends of vegetables you may have.

> *15 g/½ oz butter*
> *1 tablespoon olive, sunflower or corn oil*
> *1 onion, peeled and roughly chopped*
> *1 carrot, roughly chopped*
> *a couple of mushrooms or mushroom stalks, sliced*
> *1 stick celery, chopped*
> *1–2 rashers bacon, chopped*
> *25 g/1 oz flour*
> *some parsley stalks, bay leaves and thyme, or a bouquet garni*
> *300 ml/½ pint red wine*
> *600 ml/1 pint water*
> *salt and pepper*

Melt the butter and oil in a pan and briskly fry the vegetables and the bacon until they are well bronzed. Add the flour, stir well and continue to cook until the flour is also well browned but not burnt. Add the herbs, wine and water, scraping any bits off the bottom of the pan as you add the liquid. Add some salt and pepper, but not too much. Bring to the boil and simmer gently for 1–1½ hours. Strain the sauce, adjust the seasoning to taste and reheat to serve. If the sauce is to be frozen, do not do the final seasoning until it is defrosted.

To feeze, cool completely and freeze in a well-sealed container, leaving room for expansion.

Defrost at room temperature or in a microwave, reheat and adjust seasoning to taste before serving.

**Variations**
*Orange* Add the rind and juice of 2 oranges along with the liquids and complete as above. Serve with game.

*Olive* Complete as above and add 75–100 g/3–4 oz stoned black or green olives to the sauce 5 minutes before serving. Serve with duck or beef.

*Anchovy* Add 3 chopped anchovies with a little of their oil to the vegetables at the initial cooking. Continue as above but take care not to oversalt, especially if the sauce is to be frozen.

From top to bottom: *Chilli Tomato Sauce, Gooseberry Sauce* (see page 151), *Spinach Sauce* (see page 156) *and Olive Espagnole*

# Spinach Sauce

*Serves 4*                                    *6 months*

This sauce is based on a suggestion in John Evelyne's *Acetaria* published in the mid-seventeenth century. He suggests it be given to the 'sick and aged' for as he says 'tis laxative and emollient'. However, it is also delicious for the young and able-bodied and can be used with meat, fish or vegetables. It works well too as a supper dish with hard-boiled eggs or on toast.

> *225 g/8 oz fresh spinach, washed and finely chopped,*
>   *or frozen leaf spinach (see below)*
> *grated rind and juice of 2 oranges*
> *1 tablespoon cider or wine vinegar*
> *25 g/1 oz butter*
> *salt and pepper*

Put the spinach in a pan or in a microwave dish with the orange rind and juice and the vinegar. Cook it gently on the hob for 15–20 minutes or in the microwave for 4–6 minutes or until the spinach is cooked almost to a purée. Add the butter, stir well together and season to taste. Serve the sauce warm or cold.

If it is to be frozen, do not season the sauce but let it get quite cold, then pack it in a well-sealed container to freeze.

Defrost at room temperature or in a microwave, season to taste and serve as above.

NOTE: If you do use frozen leaf spinach, drain it very thoroughly and reduce the cooking time slightly. Canned spinach should really be avoided as the flavour is not nearly so good.

# Black Mushroom Sauce

*Serves 4*                                    *6 months*

This mushroom sauce is made from the black field mushrooms and has a very distinct mushroomy taste. It can be used either hot or cold, as an unusual salad dressing or dip.

> *100 g/4 oz onions, roughly chopped*
> *225 g/8 oz field mushrooms with stalks, wiped and*
>   *roughly chopped*
> *40 g/1½ oz butter*
> *25 g/1 oz cornflour*
> *2 tablespoons brandy*
> *600 ml/1 pint chicken or beef stock*
> *salt and pepper*
> *1–2 tablespoons mushroom ketchup*

Chop the onions and mushrooms very finely in a food processor but do not turn them into a mush. Melt the butter in a pan and cook the vegetable mixture slowly for about 10 minutes until the onions are soft. Add the cornflour and stir together for a minute or two, then add the brandy and, gradually, the stock. Bring to the boil, stirring to make sure the sauce thickens smoothly, and simmer for 30 minutes.

If the sauce is to be used at once, season to taste with salt, pepper and the mushroom ketchup. Use at once hot, or leave to get cold and use cold but not chilled.

If the sauce is to be frozen, cool it completely without adding the seasoning or ketchup, then freeze it in a well-sealed container, leaving room for expansion.

Defrost at room temperature or in a microwave, reheat and finish as above.

# Bolognese Sauce

*Serves 6*                                    *6 months*

> *4 tablespoons olive oil*
> *2 large cloves garlic, finely chopped or crushed*
> *2 medium onions, finely chopped*
> *½ red pepper, finely chopped*
> *350 g/12 oz minced beef*
> *225 g/8 oz mushrooms, sliced or chopped*
> *2 tablespoons tomato purée*

*1 large can (900 g/28 oz) tomatoes*
*1 tablespoon fresh thyme, or ½ tablespoon dried*
*300 ml/½ pint red wine*
*150 ml/¼ pint double cream*
*salt and pepper*

Melt the oil in a large pan and gently fry the garlic, onions and pepper until they are beginning to soften. Turn up the heat, add the minced beef and fry it briskly for a couple of minutes. Reduce the heat again and add the mushrooms. Cook for about 5 minutes, then stir in the tomato purée, followed by the tomatoes, thyme and red wine. Bring to the boil and simmer gently, uncovered, for 1–1½ hours. Add the cream and season to taste.

If it is to be frozen, cool it once it is cooked, before adding the cream or seasoning. Freeze in well-sealed containers in 'useful' sizes, leaving room for expansion.

Defrost at room temperature.

# Creamy Mint Sauce

*Serves 6*         *3–4 months*

I find the traditional mint sauce really too powerful with lamb, so I set about inventing an alternative that would let through the flavour of the mint without killing the lamb.

*2 large handfuls fresh mint, finely chopped*
*5–6 spring onions, very finely chopped*
*300 ml/½ pint milk*
*600 ml/1 pint chicken or veal stock*
*25 g/1 oz butter*
*25 g/1 oz flour*
*120 ml/4 fl oz double cream*
*2–3 tablespoons lemon juice*
*salt and pepper*

Put the mint and spring onions in a pan or a bowl with the milk and the stock and bring them slowly to the boil either over a low heat or in a microwave. Remove from the heat and leave to infuse for 20–30 minutes. Melt the butter in a pan, add the flour, stir together for a couple of minutes, then gradually add the milk and stock mixture. Bring slowly back to the boil, stirring to ensure a smooth sauce. Cook for 2–3 minutes.

If the sauce is to be used at once, add the cream and then season to taste with the lemon juice, salt and pepper.

If the sauce is to be frozen it should be cooled before adding the cream and seasoning, then frozen in a well-sealed container, leaving room for expansion.

Defrost at room temperature or in a microwave and reheat, then finish and serve as above.

# Salmon Sauce

*Serves 4*         *6 months*

Although this sounds expensive, it need not be if you can get an offcut of tail. It is delicious served with sole (or any other white fish) and is a lot cheaper than serving salmon with a sole sauce.

*175–225 g/6–8 oz salmon*
*2 spring onions, chopped*
*½ lemon, sliced*
*25 g/1 oz butter*
*90 ml/3 fl oz dry white wine*
*60 ml/2 fl oz water*
*60–90 ml/2–3 oz double cream*
*salt and pepper*

Put the salmon with the onions, lemon, butter, wine and water in a pan. Bring them slowly to the boil and simmer for about 15 minutes or until the salmon is cooked. Discard the lemon, then take out the salmon and remove the skin and bone. Put the salmon with the cooking ingredients in a food processor or liquidizer and purée them, then return them to the cleaned saucepan. Add the cream and season to taste. If the sauce is too thick (it should be a thick coating consistency), you may need to add a little more milk or water to thin it down. The sauce can be spooned over the fish or served with it and is as good hot or cold; you can also use any that is left over as a dip.

If the sauce is to be frozen, freeze it before you add the cream and seasoning. Freeze in a well-sealed container.

Defrost at room temperature or in a microwave and finish as above.

NOTE: See also Plum and Chilli Sauce (page 34).

*Peanut and Curry Sauce served as a dip for fresh vegetables*

# Peanut and Curry Sauce

*Serves 8*                                      *3 months*

As the Irish would say 'there's eating and drinking' in this sauce, but it has buckets of flavour and is very useful for cheering up a rather boring piece of meat. It is also good cold as a salad garnish or a dip and delicious warm and mixed with hard-boiled eggs as a supper dish.

*100 g/4 oz onions, roughly chopped*
*4 cloves garlic*
*100 g/4 oz dry roast peanuts*
*50 g/2 oz cooking apple or tart eating apple, peeled*
  *and chopped*
*1 tablespoon good vegetable oil*
*2 tablespoons curry paste*
*450 ml/¾ pint chicken, veal or vegetable stock*
*salt and pepper*
*4 tablespoons plain yoghurt (optional)*

Put the onions, garlic, peanuts and apple into a food processor or liquidizer and chop them very finely without puréeing them. Heat the oil in a pan and add the chopped mixture. Cook fairly briskly for a couple of minutes, then add the curry paste and, gradually, the stock. Bring the mixture to the boil and simmer for 10–15 minutes to get all the flavours well amalgamated.

If the sauce is to be used at once, season to taste with salt and pepper. If you wish to use the yoghurt (which will tone down the flavour), draw the sauce off the heat before adding it to prevent it separating. Serve warm or allow to cool and use cold but not chilled.

If the sauce is to be frozen, cool entirely before seasoning or adding the yoghurt and freeze in a well-sealed container, leaving room for expansion.

Defrost at room temperature or in a microwave and finish as above.

# Fruit Purées

*6–12 months*

All soft fruits purée well and keep excellently in the freezer – this method is especially useful for fruit that is slightly overripe or damaged. I find it is better to simply purée the fruit in a processor or liquidizer and freeze it with no extra additions – this leaves you free to use it for whatever you want when it is defrosted (below are a few suggestions). Freeze it in relatively small quantities so that you can get out as little as you need when you need it. The storage time will depend on the fruit.

Freeze in well-sealed containers, leaving room for expansion.

Defrost at room temperature or in a microwave and:

1 Use exactly as it is – an excellent sauce with a vanilla or fruit ice cream.

2 If you wish to make it a little smarter, add a couple of tablespoons of liqueur to the defrosted purée.

3 If the fruit was very tart, add a little sugar and/or cream to it.

4 Use the purée with whipped cream and whisked egg white to make a fruit fool or the filling for a meringue flan.

5 Use the purée cooked in flans or fruit pies.

6 Add the unsweetened purée to savoury sauces to give them an unusual flavour.

7 Dilute with water or fizzy water to make a refreshing drink.

8 Use as a basis for home-made milk shakes.

*Milk shake made with fruit purée*

# Brandy Butter

*Serves 10*          *3 months*

The best way to get a really frothy brandy butter is to whip it by hand, but I warn you that this is very hard work – if you cannot face the thought, an electric mixer will provide a perfectly acceptable substitute. It is worth making a reasonable amount at one time as there is nothing worse than running out!

*175 g/6 oz soft lightly salted butter*
*100–175 g/4–6 oz caster sugar*
*4–6 tablespoons brandy*

Put the butter in a bowl at least twice its size with a little of the sugar. Either with your hand or with an electric beater, start to whisk it, adding a little more sugar as you go. Continue to whisk it, gradually adding up to 100 g/4 oz of the sugar, until it is smooth and very pale; this can take 10–15 minutes of hand whipping or 5–10 minutes of electric beating. When you are satisfied that it is nearly done, gradually add the brandy, tasting when you have added 4 tablespoons. How much more brandy and sugar you add after that will be a matter of taste. When it is done, you can either pile it in a bowl or chill it slightly and roll it into butter balls or cut it into squares.

The butter can be frozen in balls or squares (packed in a well-sealed container) or piled into a bowl or container.

Defrost at room temperature (not in a microwave in case you overdo it) and served piled in a bowl or in balls or squares as above.

# Eliza Acton's Apple Sauce

*Serves 4*          *6 months*

Miss Acton, whose book, *Modern Cookery*, came out in 1845, maintained that apple sauce made with baked rather than boiled apples was infinitely superior – and I have to agree with her. It is excellent with meats, both hot or cold, or as a dessert sauce – or on its own as a pudding!

*450 g/1 lb cooking apples*
*1 tablespoon water*
*15 g/½ oz butter*
*a little sugar (optional)*

Peel and chop the apples and put them either in an ovenproof casserole or pie dish or in a microwave dish with the water and the butter. Cover the dish and bake them in moderate oven (180°C/350°F/Gas Mark 4) for 35–45 minutes, or microwave them on high for 4–6 minutes – in either case they need to be completely mushy. Remove the dish, stir the sauce well with a fork to ensure that it is smooth, and taste. If the apples were very tart, you may need to add a little sugar to take the edge off them. Use either hot or cold.

To freeze, cool completely, then freeze in a well-sealed container, leaving room for expansion.

Defrost at room temperature or in a microwave and reheat or not according to your needs.

**Variations**
*Orange* Add the grated rind and juice of one or two oranges and salt and pepper to taste – this is very good with duck. Alternatively, leave out the seasoning and add a little orange liqueur (Grand Marnier or Cointreau) and use it as a dessert sauce.

*Ginger* Add a little chopped fresh ginger root to the apple when you cook it or a couple of tablespoons of ginger wine when it is cooked –this is good as a dessert sauce.

*Calvados* This is the traditional liqueur to use with apples. Add a couple of tablespoons to the sauce and use it with pork or pheasant.

# Chocolate Sauce

*Serves 6*          *3 months*

*175 g/6 oz good quality dark chocolate*
*8 tablespoons water*
*1–2 tablespoons brandy or rum (optional)*

Break the chocolate in a bowl over hot water or in a double saucepan or boiler. Add the water and melt the two together, stirring until they form a smooth sauce. Add the brandy or rum if you are using it, stir to amalgamate and pour into a jug to serve. This can be used hot or cold.

Freeze this sauce in convenient-sized, well-sealed containers.

Defrost at room temperature and reheat gently if you want the sauce hot.

# GENERAL RECIPES

## Hot Water Crust Pastry

*Makes enough for 1 raised pie*

This cannot be frozen on its own but can be frozen once it has been made up into a dish.

> 450 g/1 lb plain white flour or white and wholemeal
>   flour mixed
> a pinch of salt
> ½ teaspoon icing sugar
> 100 g/4 oz lard
> 210 ml/7 fl oz water

Sift the flour, salt and icing sugar into a bowl and make a hollow in the middle. Heat the fat in the water until the former has melted and the latter is boiling. Pour it into the well in the flour, stirring continuously with a wooden spoon to draw in all the flour. Knead with your hand until the paste forms a compact ball. Cover with a cloth and leave to cool slightly before pressing into shape. Do not allow the paste to cool too much or it will be impossible to handle.

## Choux Pastry

*Makes 10–12 large éclairs*          *3 months*

> 75 g/3 oz butter
> 240 ml/8 fl oz water
> 100 g/4 oz plain flour
> 3 small or 2 large eggs

Melt the butter in the water and bring it to the boil. Sift the flour into a bowl, make a well in the middle and pour in the boiling liquid. Beat well until the mixture is well amalgamated but do not overbeat or the texture of the final choux pastry will be granular. Add the eggs one by one and beat until shiny; take care not to add too much egg or you will get a runny mixture which will not hold its shape properly. Spoon or pipe the mixture onto a baking tray and bake for 15–20 minutes in a moderately hot oven (190°C/375°F/

Gas Mark 5) – smaller ones will take slightly less time. The choux pastry should be risen, tanned and firm to the touch. Remove from the oven and cool on a wire tray. The larger éclairs or profiteroles may need their soggy middles removed before they are stuffed.

If the éclairs or profiteroles are to be frozen, pipe the mixture onto foil or a baking tray and open freeze them immediately. Once they are frozen, remove them from the tray and pack in well-sealed bags.

Bake from frozen allowing a little extra time for the defrosting.

NOTE: If you are making profiteroles, you will get 15–20 large and about 40 mini or cocktail size.

## Shortcrust Pastry

*4–6 weeks*

If you use all wholemeal flour, this will tend to give you a slightly less crisp, 'breadier' texture but it will have more flavour and be better for you. If you want the best of both worlds, use half white and half wholemeal flour. You can substitute low fat margarine for either the butter or both fats.

This quantity will be enough for two pie lids or flan cases, or one pie with pastry top and bottom.

> 225 g/8 oz plain white or wholemeal flour
> 50 g/2 oz butter
> 50 g/2 oz lard
> 2–4 tablespoons water

Sieve the flour into a bowl. Cut the fat into the flour with a knife until the pieces are quite small. Rub the fat into the flour with your fingers, raising the mixture and letting it fall back into the bowl so as to incorporate as much air as possible. Do not continue to rub if the mixture gets even remotely greasy; chill it in the fridge for half an hour and then finish mixing. It should end up like coarse breadcrumbs. It is better to undermix than overmix: undermixing will correct itself in the cooking; overmixing will make the pastry leaden. Add the water and mix as lightly as possible into a dough. Roll out and use.

To freeze, make into a neat ball, wrap in plastic cling film and pack in a well-sealed bag.

Defrost at room temperature.

# Basic Pancakes

*Makes about 20 small pancakes*                    *3 months*

Pancakes, alone or stuffed with almost anything, freeze excellently. Although you can use almost any recipe for the batter, they will become less dry if it incorporates a little melted butter (see below). Stuffed pancakes are normally better if served with a sauce, as they dehydrate slightly in the freezer. In most cases they can be frozen alone (with the sauce frozen separately) or frozen coated with the sauce. When possible, it is easier to freeze the sauce separately, as you can then pack the stuffed pancakes into foil containers rather than losing dishes in the freezer, and you get a chance to make sure the sauce has not separated and do any last minute adjustments before finally committing it to the pancakes.

> 2 eggs
> 50 g/2 oz melted butter
> 225 g/8 oz plain flour
> 300 ml/½ pint milk
> 150–240 ml/5–8 fl oz water
> a little extra butter

If you have a food processor, put all ingredients together in a bowl and turn on to full power for about 1 minute. (Do not put all the water in until the mixture is amalgamated and you can see how thick it is. The amount of water you use will depend on what you need the pancakes for and therefore how thin you want them.) The batter is then ready to use. If you are using a beater, put the eggs and butter in a bowl and then gradually add the flour and liquid until you get a smooth cream. It is safer to leave this to 'rest' for half an hour before using.

Heat a little butter until it sizzles in a flat, small pan – which is, ideally, kept for pancakes. Pour in just enough batter to cover the bottom of the pan – some people prefer to pour from a jug; some from a ladle – and leave it to cook until it starts to bubble in the middle. Raise the edges of the pancake with a spatula and the whole pancake should lift off easily and can then be turned. If it sticks, throw that one out, clean the pan very thoroughly with some kitchen paper towel (*not* soap and water) and start again. It may take your pan a few pancakes to get 'worked in'. If the pancakes are to be used immediately, they can be stacked on top of each other.

If the pancakes are to be frozen, layer them with plastic cling film or greaseproof paper so that you can peel off as many or as few as you need.

Defrost at room temperature.

# Meringues (Various)

*Makes about 10 large,*
*20 small or 1 large flan case*                    *6 months*

> 3 egg whites
> 150 g/6 oz sugar
> 15–25 g/½–1 oz grated dark chocolate, ground
>    hazelnuts or other basically dry and light
>    flavouring

Whisk the egg whites until they are pretty stiff, then add the sugar and continue to whisk until they are very shiny and stiff enough to stand in very spiky peaks. If you are whisking by hand, this can take some time, but it is very important that they are sufficiently whisked; too little whisking and the texture will be granular. You cannot whisk them too much. Fold in your flavouring and spoon or pipe the mixture onto a sheet of foil. Cook in a very low oven (120°C/ 250°F/Gas Mark ½) for 2–4 hours (or the lower oven of an Aga all night) depending on whether you like them cooked right through or slightly tacky in the middle. Remove from the oven and gently peel off the foil.

Freeze the meringues in well-sealed containers (they tend to break in bags).

Use direct from the freezer.

# FREEZER FILLERS AND MENUS

## Buffet Parties

### Summer × 20
Gazpacho (page 14)
Chicken and Almond Mould (page 44) or Terrine of Chicken and Crab (page 20)
Smoked Fish Sausages (page 40) or a platter of frozen shellfish (defrosted) served with mayonnaise dips
Stuffed Breast of Veal with Spinach and Sausagemeat (page 72) or Rolled Breast of Veal with Allspice (page 71) or Spiced Ham Salad (page 85)
Green Beans in vinaigrette (they should be lightly cooked and dressed while still warm)
Spiced Aubergine Salad (page 97)
Strawberry Mousse (page 122)
Rum and Macaroon Mould (page 125)

### Winter × 40
Spinach and Mushroom Pâté (page 17) or Terrine of Crab, Mushroom and Liver (page 21)
Blanched frozen vegetables served with dips
Smoked Mackerel and Cockle Flan (page 32) or Smoked Trout Mousse (page 36)
Boned, Stuffed Chicken (page 48)
Pickled Beef (page 63)
Cooked Cabbage and Plum Salad (page 112)
Spiced Aubergine Salad (page 97) or Carrot Soufflé (page 109)
Italian Baked Cheesecake (page 128) or Chocolate Brandy Gâteau (page 128) or Chocolate Meringue Gâteau (page 124)
Tia Maria Ice Box Cake (page 132)

## Dinner Parties

### Spring
Rhubarb Soup (page 9)
Scallops with Cream and Orange (page 29) or Rolled Fillets of Sole Stuffed with Spinach and Almonds (page 32)
Rice or fresh noodles and green salad
Rum and Macaroon Mould (page 125)

### Summer
Avocado and Mint Ice Cream (page 9)
Carrot Soufflé (page 109)
Escalopes of Veal with Spinach and Anchovies (page 69) or Veal Chops with Gooseberries and Cucumber (page 72)
New potatoes and French beans or mange-tout
Strawberry Mousse (page 122) or Summer Pudding (page 117)

### Autumn
Crab, Ginger and Almond Soufflé (page 40)
Chicken with Orange and Water Chestnuts (page 45) or Chicken with Leek, Grapefruit and Orange (page 42) or Coq au Vin Blanc (page 50)
Broccoli, Rice and Water Chestnut Casserole (page 113)
Amaretto Ice Cream Bombe (page 134)

### Winter
Chicken Liver and Tomato Pâté (page 16) or Chicken Liver and Curd Cheese Pâté (page 16)
Clear Onion and Mushroom Soup (page 14)
Casseroled Pigeon with Apple and Spices (page 58) or A Dark Venison Stew (page 57)
Celeriac and Spinach Bake (page 98)
Game Chips
Stem Ginger Ice Cream (page 131)

## Vegetarian Menus

### Summer
Avocado and Mint Ice Cream (page 9) or Tomato Ice (page 8) or Gazpacho (page 14)
Vine Leaves Stuffed with Potgourri Milanese (page 96)
Pepperonata (page 102)
Cooked Cabbage and Plum Salad (page 112) or A Cold Bean Pot (page 101)
Strawberry Mousse (page 122) or Berry and Watermelon Ice Cream Sorbet (page 131) or Summer Pudding (page 117)

### Winter
Spinach and Mushroom Pâté (page 17)
Rice, Chilli and Bamboo Shoot Casserole with cheese (page 112)
Stewed Radishes with Baby Corn (page 110)
Upside-down Gingerbread (page 116) or Chocolate and Orange Curd Tart (page 120)

# Dishes for Working Cooks

Any soup, pâté (preferably defrosted in the fridge for 24 hours to preserve its texture) or mousse (turn out while frozen and defrost in the fridge for 12 hours) is ideal. All the fish dishes, except Crab, Ginger and Almond Soufflé, are quick to prepare, as are any of the vegetable or vegetarian dishes or meat dishes, with the exception of Tongue and Ginger Pancakes.

The only dessert that will take time to prepare is the Crêpes Suzettes, but all the breads and cakes are no trouble at all.

# Cheap, Cheerful and Filling Dishes

Here are a few of the recipes that fall into this category.

Kidney Soup; Curried Parsnip and Apple Soup; Ajwar; Bacon, Apple and Sausagemeat Flan; Cod, Cream and Caper Pie; Kedgeree; Turkish Prawn Pilaff; Vegetarian Stuffed Peppers; Rice, Chilli and Bamboo Shoot Casserole; Mr Janssen's Temptation; Beef and Corn Hash Pie; Pork and Bean Pot; Seventeenth-century Apple Cake; Blackcurrant and Pear Cobbler; Steamed Ginger Pudding; Banana Bread; Lemon Brandy Cake.

# Emergency Dishes

All hot soups can be defrosted quickly in a pan or microwave and flans can be defrosted in an oven. However, do not try to defrost pâtés or mousses quickly as they will disintegrate. Some fish dishes, including Pickled Mackerel and Fish Quenelles, can be defrosted in a microwave and then reheated in an oven or microwave, but shellfish tend to lose flavour if defrosted in a hurry.

All made-up meat dishes will defrost quickly in a microwave or pan, although you do need to ensure they have been well cooked to begin with or you risk tough meat. Joints do not defrost well fast, and pies will need to be crisped up in an oven or, if desperate, under a grill.

Fruit pies and crumbles will defrost in a microwave but again will need crisping up, and ice creams are obviously excellent for emergencies.

Any bread will defrost in the oven but will not keep as long afterwards. Light sponge cakes (which can be layered with cream and topped with fruit) and biscuits defrost rapidly at room temperature.

# Picnics

Any soup, either hot or cold, is ideal for picnics and, although sandwiches (*without* mayonnaise or salad vegetables) are always popular, you might like to try blanched vegetables or shellfish with dips for a change. Below are some of the recipes that are particularly suitable.

Smoked Mackerel and Cockle Flan; Bacon, Apple and Sausagemeat Flan; Chicken and Almond Mould; Tuna Fish Loaf; Smoked Fish Sausages; Steak and Kidney Pie; Cumberland Mutton Pie; Stuffed Breast of Veal; Pickled Beef; Bobotie; Beef Tomatoes Stuffed with Bulgar Wheat and Chorizo; Spiced Aubergine Salad; Pepperonata; Chocolate and Orange Curd Tart; Lemon Cheesecake.

# Meals for One Person

Most dishes can be prepared for two or three people rather than six and then divided into individual portions before they are frozen. Whole fish can be filleted once they are cooked and frozen in portions; soufflés can be frozen in individual pots (allow slightly less time for cooking); stuffed pancakes can be frozen individually; pies can be made in individual dishes and topped separately. Cakes and gâteaux and most desserts can be made for two or three people and portioned once they are cooked. They will keep better if the portions are interleaved or separated with foil or greaseproof paper and then packed in their original shape.

# Baby Food

Any white fish, poultry, vegetable or fruit dish made for adults can be puréed and frozen in yoghurt or cream containers or ice trays for small babies. Remember to remove the babies' portions before seasoning and do not include any particularly strong or spicy flavours (chillies, curry, etc.). Make sure to observe maximum hygiene.

For slightly older children, small quantities can be frozen without puréeing.

Do not freeze high milk content dishes (blancmange, milk puddings, etc.) as they will separate on defrosting.

# NOTES ON FREEZING

## Usefulness of freezers

For people who do grow their own fruits and vegetables, have access to whole animals, freshly caught fish and so on, a freezer provides a first-class way of preserving their own produce. It enables you to be sure exactly what you are eating (which is not easy when you buy from shops) and to feed your family reasonably cheaply.

Apart from basic stores (vegetables, fruits, raw meats, fish, etc.), freezers can also store prepared meals, bought or home cooked, extremely well. This can be an enormous convenience to harrassed parents with large families, working people with little time for cooking, enthusiastic hosts, people living on their own, those who live far from late night or indeed any kind of shops, and anyone with access to a 'cash and carry' or cheap, bulk supermarket where they may get considerable bargains if they can buy in bulk.

Freezers are also invaluable for storing leftovers and small bits and pieces for decoration, flavouring and so on.

## Choosing a freezer

However, having read about the uses of freezers, if you do not already own one, think carefully about your own needs before you rush out to buy one. Like all good gadgets (as opposed to the expensive ones you buy, put in a cupboard, and forget ever to use), you will almost inevitably use your freezer more than you expect to. Be wary therefore of buying one that will only just fit what you think you will need; on the other hand, do not get carried away and buy something that would hold the contents of a supermarket and that will take up half your kitchen.

## Types of freezer available

Think seriously also about what shape and size you will need. They vary from a freezer compartment in the top of the standard fridge, a freezer on top of a standard fridge, through a half-and-half fridge/freezer, a complete cabinet upright freezer, to various sizes of chest freezer. Whichever shape you decide to buy, make sure that it has the correct star symbols. To enable you to freeze food from fresh your freezer must have the four **** symbol, */** on their own indicate that already frozen food can be stored for a certain length of time, not that you can freeze from fresh. If you plan to freeze a lot of fresh foods (as opposed to buying frozen), you should buy a freezer with a fast freeze switch or compartment to enable you to lower the temperature of the whole freezer or the area that is to receive the fresh food to be frozen.

It is wise to buy a freezer with a lock, especially if it is going to stand in an outhouse or garage. If you have young children, try also to find a model with relatively childproof – or at least out of reach – controls.

## Siting and installing freezers

Wherever you decide to put the freezer you choose to buy, make sure that there is a convenient socket; you do not want trailing wires tripping people up and fusing the freezer. If there is not one convenient, it would be worth having a separate socket fitted; this could even be on a separate circuit so that if you wanted to turn off the electricity in the rest of the house when you went away you could do so without affecting the freezer.

As a safety precaution against a careless kick as well as an inquisitive child, it is worth taping up the switch so that it cannot be turned off by accident. This is particularly worth doing if it is to be plugged into half a double socket, the other half of which is frequently turned on and off; it is all too easy to turn off the wrong one.

Make sure that the freezer has the correct amount of breathing space behind it to prevent overheating, and that it is level. Many freezers have individually adjustable feet. If not, the relevant foot should be raised with a small piece of hardboard or plywood.

A chest freezer in an upstairs bedroom should be positioned across the joists so as not to strain the floor. You must also ensure that it is level, as too much of an angle can cause an airlock in the coolant. A chest freezer in a garage should be raised from the ground so that it does not get damp or rusty. It should also be wiped over with a silicone polish fairly often to prevent any damage to the casing through damp.

## Power cuts and breakdowns

Disasters do occur even in the best regulated families, so be prepared. If the freezer ceases to work for no apparent reason, first of all check whether there is a power cut. Secondly, check whether there is a fuse in the plug – if there is, put a new fuse in to see if it works; if not, check whether the socket is working by plugging in another piece of equipment. If it is not, check the power fuse. If you have no joy, it will probably be a job for an electrician.

To check whether the compressor is working, turn on the fast freeze. If it does not grind into action, you will need a service engineer.

If the freezer seems too cold, you may have left the fast freeze switch on; if it is very noisy, you may have pushed it too close to the wall or it may not be level.

If you know about a power cut in advance, fill any gaps in the freezer with newspaper, old towels or plastic boxes filled with water, then turn on the fast freeze switch so as to get the contents as cold as possible. Cover the freezer with a blanket or rug to increase insulation, but do not cover the condenser or pipes at the back.

Once the power has gone off, do not on any account open the freezer. You should have between two or three days grace for a chest freezer (about 12 hours less for an upright), depending on the weather and the ambient temperature around the freezer, before the food starts to deteriorate seriously. Once the power comes back on or the machine is repaired, turn on the fast freeze and leave it on for at least 12 hours.

Remove any uncooked food that you suspect may have defrosted unacceptably (especially meat or fish, where the bacteria may have defrosted sufficiently to start work) and cook them. You can perfectly well refreeze them as cooked dishes. Any cooked food that has defrosted by more than 30 per cent should be defrosted completely in the fridge and used as soon as possible.

## Defrosting and cleaning

A freezer should be defrosted when the frost or ice on the shelves and interior has reached a thickness of 5 mm/¼ inch. How long this takes will depend entirely on how often you open the freezer, where it lives, and the temperature at which you keep your house. It can be as often as once a month or as infrequently as once a year.

Try to defrost when your freezer stocks are low and the weather is cold – and work quickly! Remove all the food and pack it in cold bags. If you do not have enough – or any – pile it in a heap and cover it with newspapers, a blanket or rug to reduce temperature loss.

Turn off the freezer at the socket and use bowls of hot water or a hair dryer held 20–25 cm/8–10 inches away from it to help melt the ice. You can also scrape or chip it off with a plastic spatula – do not use anything metal or you will damage the inside of the freezer. Once it is frost free, wash it out with a solution of 1 tablespoon of bicarbonate of soda or a cup of vinegar mixed into approximately 1.2 litres/2 pints of water, and wipe it dry with a soft cloth or kitchen towel. Turn on to fast freeze for an hour before you put the food back.

The outside can be washed with warm water and washing-up liquid and polished occasionally with an all-purpose silicone polish to protect the surface. This is particularly relevant if the freezer stands in an outhouse or garage.

## *Freezer Management*

Having got a freezer, the next thing is to learn to use it efficiently, and to do that you do have to be organized. It is all too easy to lose packages of food at the back or bottom, particularly in a chest freezer. If you do not have some means of 'stock control', you will waste food by failing to use it when it is as its best and finally having to throw it out because its label has fallen off and you cannot remember what it is!

## Labelling

It is absolutely essential to label everything that goes into the freezer with *a name, a date, and a quantity* – either the weight or the number of portions. It is also important to ensure that you use labels that remain stuck on and do not run. The most failsafe methods are to use polythene bags with labelling panels, or foil containers with cardboard tops on which you write with a water-proof felt pen or chinagraph pencil. The next best method is label ties – although even these can disintegrate if left in the freezer for too long. If you use stick-on labels, make sure that they were designed for the freezer and will not unstick when they freeze.

## Listing

You also need an efficient – and up-to-date – list of what is in your freezer at any time. The best way is to keep a looseleaf file or book, which hangs or sits close to the freezer with a pen or pencil attached to it. It should be sectioned into types of food (raw meats, raw fish, casseroles, uncooked vegetables, cakes, etc.) and in it you should enter everything that you put in the freezer and cross out everything that you take out. This will mean that you will always know what you have available – and how long it has been there. Ideally, you should try to circulate the foods in the freezer so that everything gets used up within its optimum freezer time.

## Packing the freezer

Upright freezers are relatively easy to deal with as they have shelves of manageable size, each of which can be devoted to a different kind of food – raw meats, cooked dishes, baking, vegetables, etc. Try to establish a system and mark which shelf is which on the freezer in the hope that your family will have some respect for your beautiful organization and occasionally put things where they belong!

Chest freezers are more difficult to cope with, but dividing trays and baskets are a great help. Again, try to devote each basket or area to a specific type of food and keep it that way so you do not have to heave everything out to find one packet of sausages.

To maximize the efficiency of your freezer, you should keep it as full as possible. This is both making the best use of your investment and making it work at maximum efficiency level. You will find it much more capacious if you pack your food into square or oblong packets, which will stack beside or on top of each other. Most freezer shops and suppliers sell a multitude of plastic boxes and foil containers of all shapes and sizes,

which are invaluable. However, if you do not want to make too major an investment in plastic boxes, you can always use the *'preforming'* method of freezing. 'Line' a plastic container with a polythene bag of approximately its capacity. Spoon or pour the cold food to be frozen into the bag in the box and put the whole thing in the freezer. Once it is frozen you can remove the food, frozen in its bag, out of the box, tie it and pack it away neatly, while the box can be used again and again.

However, not everything will obligingly fit into a square or oblong. Pieces of meat (especially if they still have the bone in), bread rolls, whole salmon (if someone is generous enough to catch and give you one) are amazingly awkward shapes and there is little you can do about them. They should be really well wrapped in foil to prevent sharp bits sticking out, then packed in heavyweight polythene bags or overwrapped and sealed in more foil or heavy polythene. (Also see Ice glazing (page 169). It is most important to ensure that everything is well wrapped as a bone sticking through the packaging will allow in air, which will cause dehydration and deterioration in the quality of whatever you are freezing. It is usually as well to keep one bit of the freezer for such unwieldy packages, so they do not disrupt your neat stacking elsewhere.

## Packaging Materials

Foil, foil containers, plastic boxes (not round if possible), reasonably heavyweight polythene bags and freezer film are all good for packing frozen food. All of these are easily available in freezer shops, large supermarkets, department stores and often, in limited quantities, in the smaller local and late-night shops as well. Used yoghurt or cream containers, well cleaned, also make excellent containers for small amounts of foods.

Foil containers, plastic boxes and heavyweight polythene bags can all be used more than once, but should be well cleaned and checked before being returned to service. Since one of the most important elements in good freezing is keeping unwanted dry and dehydrating air out, any damage or puncture to the container or bag will render it unsuitable for further freezing. You should avoid *glass* containers, some of which will shatter under extreme temperatures, especially glass jars with sloping sides and screw-on lids. If you freeze liquid in them and it expands, it will shatter the glass if it cannot expand upwards. For the same reason, you should never freeze bottles of any liquid, especially fizzy liquids which will explode if put under pressure. If you do have to put a bottle of wine or can of beer in the freezer in an emergency, *remember that it is there!*

Most metal, pottery, earthenware, stoneware and porcelain will stand a freezer, but it would be foolish to freeze a delicate or valuable plate. If you want to freeze food in a casserole or pie dish, you can usually line the dish with foil, then, when it is frozen, slip the food in its foil lining out of the casserole and pack it in a polythene bag, releasing your casserole for other purposes.

## Packaging the food

Remember that liquids expand by approximately one-tenth of their bulk as they freeze, so you must leave head room for expansion. Always pack boxes or containers as full as possible so as to exclude as much air as you can. If you are packing in polythene bags, you can suck the air out either with a vacuum pump or by sticking a straw into the bag, sucking out the air and tying it immediately.

If freezing solids plus liquids (such as casseroles or fruits in syrup), make sure that the solids are submerged in the liquids to prevent the bits that stick out drying up. You can fill the space in the top of the container with crumpled grease-proof paper or foil, which will both take up the air space and keep the solids submerged.

Delicate foods, such as meringues or short biscuits, can easily get broken in a full and busy freezer, so it is better to pack them in fairly rigid containers for protection, rather than just piling them into bags.

## Portioning

Before filling your freezer, decide in what sort of quantities you are going to need the food. Depending on the size of your family, it may be best to pack ready-cooked foods in portions for two, four, six or even – if you really have a large family – a dozen. Vegetables and fruits are better packed in smallish quantities, even when they have been frozen 'free flow'; it does not improve

them to be constantly taking them out of the freezer in large bagfuls just to get out a small quantity.

Unless you are sure you will want to use the whole thing, it is often better to portion tarts, gâteaux and cakes so that you can just take out one or two slices when you need them. The portions can either be interleaved with foil or plastic cling film and then the whole thing packaged complete, or the individual slices can be separately packed to be taken out when needed.

Stocks, sauces, baby foods, herbs, grated cheese, etc. are all useful in small quantities – even frozen in ice trays so they come out in small blocks. It is possible to take out a gallon block of stock and hack off what you need with a knife, but it is very laborious – and bad for the knife. You may also find that it pays to subdivide bulk-bought, commercially frozen food – ice creams, for example, do deteriorate when taken constantly in and out, so would be better repacked in smaller containers.

## Buying for the freezer

The fact of buying a freezer does not necessarily let you in for an endless labour of cooking, blanching and packing to fill it. You can perfectly well fill it almost entirely with commercially frozen foods – many of which are excellent. If you do intend to buy in a lot of your frozen food, you would be wise to search out a good bulk freezer centre as you can make very appreciable savings at many of them. You will also find that you can make use of seasonal gluts in fresh foods to stock up your freezer. 'Pick your own' farms now abound, and one afternoon's hard work will provide you with a six month stock of beans or fruits very cheaply.

When you get your purchases home, unpack them, reportion them if you need to, and get them into your own freezer as fast as possible. It is a wise precaution to turn on your fast freeze switch before you go on your shopping spree so that any loss of chill can be made up as soon as possible.

## How to freeze

A prerequisite of well-frozen food is that it should be frozen fast – the greater the speed at which the temperature of the food is reduced, the better will be the result. In addition to that, the failure to exclude as much cold, dry air as possible from the frozen item will, over a period of time, cause it to dehydrate and deteriorate – but that is a packing rather than a freezing problem.

Bearing in mind the importance of reducing the food temperature fast, the food that you put into the freezer should always be as cold as possible. Never try to freeze hot food – not only will it take much longer to freeze, but it will greatly increase the temperature inside the freezer, thereby partially defrosting other foods close to it. You should also limit the amount of food that you freeze in one session. The more unfrozen food you put in the freezer at one time, the more you will increase the temperature inside the cabinet, and the longer it will take to reduce the temperature of the new food. Remember too, that small packages freeze faster than large ones and that flat packs will freeze faster than square ones.

If you want to achieve the optimum result, you should never attempt to freeze more than one-tenth of your freezer's capacity in any 24 hours.

### Ways of freezing

*Open freezing* This merely means that you do not package the item until it is fully frozen. It can be frozen in the dish in which it was cooked, then unmoulded and packed for storage. Alternatively, small individual items can be spread on a tray and frozen separately, then packed. This is a particularly useful method for fruits and vegetables (peas, Brussels sprouts, raspberries, etc.) as they retain their shape and texture far better than if squashed into a bag or box. It also means that they remain separate when packed so that you can extract as few or as many as you need when you need them. Open freezing can also be used very successfully for larger items.

*Packaged freezing* The cold food is packed into its storage container, sealed, labelled and put into the freezer where it will remain until used.

*Ice glazing* This technique is useful for large items, like whole fish, which will be very difficult to seal properly. The item is open frozen and then taken out of the freezer, dipped in cold water and immediately returned to the freezer for a further half hour or so. If this technique is repeated two or three times, you will build up an all-enveloping coating of ice which will seal the food against air better than any bag. The fish or whatever it is can then be wrapped and stored as usual.

### Storage

Once food is frozen, as long as it remains totally frozen and airtight it can be virtually kept for ever. However, after a certain length of time, texture, flavour and food value, particularly in certain foods, can start to deteriorate – although to many people the change will be almost undetectable. Moreover, food in most domestic freezers is subject to certain fluctuations in temperature (as the freezer is opened and shut, the food is taken out for defrosting, etc.) and, even with careful packing, all air is not always excluded, so eventually the perfect freeze will be broken.

As long as the food remains frozen, even if not perfectly, it will not become a health hazard. However, it may lose some of its initial charm. Since it is not possible to gauge the efficiency of each person's freezer, let alone the conscientiousness of their packaging, I have given conservative ideal times for which foods should be kept. These are the optimum freezer times, after which I suspect that the flavour or texture of the food may start to deteriorate.

### Thawing

As a general rule, the slower the frozen food is thawed, the less the damage there will be to its texture and flavour. However, in the course of the thaw liquid may seep from the frozen food which will contain both flavour and nutrients from that food – it is important therefore to preserve it (by defrosting the item in its original wrapper or in the dish in which it is to be served, or by cooking the food from frozen) and to use the juices with the food concerned. This is especially the case with something like prawns, which have little flavour when separated from their juices.

Slow defrosting usually means either in a fridge or at room temperature. However, one of the conveniences of frozen food is that it is instantly accessible, so a speedier method of defrosting may be called for. Many foods (casseroles, pies, etc.) can go straight from the freezer to the oven and be defrosted and reheated in one operation.

# A–Z DIRECTORY OF FREEZING

○ CAN YOU FREEZE IT AND IS IT WORTH FREEZING?

☀ PREPARATION AND PACKING

⬥ HOW TO THAW/DEFROST

NOTE: Although some recipes are referred to in this section, please check the index for further recipes.

## Apples

○ Since bought apples are available all year, the only reason to freeze them is if you have no convenient place to store home-grown or cheaply-bought seasonal crops, or if you want a stock of pre-prepared apple for pies, flans, sauces, etc. Once frozen, use apples only for cooking. *See also* Fruit
Baked apples freeze excellently.

**Recipes:** Seventeenth-century Apple Cake (page 114); Apple Pie with Orange (page 116); Baked Apples (page 117); Guernsey Apple Cake (page 138).

☀ SLICES, DICE OR RINGS Peel, core, slice, dice or ring the apples into a bowl of cold water with plenty of lemon juice. Blanch in boiling water for 1 minute. Drain, cool and dry.
   *Free flow:* spread apple pieces on a tray, open freeze, then pack in well-sealed bags or containers.
   *Dry sugar pack:* allow 450 g/1 lb sugar per 2 kg/4 lb fruit. Mix the apple pieces with sugar and pack in well-sealed bags or containers, leaving room for expansion.
   *Cold syrup:* dissolve 300 g/10 oz sugar per 600 ml/1 pint boiling water. Cool. Pack the apples in containers, submerged in syrup and leaving room for expansion.
PURÉE Cook and purée as normal, with or without sugar. Cool and pack in well-sealed rigid containers, leaving room for expansion.
BAKED Bake as normal. Cool completely, then open freeze and pack in individual bags or containers with their juices.

**Storage time:** *dry pack rings, slices, etc:,* 8–12 months; *syrup pack or purées,* 6–8 months; *baked apples,* 3 months.

⬥ Defrost at room temperature or in a microwave.

## Apricots

○ Use only for cooking. They are worth freezing if you have home-grown or bulk-bought crop. *See also* Fruit.

☀ Halve and stone but do not peel the fruit and keep in acidulated water until ready to freeze. Blanch briefly, cool and dry.
   *Dry sugar pack:* allow 100 g/4 oz sugar per 450 g/1 lb fruit. Mix fruit well in the sugar and pack in well-sealed bags or containers, leaving room for expansion.
   *Cold syrup:* melt 225 g/8 oz sugar in 600 ml/1 pint water. Cool and pour enough over the apricot pieces to submerge them. Add ¼ teaspoon ascorbic acid melted

in a little water or the juice of 1 lemon to the sugar syrup just before freezing to help to retain colour. Leave room for expansion and seal well.
   *Cook in syrup:* Underripe fruit is best cooked in syrup (as above) until it is soft but retains its shape. Cool completely and pack in rigid containers, leaving room for expansion.
   *Purée:* Overripe fruit is better puréed. Cook with or without sugar in just enough water to prevent sticking, then purée. Pack in rigid containers, leaving room for expansion, and seal well.

**Storage time:** *dry pack and syrup,* 8–12 months; *purée,* 4 months.

⬥ Defrost at room temperature or in a microwave.

## Artichokes, Globe

○ Both whole artichokes and hearts freeze well.

**Recipes:** Artichoke Heart, Date and Almond Pie (page 110).

☀ WHOLE ARTICHOKES Trim and pull off outer leaves, wash well and blanch for 7 minutes in boiling water (time from when water returns to the boil). Cool artichokes immediately in iced water. Drain them well upside-down and squeeze out any excess water. Pack in well-sealed bags.

HEARTS Boil whole artichokes until tender, pull off leaves and discard, remove choke with a spoon. Cool hearts, then pack, interleaved with foil, seal well and freeze.

**Storage time:** 6–9 months.

⬥ Thaw in containers at room temperature or in a microwave. Whole artichokes should then be boiled until tender and served as normal.

## Artichokes, Jerusalem

○ Home-grown artichokes keep well in the ground, so there is little virtue in freezing them unless you want to store them ready cleaned or puréed. Bought artichokes are not always obtainable, so it is worth buying and freezing them when they are available and cheap. They freeze well both sliced and puréed.

**Recipes:** Jerusalem Artichoke and Brussels Sprout Purée (page 106).

❄ SLICED  Scrub or peel and put in acidulated water. Slice and blanch for 1 minute. Cool rapidly, dry, and pack in well-sealed bags or containers.

PURÉED  Scrub or peel and cook in boiling water until tender. Purée, cool, pack and seal well in rigid containers, leaving room for expansion.

**Storage time:** 3 months.

💧 SLICED  Thaw in containers at room temperature or in a microwave and use raw on salads, or thaw and cook as usual.

PURÉED  Thaw at room temperature or in microwave.

## Asparagus

○ This must be absolutely fresh to be worth freezing, so only do so if you grow it and have a glut. Asparagus freezes well because it contains so little water.

❄ Trim stems and scrape scales from lower part. Leave stems loose. Blanch thin stems for 2 minutes; thick stems for 4 minutes. Cool, drain and dry well. Pack carefully in rigid containers to freeze.

**Storage time:** 9 months.

💧 Defrost thin stems on kitchen paper towel, then cook in boiling water for 2–4 minutes. Thicker stems are better cooked from almost frozen.

## Aubergines (Eggplant)

○ Aubergines freeze well for cooking but should only be frozen when they are fresh, shiny and resist squeezing.

**Recipes:** Spiced Aubergine Salad (page 97)

❄ UNCOOKED  Wash and slice fairly thickly or cut in half. To avoid discolouration add 2 teaspoons ascorbic acid or the juice of a lemon to the blanching water. Blanching time – 4 minutes. Cool rapidly and dry. Open freeze, then pack in well-sealed bags or pack in rigid containers interleaved with foil or plastic cling film.

COOKED AS PART OF A DISH  If the aubergines are to be cooked as part of a moussaka or a similar dish, slice them into a colander, salt and leave for 30 minutes to draw out the excess water. Rinse thoroughly, dry, then fry and continue with the recipe.

**Storage time:** 12 months.

💧 They can be cooked from frozen or defrosted at room temperature or in a microwave.

## Avocados

○ Avocados lose some texture and flavour in freezing. Purée and use in a made-up dish before or after.

**Recipes:** Avocado and Mint Ice Cream (page 9).

❄ Purée the flesh and add 1 tablespoon lemon juice or a pinch of ascorbic acid for each avocado to prevent discolouration. Pack in rigid containers, seal, leaving

**Storage time:** 2 months.

💧 Defrost at room temperature or in a microwave and use immediately to avoid discolouration.

## Baby Foods

○ It is a good way to save time and money by cooking batches of baby foods or puréeing foods already cooked for adults and storing in small quantities.

❄ Store foods in small cartons, yoghurt pots, etc., or freeze puréed foods in ice trays, then wrap and pack cubes. Always observe maximum hygeine and sterilize all containers.

**Storage time:** 1 month (try to use within the month to avoid any nutritional loss).

💧 Cook from frozen in a non-stick saucepan, or defrost and heat in a microwave.

## Bacon and Salt Pork

○ Because of the heavy fat and salt content, neither bacon nor salt pork freezes well and should only be kept in a freezer for a limited time. They should be very well wrapped or they will flavour everything else in the freezer. Freeze only very fresh, mild cure bacon, preferably vacuum-packed for maximum air exclusion. Smoked bacon will keep better than unsmoked.

❄ VACUUM-PACKED BACON  Freeze in its pack, sealed in a plastic bag if the pack is damaged.

BACON RASHERS  Interleave with plastic cling film or foil to help get them apart when defrosting. Pack tightly, excluding all air, and seal well.

BACON JOINTS/SALT PORK  Wrap tightly in foil and then seal in bags, excluding as much air as possible, and freeze as rapidly as possible.

**Storage time:** *unsmoked rashers/joints*, 3–4 weeks; *smoked rashers/joints*, 8 weeks; *vacuum-packed rashers/joints*, 20 weeks.

💧 Unwrap and defrost as slowly as possible. Rinse or soak and dry the rashers or joints before cooking if salty.

## Bananas

○ These do not freeze well whole or in their skins, but can be frozen mashed with lemon juice and sugar or mixed into a dish – bread, etc.

**Recipes:** Banana Bread (page 140), Banana Ice Cream (page 132).

❄ Mash with lemon juice and sugar to taste and freeze in small, well-sealed containers.

**Storage time:** 6–8 months.

💧 Defrost in container at room temperature or in a microwave and use immediately to avoid discolouration.

### Beans – Broad/French/Runner

○ All beans freeze well, but since there are excellent commercially frozen beans available, it is only worth freezing them if you grow your own or have access to cheap, really fresh seasonal crops. Only freeze young and top quality beans.

❋ BROAD BEANS Pod, blanch for 3 minutes and cool rapidly. Drain, dry and open freeze. Pack loose in well-sealed bags.

FRENCH BEANS Top and tail and blanch whole for about 2 minutes (depending on size). Cool rapidly, drain, dry and open freeze. Pack in well-sealed bags.

RUNNER BEANS Top, tail, slice thickly (if sliced thinly, they go flabby) and blanch for 1–2 minutes. Cool quickly, drain, dry, open freeze and pack loose in well-sealed bags.

**Storage time:** 9–12 months.

🌢 Cook from frozen. If French or runner beans are for a salad, reduce the cooking time slightly.

### Beansprouts

○ Beansprouts, otherwise known as beanshoots, lose too much crunch in freezing to be used for salads but are fine for cooking or for freezing in an already cooked dish.

**Recipes:** Soy Pork with Beanshoots (page 82).

❋ Blanch for 1 minute, cool rapidly, dry and freeze in well-sealed bags, or cook according to recipe.

**Storage time:** 1–2 months.

🌢 Unwrap and defrost at room temperature or in a microwave. Use immediately.

### Beef

○ Beef, both cooked and uncooked, freezes well, but raw beef should be of the best quality and well hung (dull red, firm flesh, marbled with yellowish fat). Unless you can be sure of a very good bargain in top quality meat, it is not worth cluttering your freezer with half a carcase; even then it will pay you to get it properly butchered. Freezer burn through punctured wrapping will spoil the meat (although it is not harmful), so ensure that it is robustly wrapped; if necessary in a double layer of polythene or wrapped first in foil. *See also* Meat.

**Recipes:** see pages 59–68.

❋ LARGE CUTS OR JOINTS Wipe the meat with a damp cloth, trim excess fat, remove bones where possible, and cut the joint into practical, usable sizes. Wrap in polythene or foil, padding any remaining bones, and store in well-sealed bags.

STEAKS, ETC. Wipe each piece of meat, wrap separately in foil or plastic cling film and pack in well-sealed bags.

STEWING MEAT OR MINCED BEEF Trim and pack tightly in well-sealed bags, excluding as much air as possible.

COOKED CASSEROLES, PIES, ETC. Trim meat of any excess fat. Slightly undercook and underseason. Cool completely, skim off any excess fat, then pack in containers to freeze.
Alternatively, line the casserole or dish with foil before cooking so that it can be frozen in the dish then lifted out and packed in well-sealed bags, releasing the dish for other purposes.

COOKED SLICED MEAT Freeze in stock or gravy where possible to prevent drying out. Otherwise, pack and seal very well, interleaving slices with plastic cling film.

BEEF FAT OR SUET Fat can be cut into small pieces and packed in well-sealed bags for freezing. If it has already been rendered down into dripping, it keeps well in the fridge, so there is no need to freeze it apart from for long-term storage.
Chop or grate suet and mix with a little flour to separate the pieces; pack in well-sealed bags.

**Storage time:** *large cuts*, 8 months; *steaks and stewing beef*, 6 months; *minced beef*, 3 months; *cooked casseroles, pies, etc.*, 3–4 months; *sliced meats*, 1 month; *fat and suet*, 1–2 months.

🌢 RAW MEAT This can be cooked from frozen, but with large pieces there is a risk that the outside will be overcooked before the centre is cooked; it will also take almost twice as long. Flavour and texture is usually better if it is defrosted, in its wrappings, in a fridge (4-6 hours per 450 g/1 lb), at room temperature (2 hours per 450 g/1 lb) or in a microwave.

COOKED MEAT This can also be reheated from frozen but will take nearly 2 hours in a hot oven for a casserole for 6. Alternatively, defrost in a fridge, at room temperature or in a microwave and reheat gently in an oven, pan or microwave.

### Berries

○ The smaller the berry and the lower its water content, the better it will freeze. Open freezing is the most flexible method for good quality, just ripe fruit, although dry sugar and cold syrup can also be used. Slightly damaged or overripe fruit should be puréed or cooked. All berries freeze well in made-up dishes. *See also* Fruit.

**Recipes:** Strawberry Mousse (page 122); Summer Pudding (page 117); Berry and Watermelon Ice Cream Sorbet (page 131); Blackberry or Rapsberry and Pear Cobbler (page 124).

❋ *Dry pack:* do not wash berries unless absolutely necessary and if so dry thoroughly. Open freeze on flat trays, then pack in well-sealed bags.
*Dry sugar pack:* mix fruit with approximately 100g/4 oz sugar per 450 g/1 lb fruit and pack in containers; seal, leaving room for expansion.

*Cold syrup:* put fruit in rigid containers, submerge in syrup made from equal quantities of sugar and water, and seal, leaving room for expansion.

*Purée:* purée fresh fruit and freeze in well-sealed containers, leaving room for expansion.

*Cooked:* cook berries with or without sugar in a little water, pack in containers and seal, leaving room for expansion.

**Storage time:** 12 months.

◌ If dry pack berries are to be used straight or for decoration, use them partially frozen so they retain a little crispness and do not leak into whatever they are decorating. Otherwise, defrost at room temperature or in a microwave.

## Biscuits

○ Biscuits freeze well, especially those with a high fat content. If you have airtight storage tins, there is little advantage in putting cooked biscuits in the freezer unless for long-term storage; uncooked dough freezes well and can be cooked quickly into fresh biscuits.

**Recipes:** see pages 136–149.

✳ COOKED BISCUITS Cool, then pack in rigid containers to prevent breakage and seal well.

UNCOOKED DOUGH Roll dough in foil in a sausage shape and pack in a well-sealed bag or, for soft mixtures, pipe or spoon dough onto a tray and open freeze. When frozen, remove with a metal spatula and freeze in well-sealed bags.

**Storage time:** 4–6 months.

◌ COOKED Defrost at room temperature or in microwave. They may need to be 'crisped' in a microwave or conventional oven, but take care not to burn.

UNCOOKED Take the roll from the freezer and allow to soften just enough to cut off the required number of biscuits. Refreeze roll. Bake biscuits from frozen. Bake individually frozen biscuits from frozen.

## Bread

○ Bread freezes well both baked and unbaked, but must be very well packed to avoid dehydration. Crusty breads have disproportionately short freezer lives as the crust flakes off on defrosting after about a week.
Flavoured breads (garlic, herb, anchovy, etc.) freeze well but risk losing their crust if kept over 1 week.

**Recipes:** see pages 136–149.

✳ UNBAKED DOUGH To ensure proper rising it is wise to slightly increase the amount of yeast in the dough. The dough can be frozen either before or after rising.

*Before rising:* make dough and put in a large greased bag. Seal and freeze.

*After rising:* put dough in a large greased bag, seal at the top and allow to rise. Knock down, knead, return to the bag and freeze.

PART BAKED BREAD Home-made or bought bread can be frozen half baked, wrapped in well-sealed bags.

BAKED LOAVES, BAPS, ROLLS AND SLICED BREAD Wrap very well, in double bags if necessary, and seal to exclude all air.

FLAVOURED BREADS (garlic, etc.) Slice the loaf almost through and cover both sides of each slice liberally with the flavoured butter. Reassemble the loaf and wrap it tightly in foil. Pack in well-sealed bags.

**Storage time:** *unbaked dough (unrisen), plain,* 1 month, *enriched,* 3 months; *risen dough, plain or enriched,* 2 weeks; *part baked bread,* 3–4 months; *baked loaves or rolls, plain shop or home baked (sliced or whole),* 6 months; *enriched shop or home baked,* 3 months; *crusty loaves or rolls, or flavoured breads,* 5–7 days.

◌ UNBAKED DOUGH (unrisen) Open bag and reseal at top, then leave dough in a warm place to rise and bake as normal; (risen) defrost and bake as normal.

PART BAKED BREAD Bake direct from frozen (a loaf should take about 30 minutes in a hot oven).

BAKED BREAD AND ROLLS Defrost at room temperature or, to crisp the crust, in a hot oven. However, bread that has been defrosted in an oven will get stale very quickly.

FLAVOURED BREADS Remove from the bag and bake in the foil in a hot oven from frozen for 10–15 minutes. Open foil for the last 5 minutes to crisp the crust.

## Broccoli

○ This freezes very well.

**Recipe:** Broccoli, Rice and Waterchestnut Casserole (page 113).

✳ Use young, tender stalks and grade according to size. Blanch for between 1 and 3 minutes depending on thickness of stem. Cool rapidly and dry. Open freeze and then pack in well-sealed bags or, to protect heads, freeze head to tail in rigid containers.

**Storage time:** 12 months.

◌ Cook from frozen.

## Brussels Sprouts

○ Small sprouts freeze very well; large sprouts contain too much water to freeze satisfactorily. Freeze them as a cooked purée.

**Recipe:** Jerusalem Artichoke and Brussels Sprout Purée (page 106).

✳ Wash and trim sprouts. Blanch for 2–4 minutes depending on size, cool rapidly, dry and open freeze. Store in well-sealed bags.
Freeze purée in containers, leaving room for expansion.

**Storage time:** 12 months.

◌ Cook from frozen.

## Butter

○ This freezes well but must be well packed so that it is not affected by other strong smells in the freezer. Unsalted butter keeps longer than salted. Frozen butter will not keep as long after defrosting as unfrozen.
Butter balls or curls are useful to keep stored for emergency use.
FLAVOURED BUTTERS (garlic, anchovy, parsley, herb, brandy, etc.) These freeze well in blocks, curls or balls and are useful to keep in small quantities.

❇ Freeze as fresh as possible. Double wrap in well-sealed bags.
Freeze balls, curls, etc. in rigid containers to avoid damage.
Freeze flavoured butter in rolls so that you can cut off only what you need.
**Storage time:** *unsalted*, 6 months; *salted or flavoured*, 3 months.

◖ Defrost plain butter in the fridge, at room temperature or, with great care, in a microwave – it is very easy to melt rather than thaw.
Flavoured butters (except brandy butter) and butter balls or curls can be used from frozen.

## Cabbage

○ All cabbages freeze well cooked or for subsequent cooking, but since most are available all year it is only worth freezing special varieties (red, some Chinese cabbages, etc.), which you may not always be able to get.
**Recipes:** Cooked Cabbage and Plum Salad (page 112); Red Cabbage and Apple Casserole (page 109); Braised Red Cabbage Salad (page 95).

❇ Wash, shred and blanch for 1–2 minutes. Cool rapidly, drain, dry and pack in well-sealed bags, or cook according to recipe.
**Storage time:** *raw*, 12 months; *cooked*, 6 months.

◖ Cook from frozen or defrost at room temperature or in a microwave and cook.

## Cakes

○ All baked cakes freeze well, either whole or sliced for easy use. Uncooked cake mixtures, except whisked sponges, also freeze well. Ingredients should be as fresh as possible; do not use synthetic flavourings as they develop an 'off' taste in the freezer, and do not overspice as this gives a musty flavour. All cakes must be packed to exclude as much air as possible and so avoid dehydration.
Rich fruit cakes freeze well but keep just as satisfactorily, well-wrapped, in an airtight tin.
Icings with the exception of butter icing and whipped cream, do not freeze well and should be applied when the cake is defrosted.

Jam, fruit fillings, etc. should be added after defrosting as they make the cakes soggy.
**Recipes:** see pages 136–149.

❇ PLAIN SPONGES, LAYER CAKES, ETC. Cool cooked cakes completely.
*Uniced:* interleave with greaseproof paper or foil and freeze in well-sealed bags, excluding as much air as possible.
*Iced:* open freeze, then store in well-sealed bags or tightly fitting rigid containers to avoid damage in the freezer, excluding as much air as possible.
*Swiss rolls:* roll up with a little cornflour or with greaseproof paper, not sugar, and pack in a well-sealed bag, excluding as much air as possible.

SMALL ICED OR UNICED BUNS, CAKES, ETC. Open freeze, then pack in well-sealed bags or rigid containers, excluding as much air as possible.
LARGE CAKES, FRUIT CAKES, GINGERBREADS, ETC. Wrap in foil and then store in well-sealed bags. Or slice cakes, interleave slices with foil or plastic cling film and store in well-sealed bags, excluding as much air as possible.
UNBAKED CAKE MIXTURES Either line the cake tin with foil, pour in the mixture, open freeze, then pack in well-sealed bags. Or pour the mixture into rigid containers and freeze, leaving room for expansion.
**Storage time:** *sponge cakes, iced or uniced, small cakes, etc.*, 4 months; *fruit cakes, gingerbreads etc.*, 6 months; *uncooked cake mixtures*, 2 months.

◖ UNICED CAKES, BUNS, FRUIT CAKES, ETC. Defrost in their containers in a fridge, at room temperature (about 2 hours for a medium-sized sponge cake) or with care in a microwave.

ICED CAKES Remove from their wrappings or containers before defrosting so as to avoid damaging the decoration. Iced cakes, especially cream gâteaux, are easier to cut when still partially frozen.

UNCOOKED MIXTURES Defrost at room temperature or, with great care so as not to start cooking the mixture, in a microwave, then bake as usual.

## Capon – see Chicken or Poultry

## Cauliflower

○ This freezes well, whole (small heads), in florets, or in cooked dishes.
**Recipe:** Cauliflower Cheese (page 105).

❇ WHOLE HEADS Wash, blanch for 4 minutes in acidulated water to preserve the colour, then cool rapidly. Drain, dry and freeze in well-sealed bags.
FLORETS Grade according to size, wash and then blanch for 2–3 minutes in acidulated water to preserve the colour. Cool rapidly, drain, dry and open freeze,

then pack in well-sealed bags.
COOKED Prepare and freeze according to recipe.
**Storage time:** 6 months.

🌢 Cook from frozen; lightly if it is to be used for salads.

## Celery

○ Celery loses its crispness when frozen but is fine cooked or for use in other cooked dishes.

**Recipes:** Celery with Spring Onions or Green Beans (page 105); Celery and Water Chestnut Casserole (page 108).

✳ Wash thoroughly, remove any tough strings and chop into shortish lengths. Blanch for 3 minutes, cool rapidly, drain, dry and freeze in well-sealed bags.

**Storage time:** 6–9 months.

🌢 Cook from frozen in water, butter or a composite dish.

## Cheese

○ Most hard cheeses freeze well, although they will become crumbly if kept in the freezer for more than a couple of months. Grated hard cheese is particularly useful as it remains separated, allowing you to take out small quantities as needed.
Soft cheeses can be frozen successfully but it depends on the condition of the cheese at the time of freezing. Unless you have a surplus it is not advisable.
Cream cheeses with over 40 per cent butter fat freeze well; cream cheeses with a lower proportion of fat and cottage cheese only freeze well if mixed with another ingredient in a composite dish (e.g. cheesecake).
Blue cheeses do freeze but become very crumbly.

**Recipes:** Cheese Sables (page 22).

✳ HARD, SOFT AND BLUE CHEESE Wrap sections of hard, soft and blue cheese well in foil or plastic cling film, then pack in well-sealed bags.
CREAM CHEESE Pack in cartons or small containers and freeze.

**Storage time:** *hard cheese*, 3–6 months; *blue cheese*, 2–3 months; *soft and cream cheese*, 1–2 months.

🌢 HARD, SOFT, CREAM AND BLUE CHEESE Defrost in wrapping or container as slowly as possible. Cream cheese may need stirring when defrosted.
GRATED CHEESE Can be used from frozen.

## Cherries

○ All cherries freeze well, although the red keep their colour best. They should be pitted, unless you like the slightly almondy flavour the stone will leave in the cherries after prolonged freezing. *See also* Fruit.

✳ Wash the fruit, remove stalks and stones (optional), dry them well, then:

*Open freeze:* freeze on a tray; pack in well-sealed bags.
*Dry sugar pack:* allowing approximately 225 g/8 oz sugar to 1 kg/2 lb cherries, mix the cherries and sugar well and pack in well-sealed bags.
*Sugar syrup:* make with 450 g/1 lb sugar per 1 litre/ 2 pints water, plus ½ teaspoon ascorbic acid or the juice of a lemon to help retain the colour. Pack the cherries in rigid containers and ensure they are submerged in the syrup. Seal, allowing room for expansion and freeze.
**Storage time:** 12 months.

🌢 Defrost in their containers at room temperature or in a microwave. Do not expose them to the air before you want to use them as they will lose colour.

## Chicken

○ There are such a wide range of good-quality, reasonably-priced frozen chickens on the market that it is only worth freezing your own if you have access to really fresh, cheap birds, or if you are trying to store surplus. Chickens should be prepared for the freezer as for the oven but should be stuffed on defrosting as most stuffings have a shorter freezer life than the birds. Only roast tender young birds; use the older birds for casseroles, soups or pâtés.
Cooked chicken dishes also freeze well; follow appropriate recipe. *See also* Poultry.

**Recipes:** see pages 42–52.

✳ WHOLE BIRDS Pluck, draw and clean the bird and leave hanging in a fridge for 2–3 days. Truss it carefully but do not use skewers, pad the legs with foil and wrap in well-sealed bags, extracting as much air as possible.

CHICKEN JOINTS Wrap each joint in foil or freezer paper, then pack in well-sealed bags, extracting as much air as possible.
NOTE: Pack giblets separately as they have a shorter freezer life.

**Storage time:** 12 months. Giblets 1–2 months.

🌢 Defrost very thoroughly in the wrapping at room temperature or in a microwave and use as usual.

## Chocolate

○ Chocolate freezes well both on its own and as a flavouring in cakes, desserts, etc. Plain chocolate may get a slight 'bloom' in the freezer but that will not affect its flavour or texture. It can be useful to keep chocolate leaves, squares or curls in a rigid container in the freezer.

**Recipes:** Chocolate and Pear Meringue Pie (page 118); Chocolate and Orange Curd Tart (page 120); Chocolate Brandy Gâteau (page 128); Chocolate Sesame Biscuits (page 149).

✳ LEAVES Melt some chocolate in a double saucepan or boiler. Spread the melted chocolate thinly, with a palette knife or spatula, on the underside of any well-shaped, well-washed leaf. Leave to set on non-stick paper, then carefully peel off leaves and freeze in a small rigid container or carton.

SQUARES Spread melted chocolate thinly on non-stick paper and leave until almost set. Cut into squares and leave until quite set. Slide the paper to the edge of the table or surface, pull it downwards and peel off the squares. Freeze in cartons or rigid containers.

CURLS Melt chocolate and spread on a cold work surface. When it is just setting, peel off curls with a thin, sharp knife. You may also be able to shave curls off the side of a softish block with a vegetable peeler. Freeze in well-sealed, rigid cartons or containers.

**Storage time:** 2–3 months.

🌢 Use from frozen as decoration.

## Choux Paste – Profiteroles, Eclairs
○ Choux paste freezes well both cooked and uncooked (see recipe page 161).

❋ UNCOOKED Make paste as usual, then pipe into profiterole or éclair shapes on a baking tray or non-stick paper. Open freeze, then store in well-sealed bags.
COOKED Cook profiteroles or éclairs as normal. Take out of the oven, pierce or slit and remove any soggy middle as usual and cool on a rack. Open freeze, then pack in well-sealed rigid containers.
**Storage time:** *uncooked*, 3 months; *cooked*, 6 months.

🌢 UNCOOKED Bake from frozen, allowing 5–10 minutes longer than usual according to size.
BAKED Defrost by crisping the profiteroles or éclairs for 5–10 minutes in a moderate oven (180°C/350°F/Gas Mark 4), but take care they do not burn. Do not microwave as they will just go soggy.

## Citrus Fruit
○ Citrus fruits freeze well and it is useful to be able to freeze some of the seasonal or more unusual varieties when they are available. Depending on what they are to be used for (fruit salads, marmalade, composite desserts, cakes, etc.), they can be frozen whole or in sections.
Frozen citrus fruit peel is always useful.
Frozen citrus fruit juice also freezes well and is useful to keep as a standby.

❋ WHOLE FRUITS Unless they are to be cooked (e.g. marmalade oranges), large fruits (oranges, grapefruit, etc.) and those with loose skins (clementines, mandarins, satsumas, etc.) are better sectioned.
The smaller fruits (kumquats, lemons, limes, etc.) freeze well whole and can then be squeezed, cooked, preserved or served raw.
Open freeze the whole fruits, then wrap in foil or plastic cling film or pack straight into well-sealed bags.

PEEL Remove the peel thinly with a vegetable peeler or a grater, depending on what it is to be used for. Freeze in well-sealed cartons, twists of foil or bags.
SECTIONS Section the fruits, removing any pith. Then:
*Open freeze:* freeze on a tray and store in well-sealed bags or containers.
*Dry sugar pack:* allowing 100–175 g/4–6 oz sugar for every 450 g/1 lb fruit, mix thoroughly together and store in well-sealed containers.
*Cold syrup:* make with 225 g/8 oz sugar per 600 ml/ 1 pint water. Pack the sectioned fruit in rigid containers and pour over enough syrup to submerge the fruit. Seal well, leaving room for expansion.

JUICE Squeeze the fruits and freeze the juice, sweetened or unsweetened, in containers, leaving room for expansion.
**Storage time:** 9–12 months.

🌢 WHOLE OR SECTIONED FRUIT Can be defrosted at room temperature or in a microwave.
PEEL Can be used from frozen.
JUICE Can be defrosted at room temperature or in a microwave.

## Courgettes (Zucchini)
○ Courgettes freeze well whole, sliced or puréed.

❋ Wash small courgettes, blanch them whole for 1 minute and cool rapidly. Drain, dry and pack in well-sealed bags. Slice larger courgettes thickly, blanch for 1 minute and cool rapidly. Drain, dry and open freeze. Pack in containers or well-sealed bags.
Alternatively, cook courgettes in boiling water or sweat in butter and purée. Freeze the purée in well-sealed containers, leaving room for expansion.
**Storage time:** 6–9 months.

🌢 Cook courgettes from frozen, or defrost at room temperature or in a microwave and cook in butter. Defrost purée at room temperature or in a microwave.

## Crab
○ Like all shellfish, crab must only be frozen when it is absolutely fresh: caught, cooked and frozen on the same day. *See also* Shellfish.
**Recipe:** Crab, Ginger and Almond Soufflé (page 40).

❋ Dress crab as normal. Either pack brown and white meat into separate containers or return it to the cleaned crab shell. Cover tightly with plastic cling film, then pack in well-sealed bags.
**Storage time:** 1 month.

🌢 Defrost as slowly as possible in the fridge in its wrappings. Use as soon as it is defrosted.

## Cream

○ Cream with over 40 per cent butter fat (Devonshire, Jersey, double and some whipping creams) will freeze satisfactorily. Creams with lower butter fat content will separate on defrosting. Cream will normally keep better if chilled and lightly whipped before freezing, or if a little sugar is mixed in. However, it must be very fresh when frozen.
Rosettes of whipped cream can also be frozen and used to decorate desserts.

❋ Chill the cream thoroughly, then whisk lightly and pack in well-sealed cartons or containers, leaving room for expansion. Alternatively, stir approximately 1 teaspoon sugar into each 150 ml/¼ pint cream before freezing.
ROSETTES Whisk cream until it is just thick enough to pipe. Pipe it in rosettes or whirls onto non-stick paper or a baking tray and open freeze. When frozen, store the rosettes in rigid containers, each layer protected by a sheet of foil or greaseproof paper.
**Storage time:** 3 months.

◗ Defrost as slowly as possible and use as fresh.

## Croûtons

○ Croutons freeze very well and, since they remain separated when frozen, are easy to use. They must be frozen when freshly made.

❋ Make croûtons as usual. Cool completely and freeze in well-sealed bags.
**Storage time:** 1–3 months, depending on whether and what they are flavoured with.

◗ Crisp from frozen in a hot oven (200°C/400°F/Gas Mark 6) for 5–10 minutes.

## Cucumber

○ Cucumber does not freeze well as a salad vegetable but is fine cooked, in a composite dish, or puréed raw.

❋ Cube the cucumber, remove the skin, and put the pieces in a colander with some salt to draw out some of the water. Sweat in butter or cook in a composite dish. Alternatively, purée the cucumber raw. Freeze in well-sealed containers.
**Storage time:** 2 months.

◗ Defrost at room temperature or in a microwave.

## Currants – Red or Black

○ Both red and blackcurrants are well worth freezing as their season is so short. Open freezing is the most flexible way to freeze them. *See also* Fruit.
**Recipes:** Summer Pudding (page 117).

❋ Pick over, wash and dry the currants as well as possible. Then:
*Open freeze:* freeze on baking trays, then pack in well-sealed bags.
*Dry sugar pack:* allowing approximately 225 g/8 oz sugar per 450 g/1 lb currants, mix the fruit and sugar thoroughly, then freeze in well-sealed bags, leaving a little room for expansion.
*Cooked and/or puréed:* cook the currants with a little water and sugar to taste. Cool completely and either freeze in well-sealed containers as they are, or purée the fruit in a processor, sieve and pack in well-sealed containers. In both cases leave some room for expansion.
**Storage time:** 12 months.

◗ Use open freeze currants from frozen. Defrost sugar packed or puréed in their containers or bags at room temperature or in a microwave.

## Damsons – see Plums

## Dripping – see Fat

## Duck

○ Ducks freeze well, cooked or uncooked. *See also* Poultry. If freezing your own duck, freeze only young ducks; make older ones into casseroles or pâtés before freezing. It is better to stuff the ducks after they are defrosted, as heavily-herbed stuffings can get 'musty' after a couple of months.

❋ Prepare as normal. Chill before wrapping and freezing. Pad legs with foil and extract as much air as possible from the bag. Freeze giblets separately.
**Storage time:** *birds*, 6 months; *giblets*, 2 months

◗ Defrost very thoroughly in wrappings at room temperature.

## Eggs

○ Eggs freeze very well incorporated in almost any dish, cooked or raw. Raw eggs can be frozen satisfactorily out of their shells, either separated or together but there is no great virtue in doing so unless you have spare freezer space and access to really fresh, cheap eggs. It is useful to be able to freeze leftover whites or yolks rather than leave them hanging around in the fridge.
Cooked whites do not freeze well as they become leathery. Cooked yolks freeze all right if they are incorporated in another dish.

❋ WHOLE RAW EGGS Stir eggs together but do not whisk. Add ½ teaspoon salt or sugar to every 4–6 eggs (depending on size) to prevent them thickening. Pack in well-sealed cartons or containers and label to indicate how many eggs and whether sweet or savoury.

RAW EGG YOLKS Mix with a pinch of sugar or salt per yolk and freeze in cartons or ice trays. Pack in a well-sealed bag and label for quantity and whether sweet or savoury.

RAW EGG WHITES Freeze as they are in cartons or ice trays, then pack in a bag and label for quantity.

**Storage time:** 6 months.

◊ Defrost at room temperature and use at once.

## Fat or Fats

○ Animal fat does not freeze well as it turns rancid relatively quickly and will contaminate anything it comes in contact with. Remove as much fat as possible from any meat to be frozen, and remove any excess fat from casseroles that are to be frozen. Remember also that including bacon or belly of pork in a dish that is to be frozen will shorten its freezer life.
Butter, margarine, lard and shortening all freeze well provided they are very well wrapped.

**Storage time:** 3 months.

◊ Use from frozen, or allow to defrost at room temperature.

## Fish (Fresh)

○ Really freshly frozen fish (ideally within 12 hours of the catch) is almost indistinguishable from fresh, but unless you can be sure that it is really fresh it is not worth freezing raw. You would do better to buy commercially frozen fish, which is frozen in ideal conditions on the trawlers at sea. Fresh fish can be cooked and frozen successfully.
Whole fish can be frozen straight from the water or gutted. In terms of flavour, the first is marginally better, but it does mean that you have to wait until the fish is completely defrosted before you can use it rather than working from frozen or partially frozen.

**Recipes:** see pages 28–41.

✻ WHOLE LARGE FISH (salmon, etc.) Clean the fish or not, as preferred. For relatively short storage, open freeze the fish. Once frozen, dip in water so as to form a film of ice over the top and return to the freezer. Repeat the process twice so as to form a completely airtight layer of ice. Put in a bag and seal for storage.
LARGE FILLETED FISH Large fish may be more useful in fillets or steaks. Cut into the size required and freeze in well-sealed rigid containers, interleaved with foil or greaseproof or freezer paper.
SMALL FISH Gut (except in the case of tiny fish like whitebait), wash well in cold water, dry and freeze wrapped in well-sealed individual bags. Tiny fish can be open frozen then stored in well-sealed bags so that they remain separate.
COOKED FISH Cook and freeze according to recipe.

**Storage time:** *white fish*, 3 months; *oily fish*, 2 months; *cooked fish dishes*, 1–3 months.

◊ Always defrost fish in the container, reserve the juices and use them where possible in the cooked dish as they will retain much of the flavour of the fish.
WHOLE LARGE FISH Defrost at room temperature (about 24 hours).
WHOLE SMALL FISH, FILLETS, ETC. These can be cooked from frozen or defrosted in a fridge, at room temperature or in a microwave (with care), and then cooked as normal.
COOKED FISH DISHES These can be reheated from frozen or defrosted and reheated.

## Flans – see Pastry

## Fruit

○ Most fruits freeze excellently, as long as they are in good condition when frozen. The fruit should be just ripe and undamaged. Damaged or overripe fruits can be stewed or puréed and still freeze well.
The most flexible way to freeze fruits is dry or free flow, without sugar. This is not ideal for all fruits, but works well with most soft and berry type fruits.
Hard, non juicy fruits (apples) and fruits that discolour easily (apples, peaches, etc.) are better frozen in a sugar syrup. Soft juicy fruits (oranges) are better frozen in dry sugar or a sugar syrup. Mixed fruits can also be frozen successfully in a light syrup to make a frozen fruit salad. Free flow frozen fruits that are to be used whole with ice creams, gâteaux, etc. should always be served slightly frozen to retain some crispness.
NOTE: Frozen fruits make excellent jams if you do not have time to make them during the season. *See also* individual fruits.

## Game

○ All game freezes well either cooked or uncooked and, in the case of slightly tough birds or animals, freezing will break down fibres and help to tenderize the flesh. Since most game has a restricted season, it is particularly useful to be able to freeze it when it is available.
Game should be frozen in the condition in which it would be cooked – hung and, in the case of birds, plucked and drawn. (It is possible to freeze birds in their feathers for a few weeks if you do not have time to prepare them.)
Water birds should be prepared and frozen as soon as possible to prevent them developing a fishy flavour. Remember to remove the oil sac from the base of the tail.
Only young game (animals or birds) should be frozen for roasting; use old, tough or badly shot animals or birds for casseroles, soups or pâtés. Game can be marinated before freezing and frozen in its marinade; this will help to tenderize the meat and will damp down its gamey flavour. However, it is better not to stuff the game until

it is defrosted as most herby or garlicky stuffings have a shorter freezer life than the game.
Cooked game dishes also freeze well – just follow the recipe. *See also* individual birds and animals.

## Gammon – see Bacon

## Garlic
○ Fresh garlic keeps perfectly well hanging in a cool corner of the kitchen.
Garlic flavouring in dishes can develop an 'off' taste if frozen for more than a couple of months. If the dish to be frozen requires a heavy flavouring of garlic, add it when it is defrosted.

## Gâteaux - see Cakes

## Grapes
○ Grapes freeze satisfactorily for use in fruit salads or cooked dishes or cooked in a composite dish but not to be eaten fresh. They are normally available in the shops but can be expensive out of season, so it might be worth freezing a small amount for emergencies.

❅ Seedless grapes can be frozen in the bunch or loose and then packed into well-sealed bags or containers.
Large grapes should be pipped, peeled and submerged in a cold, light, sugar syrup – 225 g/8 oz sugar per 600 ml/1 pint water. Pack in well-sealed containers, leaving room for expansion.

**Storage time:** 12 months.

♦ Defrost in their containers at room temperature or in a microwave.

## Grouse
○ Grouse freeze very well both cooked and uncooked and, since the season is so short, it is worth freezing birds when they are available. Freeze young birds for roasting; use older and badly shot birds for casseroles, soups or pâtés.
Grouse should be hung for the appropriate amount of time (5–10 days, depending on weather and personal taste), plucked, drawn and cleaned before being frozen. It is better to stuff the birds after they are defrosted, as herby stuffings will leave a slightly musty taste after a couple of months. *See also* Game.

**Recipe:** Grouse Casseroled with Port and Celery (page 56).

❅ Pack legs with foil, wrap birds in foil or plastic cling film, then pack in well-sealed bags, extracting as much air as possible, and freeze. Or cook and freeze according to recipe.

**Storage time:** 6–12 months (after 6 months the gamey flavour will start to develop).

♦ Defrost in the container slowly and very thoroughly and cook as usual.

## Ham
○ Because of its high salt content, ham has a relatively short freezer life; frozen for more than 2 months it becomes unpalatably salty. However, it can be frozen raw, cooked or cooked in composite dishes for 2 months. Soaking in water or milk will reduce the saltiness but not get rid of it. *See also* Meat.

**Recipes:** see pages 83–6.

❅ RAW Uncooked ham is best frozen in the piece. Wrap in foil or plastic cling film, then freeze in well-sealed bags.
COOKED HAM Wrap pieces in foil or plastic cling film and freeze in well-sealed bags. Interleave slices with foil or plastic cling film and freeze in well-sealed bags. Or cook and freeze according to recipe.

**Storage time:** *raw*, 2 months; *cooked*, 1 month.

♦ Defrost as slowly as possible in the wrappings.

## Herbs
○ Most herbs freeze well, retaining more of their flavour and odour frozen than they would dried. Since many also have a short season, it is worth growing or buying them when you can and freezing them for later use.
They can be frozen on the sprig or chopped and suspended in ice cubes; the latter will give a longer freezer life but may not be as flexible for later use.
Herbs on the sprig with relatively tough leaves (thyme, rosemary, etc.) can be frozen blanched or unblanched; blanching will prolong their freezer life.
Herbs with softer leaves should be frozen unblanched or chopped and stored in ice cubes. Herbs should be frozen in very well-sealed bags as their aroma (especially that of the stronger herbs, such as mint) can contaminate other food in the freezer.
Most seeds can also be frozen successfully.

❅ SPRIGS Wash and blanch for 1 minute, if appropriate. Cool rapidly, drain, pat dry and freeze in very well-sealed bags.
CHOPPED Wash, dry and chop the leaves into ice trays. Freeze in suspension.
SEEDS Dry totally, then freeze in well-sealed bags or cartons.

**Storage time:** *leaves (unblanched)*, 2 months; *leaves, (blanched or chopped)*, 6–8 months; *seeds*, 8 months.

♦ The herbs should be used straight from the freezer, crushed or whole as decorations for soups, salads or made up dishes, or to flavour soups or casseroles

## Ice Creams or Sorbets

○ Freezers were obviously designed to take a large range of ice creams and sorbets, home-made and commercial, for general and emergency use. Ice creams and sorbets should not be served direct from the freezer, but should be allowed to soften for 15–30 minutes, depending on the mixture, in a fridge before serving. However, ice cream that has been allowed to partially defrost will deteriorate in texture, so if you only want to use a small amount, use an ice cream scoop dipped in hot water to remove the necessary amount and return the rest to the freezer immediately. Commercial 'soft scoop' ice cream can be served direct from the freezer.

Ice creams and sorbets will gradually deteriorate as a result of the change of temperature if constantly taken in and out of the freezer, but will last longer if always well covered when returned to the freezer. Do not attempt to refreeze thawed ice cream or sorbet as the texture will be ruined.

Commercially-bought ice creams and sorbets should be transferred to the freezer as soon as possible after purchase. If you bulk buy ice cream, it would be better to split it into smaller quantities to avoid constantly taking it in and out of the freezer.

Home-made ice creams and sorbets can be made in an ice cream maker, then transferred to the freezer, or made in the freezer. Ice creams made without an ice cream maker should be removed from the freezer when they are just starting to freeze and whisked vigorously to prevent the formation of large ice crystals. Sorbets should be removed from the freezer every half hour while freezing and stirred vigorously to prevent the formation of large crystals.

Fruits retain their flavour better in purée form than as ice cream, so store fresh fruits as purée and make into ice cream or sorbet as needed.

Bombes can be easily made by lining a mould with one flavour or colour ice cream, freezing it until hard, then filling it with a contrasting flavour or colour and refreezing. Unmould by holding a hot wet cloth over the outside of the mould and decanting it onto a plate.

**Recipes:** see pages 130–5.

❄ Wrap both commercially-bought and home-made ice cream containers in well-sealed bags to freeze.

**Storage time:** *commercial*, 1 month; *home-made*, 3 months (after 3 months the texture starts to go grainy and the flavour deteriorates).

◆ Serve slightly 'softened'.

## Icings

○ Any icing with a high proportion of fat (butter icing, frosting, etc.) keeps well in the freezer. It can be made up and frozen to be defrosted and used as needed, or used to decorate a cake, bun, etc. and then frozen. Fondant, royal, egg white and boiled icings do not freeze well as they crumble on defrosting, making it

almost impossible to spread them. They are more satisfactory when frozen on cakes, although it is better to freeze the cake and ice it when it is thawed.

## Kidneys

○ Kidneys freeze well cooked and uncooked. If raw, they must be very fresh and have all the fat and skin removed. They can also be cored before freezing. Ready-frozen kidneys should be transferred immediately to the freezer.

**Recipes:** Kidney Soup (page 12); Lambs' Kidneys with Apple and Cream (page 88).

❄ RAW  Remove all fat, skin and core, wash well and dry. Open freeze, then pack in well-sealed bags or containers.

COOKED  Cook and freeze according to recipe.

**Storage time:** 3 months.

◆ Cook from frozen or defrost in their container or opened bag at room temperature or in a microwave.

## Lamb

○ Lamb freezes well both raw and cooked. It is a good meat to bulk buy as you will be able to get a whole lamb in your freezer and still have plenty of space for other items. It will normally be sold on the bone and most butchers will pack it for the freezer for you. If you are bulk buying frozen lamb, make sure that it has not been or does not get defrosted before it gets to your freezer.

**Recipes:** see pages 71–80.

❄ Wrap joints and small cuts of lamb in foil or plastic cling film, protecting bones, etc. with foil to prevent them breaking through the bags. Freeze in well-sealed, heavy-gauge bags, extracting as much air as possible.

COOKED  Cook and freeze according to recipe.

**Storage time:** 6 months.

◆ Joints and smaller cuts can be roasted or cooked from frozen, but flavour and texture is usually better if the meat is allowed to defrost in its opened bag at room temperature or in a microwave and then cooked as usual.

## Lard – see Fat

## Leeks

○ These freeze well for cooking.

❄ Trim and wash thoroughly. Blanch small leeks whole for 3–4 minutes; cut larger leeks in thick slices and blanch for 2 minutes. Cool rapidly, drain, dry and freeze in well-sealed bags.

**Storage time:** 6 months.

◑ Cook from frozen or defrost in their opened bags at room temperature or in a microwave and cook.

## Liver

○ Both raw and cooked liver (animal or poultry) freezes well.

❅ Wash raw liver well, removing any tubes or blood and, with poultry liver, any greenish marks from the bile sac. Freeze small livers in small, well-sealed cartons or bags; slice larger livers and interleave the slices, then freeze in well-sealed bags or containers.

COOKED Prepare according to recipe.
**Storage time:** *raw,* 3 months; *cooked,* 2 months.

◑ Start to defrost in their opened bags or containers in the fridge or at room temperature. Use when they are beginning to soften. Do not defrost in a microwave.

## Lobster

○ Lobster freezes well but ideally should be frozen within 12 hours of being caught. *See also* Shellfish.

❅ Cook lobsters as usual, then either cool and freeze immediately in heavy-gauge bags or dress and freeze the meat separately in well-sealed cartons or bags.
**Storage time:** 1 month.

◑ Defrost as slowly as possible in opened bags or containers.

## Mange-tout – see Peas

## Meat

○ All fresh meats, including offal, freeze well; smoked and salted meats do not, as the flavours develop overpoweringly in a couple of weeks.
Cooked meats also freeze well but retain their flavour better if frozen in a sauce or casserole, etc., rather than dry.
RAW MEAT Although freezing will help to tenderize meat by breaking down some of the fibres, it will not improve its flavour, so only freeze best quality raw meat. This should be well hung, marbled with fat, but with any excess fat removed as this will go rancid over a couple of months. Bones should also be removed where practicable as they take up a lot of space and can pierce packaging.
It is better to stuff meat when it is defrosted as most stuffings have a shorter freezer life than the meat; herbs and garlic can taste 'musty' or 'off' after a couple of months.
Raw meat should be frozen as fast as possible to avoid loss of texture or flavour. Slow freezing causes the meat to 'drip', thus losing moisture and spoiling texture. A commercial blast freezer is the most successful way to freeze meat.

COOKED MEAT Cooked or roast joints, large or small, freeze satisfactorily if they are to be used cold, although it is better to freeze the meat raw and roast it when it has defrosted. Cooked and frozen joints do not reheat satisfactorily as they tend to get overcooked even in a microwave, and nearly always dry out in an oven. Cooked, composite meat dishes should always be frozen as soon as possible after they have cooled. Where applicable, they should have any excess fat removed to prevent it going rancid. They should be very well packed and sealed to avoid dehydration. *See also* Individual Meats, Offal, Game and Poultry.

## Melon

○ Firm, ripe melons lose some of their crispness in the freezer but can be used half defrosted with ice cream, in a fruit salad, etc. Overripe melons should be puréed or made in a sorbet. Watermelons do not freeze.

❅ Remove seeds and dice or ball the flesh.
*Dry sugar pack:* use 100 g/4 oz sugar per 450 g/1 lb fruit. Mix cubes well with the sugar and freeze in well-sealed bags or containers.
*Cold syrup:* freeze the cubes in well-sealed containers, submerged in syrup (225 g/8 oz sugar per 600 ml/1 pint water), leaving room for expansion.
**Storage time:** 9 months.

◑ Partially defrost in a fridge, at room temperature or in a microwave and use half frozen.

## Meringues

○ Meringues freeze excellently but remain delicate, so should be frozen in a rigid container to avoid breakage. Meringues can be frozen with cream fillings, although they are better if they can be filled on defrosting. Meringue toppings go soft and marshmallowy in the freezer. If you are happy with a soft top to your dessert, freeze fully made; if you would rather have a crisp topping, top when the dessert is defrosted.

❅ PLAIN Make meringues as usual and cool. Pack in rigid containers to freeze.

FILLED Make meringues as usual and cool. Whisk cream stiffly and sweeten with a little sugar. Sandwich meringues with the cream and open freeze. Pack in rigid containers, interleaved with foil.
**Storage time:** 3 months.

◑ Defrost at room temperature.

## Milk

○ Pasteurized milk will separate on defrosting; homogenized milk will freeze satisfactorily for a short period. Should it separate on thawing, heat it gently to boiling point and allow it to cool when it will reconstitute itself. Freeze in cartons, not bottles, which may shatter in the freezer.

Where milk forms a high proportion of a cooked dish, it is better to add it on defrosting, unless it is held by a firm liaison, such as a béchamel sauce. If a milk mixture should separate on defrosting, it is usually possible to reconstitute it by whisking or heating it gently.

❄ Freeze milk in cartons, leaving room for expansion.
**Storage time:** 1 month.

💧 Defrost as slowly as possible.

## Mousses
○ Both sweet and savoury mousses freeze well, although those made without gelatine may separate on thawing.

❄ Make mousse as usual. If you do not want to leave the dish in the freezer, line it carefully with plastic cling film; you may get a slight 'creasing' on the outside of the mousse but usually not enough to bother about. Open freeze the mousse in the dish, then either pack it in a well-sealed bag or decant it from the dish and pack in a well-sealed bag or container.
Decorate the mousse when it is defrosted as decorations can get damaged or deteriorate during freezing.
**Storage time:** 1–2 months.

💧 Defrost as slowly as possible to avoid any possibility of separation. If the mousse was decanted from its dish, peel off the plastic cling film carefully as soon as it comes out of the freezer, drop back into its dish and defrost as above. Decorate or unmould and decorate as usual.

## Mushrooms
○ Mushrooms freeze adequately raw provided they are cooked immediately on defrosting, otherwise they will go slimy. For long-term storage and use, it is better to cook the mushrooms in a little butter or stock before freezing.

❄ Freeze loose in bags or cook lightly, whole or sliced, and freeze in well-sealed containers.
**Storage time:** *raw*, 1 month; *cooked*, 3 months.

💧 Defrost at room temperature or in a microwave and use at once.

## Mussels
○ Mussels freeze well, with or without their shells, but must be very fresh.

❄ Clean thoroughly, rinsing several times in cold water, and discard any open or broken shelled mussels. Cook as usual, discard any mussels that did not open in cooking, cool and freeze in well-sealed containers, in their juices.
**Storage time:** 1 month.

💧 Defrost in their containers as slowly as possible.

## Offal
○ Offal freezes very well but must be absolutely fresh and cleaned when frozen. *See also* Kidneys, Liver, Sweetbreads.

## Oysters
○ These freeze well, raw or cooked, provided they are frozen absolutely fresh; ideally within 12 hours of being harvested. *See also* Shellfish.

❄ Clean and open oysters as normal, catching and reserving juices. Wash the oysters in heavily-salted water and pack in containers or cartons. Cover with their own juices, strained through muslin to remove any shell, seal well, leaving room for expansion, and freeze.
**Storage time:** 1 month.

💧 To eat raw, defrost as slowly as possible in their container. Cook from frozen but take care not to overcook.

## Pancakes
○ Pancakes, both filled and unfilled, freeze well, although care should be taken as to what filling is used – hard-boiled eggs or tomatoes, for example, are not successful. If the pancakes are to be frozen, add a little olive oil or melted butter to the pancake batter; it will help to keep them moist. Unfilled pancakes can be reheated (in a pan in a little butter or in a microwave) and used just as pancakes, but they are more successful filled or served in a sauce.
**Recipes:** Crêpes Suzettes (page 120); Seafood Pancakes (page 41); Chilli Pancakes (page 59); Curried Chicken Pancakes (page 49); Vegetarian Pancakes (page 100).

❄ UNFILLED Make pancakes in the usual way and stack them, interleaved with greaseproof paper or plastic cling film. Freeze in well sealed bags or containers.

FILLED Stack pancakes interleaved with filling to make a cake. Open freeze, then pack in well-sealed bags.
Fill individual pancakes with filling and roll or fold them into a parcel. Open freeze, then pack in well-sealed bags or containers.
Freeze pancakes and filling separately.
**Storage time:** *unfilled*, 4 months; *filled*, depends on filling.

💧 UNFILLED Remove individual pancakes as needed and defrost at room temperature. Or defrost the whole batch in the container in the fridge, at room temperature or, with care, in a microwave.

FILLED Pancake cakes or individual filled pancakes should be unpacked onto a serving dish, covered and reheated from frozen, or defrosted in the fridge, at room temperature or in a microwave and then reheated.

Unless they are to be covered with a sauce, the covering should be taken off 5–10 minutes before they are ready and the outside should be crisped or sprinkled with breadcrumbs or cheese, etc.

## Pasta

○ Fresh pasta freezes satisfactorily, raw or cooked, for a short period. However, it is so quick to cook that there is no point in freezing it cooked unless you have a great deal left over. Dried pasta keeps perfectly well in a store cupboard so there is no point in freezing it.
Pasta pieces are better added to soups, casseroles, etc. on defrosting as they can go mushy in the freezer. Composite pasta dishes freeze very well.

**Recipes;** Macaroni Pie (page 93), Lasagne (page 89).

☀ Freeze uncooked pasta in well-sealed bags. Drain cooked pasta very thoroughly, then freeze in well-sealed bags. Freeze composite dishes according to recipe.

**Storage time:** *fresh pasta, cooked or uncooked,* 1 month; *composite dishes,* 3 months.

🌢 Cook fresh pasta from frozen; reheat cooked pasta in boiling water from frozen. Bake or reheat composite dishes, covered or uncovered, from frozen in an oven or microwave. They are usually better uncovered before the end of cooking to crisp up, or sprinkled with breadcrumbs or cheese.

## Pastry

○ All uncooked pastries, commercially prepared or home-made, freeze very well; cooked pastry freezes well but needs to be crisped in an oven after freezing.
Blocks of uncooked pastry take longer to defrost than it would take to make fresh, so it is worth rolling out uncooked pastry into flan cases, pie lids, etc., and freezing them ready for use.
Cooked pastry is very fragile so should be stored in its dish or in rigid containers or otherwise protected.
Filled pies, tarts and flans can be frozen before or after they are cooked.

**Recipes:** Chocolate and Orange Curd Tart (page 120); Chocolate and Pear Meringue Pie (page 118); Walnut Tart (page 115); Apple Pie with Orange (page 116); Smoked Mackerel and Cockle Flan (page 32); Artichoke Heart, Date and Almond Pie (page 110); Chicken and Courgette Pie (page 44).

☀ UNCOOKED PASTRY
   *Shortcrust or suet crust (sweet or savoury):* make and roll out into flan cases, pie lids, useful size squares, etc. Interleave well-chilled flat pieces with double layers of foil or plastic cling film so that you can remove one without damaging the rest. Freeze in dishes, well-sealed bags or containers.
   *Puff or flaky:* prepare up to last rolling. Roll pastry into a rectangle, wrap well in foil or plastic cling film and freeze in well-sealed bags.

Uncooked mille-feuilles or vol-au-vent cases can be rolled out and open frozen, interleaved with foil or plastic cling film. Pack in well-sealed bags or containers.
COOKED PASTRY Prepare and cook pastry as normal. Cool completely, then freeze in rigid containers or in the dish in which it was cooked, if it can be spared. Pack carefully to prevent breakage and damage.
FILLED PIES, TARTS OR FLANS Pies can be frozen with the contents cooked and the pastry uncooked (e.g. steak and kidney pie), with both contents and pastry uncooked (e.g. fruit pies), or entirely cooked. Whichever way you choose, it is better to leave the pie in its dish in the freezer.
It is possible to decant it after it is frozen but difficult to do so without damaging the pie. Uncooked lids should not be slit until after they are defrosted. Cooked lids should be slightly undercooked to allow them to be crisped in an oven on defrosting.
Double crust pies should have their pastry lining baked blind before they are filled, whether or not the pie is to be baked before freezing, otherwise it will not remain even remotely crisp. They can then be frozen as above. Filled flans or tarts should also have their lining baked blind before they are filled to keep it crisp.
It is not advisable to fill vol-au-vents or mille-feuilles before freezing as it will not then be possible to crisp up the pastry.

**Storage time:** *unbaked pastry,* 3 months; *baked pastry,* 6 months; *baked and filled pastry,* depends on filling.

🌢 UNBAKED PASTRY Shortcrust and suet crust pastry should be defrosted in the fridge or at room temperature until it can be shaped for use, then cooked as usual. Flaky or puff pastry should be defrosted as slowly as possible, then cooked as usual. Ready-made vol-au-vent cases, etc., should be baked from frozen.

BAKED PASTRY Defrost at room temperature and crisp up in a moderate oven (180°C/350°F/Gas Mark 4).

FILLED TARTS, PIES, ETC. Bake from frozen, slitting pie lids once they are defrosted, and allowing 10-15 minutes extra time.

## Pâtés and Terrines

Most pâtés freeze well or satisfactorily depending on their contents; they can be frozen cooked or uncooked, provided that the ingredients are absolutely fresh. Butter-based fish pâtés freeze excellently.
Fine or puréed pâtés (chicken liver, etc.) freeze satisfactorily, although they tend to go rather soft on thawing; it is better to freeze them in small quantities where there is minimum loss of texture.
Coarse pâtés and terrines are better frozen uncooked. If cooked, they need to be very well weighted after cooking to squeeze out as much liquid as possible. When frozen, their high liquid content causes them to lose texture.

**Recipes:** see pages 16–21.

✳ UNCOOKED BUTTER-BASED PÂTÉS Freeze in well-sealed cartons or containers.

UNCOOKED PÂTÉS OR TERRINES Line dish with foil or plastic cling film. Make pâté and open freeze in dish. Decant and store in well-sealed bags, extracting as much air as possible.

COOKED PÂTÉS OR TERRINES Line the dish with foil. Cook pâté as normal, weight heavily to cool. When cold, open freeze, then decant from dish and store in well-sealed bags. extracting as much air as possible.

**Storage time:** *butter-based fish pâtés,* 2–3 months; *meat pâtés or terrines (cooked),* 1–2 months, depending on ingredients *(uncooked),* 1 month.

🌢 BUTTER-BASED FISH PÂTÉS Defrost at room temperature or, with care, in a microwave

MEAT PÂTÉS (UNCOOKED) Peel off foil or plastic cling film and drop back into the dish. Defrost at room temperature or in a microwave and cook as usual.

MEAT PÂTÉS (COOKED) Defrost in wrappings as slowly as possible to minimize loss of texture.

## Peaches

⭘ Only ripe, firm peaches are worth freezing whole, halved or sliced; overripe or damaged fruit should be puréed and used for ice creams, sauces, etc. If frozen whole, the stone can leave a slight almondy flavour after a couple of months.

✳ Skin ripe peaches, without scalding if possible, and brush with lemon juice to prevent discolouration. Freeze, whole or halved or sliced, in well-sealed containers, submerged in cold syrup (225 g/8 oz sugar and 1 tablespoon lemon juice or ¼ teaspoon ascorbic acid per 600 ml/1 pint water), leaving room for expansion.
Purée damaged fruit and freeze in well-sealed containers, leaving room for expansion.

**Storage time:** 12 months.

🌢 Defrost in their containers at room temperature.

## Pears

⭘ Pears are not worth freezing unless you have a surplus. They lose some texture and flavour when frozen raw, although they keep rather better lightly cooked.

**Recipes:** Chocolate and Pear Meringue Pie (page 118).

✳ Poach halves, quarters or slices in a medium syrup (225 g/8 oz sugar and 1 tablespoon lemon juice per 600 ml/1 pint water). Cool completely, then freeze submerged in the syrup in well-sealed containers, leaving room for expansion.

**Storage time:** 12 months.

🌢 Defrost in their containers at room temperature.

## Peas

⭘ It is only worth freezing peas if you grow your own; commercial frozen peas are picked far younger than you will buy from any greengrocer and frozen under ideal conditions. Green peas should be frozen when they are young and tender; older peas should be made into purées or soups for freezing.
Mange-tout should also only be frozen if they are really flat, young and tender; once the peas begin to swell the pods will become stringy.

✳ PODDED PEAS Shell, blanch for 1 minute (in small quantities to make sure they are evenly cooked). Cool rapidly, drain well and open freeze. Pack in well-sealed bags.

MANGE-TOUT Top and tail, and then blanch for 1 minute. Cool rapidly, drain, dry, open freeze and pack in well-sealed bags.

**Storage time:** 12 months.

🌢 Cook from frozen.

## Peppers

⭘ Unblanched frozen peppers keep their colour better and remain just about crisp enough to use in salads but their freezer life is reduced. Blanched or cooked peppers freeze well alone or in composite dishes. It is only worth freezing really fresh, firm peppers if they are to be used raw; riper peppers can be cooked.
Different coloured peppers should be frozen separately, as green stay firmer than red, yellow or purple.

**Recipes:** Pepperonata (page 102); Ajvar (page 19); Vegetarian Stuffed Peppers (page 98).

✳ Wash peppers, remove stem, seeds and membrane. Leave halved or slice, then open freeze and pack in well-sealed bags. Or blanch for 2–3 minutes, cool rapidly, drain. Dry, open freeze and pack in well-sealed bags. Or cook and freeze according to recipe.

**Storage time:** *unblanched or cooked,* 3–4 months; *blanched,* 12 months.

🌢 Defrost raw peppers as slowly as possible and use in salads, or add frozen to stews or casseroles, etc.

## Pheasant

⭘ These birds freeze well both cooked and uncooked. Freeze plump, hen birds for roasting; use cocks for casseroles, soups and pâtés. The birds should be hung (7–14 days), plucked, drawn and trussed before freezing. It is better to stuff the birds on defrosting as most stuffings have a relatively short freezer life. *See also* Game.

**Recipe:** Pheasant Braised with White Grapes (page 57).

✳ Freeze birds in well-sealed, heavy-gauge bags, extracting as much air as possible. Or cook and freeze according to recipe.

**Storage time:** 6 months.

🌢 Defrost very thoroughly, in the opened bag, as slowly as possible.

## Pies – see Pastry

## Pigeon

◯ These birds freeze well cooked or uncooked. Only young, plump birds should be used for roasting; use older birds for casseroles, pâtés, soups, etc. *See also* Game.

**Recipe:** Casseroled Pigeon with Apple and Spices (page 58).

❄ Do not hang pigeon, but pluck, draw, truss and freeze in well-sealed, heavy-gauge bags, packing any protruding bones with foil, and extracting as much air as possible. Or cook and freeze according to recipe.

**Storage time:** *uncooked*, 6 months; *cooked*, 3 months.

🌢 Defrost *very thoroughly*, in opened bags, as slowly as possible.

## Pineapple

◯ This freezes well, but only freeze really ripe fruit. *See also* Fruit.

❄ Peel and core pineapple, cutting out any eyes. Slice or dice it.

*Open freeze.* freeze slices or cubes on a tray, then pack in well-sealed bags or containers.

*Dry sugar:* mix slices or cubes well with sugar (175 g/ 6 oz per 450 g/1 lb fruit) and freeze in well-sealed bags or containers.

*Cold syrup:* freeze slices or cubes in well-sealed containers, submerged in cold syrup (225 g/8 oz sugar per 600 ml/1 pint water), leaving room for expansion.

**Storage time:** 12 months.

🌢 Defrost at room temperature or in a microwave.

## Plums, Damsons or Greengages

◯ Firm, ripe, undamaged plums, damsons or greengages freeze well in syrup; overripe or damaged fruit should be stewed or puréed. These fruits can be frozen whole, but the skins can become tough and the stones flavour the fruits after about 3 months. *See also* Fruit.

❄ *Open freeze:* wash, dry and open freeze whole fruit, then store in well-sealed bags.

*Cold syrup:* halve, stone and freeze the fruit in well-sealed containers, submerged in syrup (225 g/8 oz sugar and 1 tablespoon lemon juice or ¼ teaspoon ascorbic acid per 600 ml/1 pint water), leaving room for expansion.

*Stewed or puréed:* stew or purée fruit as usual, cool and freeze in well-sealed containers, leaving room for expansion.

**Storage time:** *open frozen*, 3 months; *in syrup, or stewed or puréed*, 12 months.

🌢 Defrost in containers at room temperature or in a microwave and use as soon as possible to avoid loss of colour.

## Pork

◯ Large and small joints of pork, crackling and cooked pork all freeze well, provided the meat is really fresh when frozen. However, their freezer life is relatively short and the animal relatively big, so unless you are addicted to pork, it may not be a good meat to bulk buy. *See also* Meat.

**Recipes:** see pages 80–6.

❄ Remove any excess fat and wrap large and small joints in foil or plastic cling film, padding any protruding bones and interleaving chops, etc. with foil or plastic cling film. Freeze in well-sealed, heavy-gauge bags, extracting as much air as possible. Prepare and freeze cooked dishes according to recipes.

**Storage time:** *uncooked*, 6 months; *cooked*, 3 months.

🌢 Cook from frozen, taking care not to burn small joints but to cook the meat thoroughly, or defrost in opened bags at room temperature or in a microwave and cook as usual.

## Poultry

◯ All poultry freezes well both cooked and uncooked. However, there is so much top quality commercially frozen poultry available that, unless you breed your own or have access to farm poultry, there is little point in freezing your own birds. Poultry portions are also now available and make the larger birds (turkeys) much more accessible to small families.

All poultry must be very fresh when frozen and must be *very thoroughly defrosted before cooking*.

To prevent the birds dehydrating, as much air as possible should be extracted from the package when freezing and care should be taken to ensure that the package does not get damaged in the freezer.

Cooked, roast poultry freezes well provided it is kept moist.

Composite poultry dishes should be prepared and frozen according to the recipe. *See also* individual birds.

## Prawns or Shrimp

◯ Prawns or shrimp freeze well provided they are frozen absolutely fresh. Unless you catch your own, you will be better off buying *top quality* commercially frozen prawns which have been caught and frozen under the best conditions. They can be frozen in or out of their shell: in gives a better flavour; out is more convenient to deal with. They also freeze well in composite dishes. *See also* Shellfish.

❋ Wash fresh prawns thoroughly and boil for 2–4 minutes or until they turn pink. Cool rapidly, remove the heads, dry and open freeze. Or, shell completely and open freeze. Pack frozen prawns in well-sealed bags or containers with as much air extracted as possible. For composite dishes prepare and freeze according to recipe.

**Storage time:** 1 month.

🌢 Use from frozen, or defrost, as slowly as possible, in their containers. Use any juices in cooking.

## Puddings, Steamed or Baked

○ All steamed or baked puddings freeze well provided they do not have too high a proportion of milk, which may cause them to separate on defrosting.
Milk puddings that are to be frozen (rice, etc.) should be made with double cream where possible rather than milk.
Steamed puddings should not have their jam or syrup put in the bottom of the bowl as it will make the pudding soggy.
Baked cake puddings, upside-down puddings, trifles, etc., all freeze well but should have cream fillings or decorations added when they are defrosted.

**Recipes:** Upside-down Gingerbread (page 116); Summer Pudding (page 117); Seventeenth-century Apple Cake (page 114).

❋ Bake puddings as usual in dishes or foil containers. If you do not wish to leave the dish in the freezer, line it with foil before making the pudding. Cool completely, then open freeze. Remove puddings from their dishes where appropriate or pack in well-sealed bags for storage.

**Storage time:** 2–4 months.

🌢 STEAMED PUDDINGS  Peel off the foil and return the pudding to the dish; reheat by steaming for 20–30 minutes, or reheat in a microwave.
BAKED PUDDINGS  Defrost at room temperature or in a microwave and use cold or reheat in an oven or microwave as appropriate.
MILK PUDDINGS  Defrost as slowly as possible and reheat in a microwave or, covered, in a low (150°C/300°F/ Gas Mark 2) oven.

## Pulses

○ There is no point in freezing dried pulses, but because they take a long time to cook, it can be useful to have some frozen cooked pulses, either on their own to be used in other dishes, or made up in composite dishes. Try to ensure that the pulses you cook are fairly fresh.

❋ Cook pulses as usual in water or stock or according to recipe. Drain well, cool and freeze in well-sealed bags or containers.

**Storage time:** 4–6 months.

🌢 Defrost at room temperature or in a microwave and use as fresh.

## Quiche – see Pastry

## Rabbit

○ Rabbits freeze well for casseroles, pies and pâtés, but only very young rabbits should be used for roasting. Whether or not they are hung before freezing is a matter of personal preference, but they should be well cleaned.

❋ Freeze very young rabbits whole in well-sealed, heavy-gauge bags with as much air extracted as possible. Joint older rabbits, wrap joints and freeze as above.

**Storage time:** 6 months.

🌢 Defrost as slowly as possible, in the wrappings.

## Rhubarb

○ Young sticks of rhubarb can be open frozen but they keep their colour better if blanched or packed in syrup. Older sticks should be stewed or puréed.

❋    *Open freeze:* wash and dry the sticks and cut into shortish lengths. Open freeze the rhubarb, then pack in well-sealed bags.
*Blanched:* blanch the sticks for 1 minute and cool rapidly. Dry, open freeze and pack in well-sealed bags.
*Cold syrup:* pack sticks in well-sealed containers, submerged in cold syrup (225 g/8 oz sugar per 600 ml/ 1 pint water), leaving room for expansion.
*Stewed or puréed:* stew or purée with or without sugar and freeze in well-sealed containers, leaving room for expansion.

**Storage time:** 12 months.

🌢 Use from frozen, or defrost at room temperature or in a microwave.

## Rice

○ Boiled rice can be successfully dry frozen, but since it takes almost as long to defrost as to cook from fresh, there is not much point unless there is surplus. Dryish, cooked rice dishes (risotto, stuffed peppers, etc.) freeze well, but rice frozen in liquid (e.g. soup) tends to go mushy and should be added on defrosting.
Rice pudding freezes successfully provided the custard is cream based; if milk based, it may separate on defrosting.

**Recipes:** Turkish Prawn Pilaff (page 33); Tomato Rice Cakes (page 104).

☀ Drain and dry boiled rice. Pack loosely in bags and freeze. When it is half frozen, remove from the freezer and shake or squeeze to separate the grains, then return and freeze completely. Prepare and freeze cooked dishes according to recipe.

**Storage time:** 2–6 months, depending on ingredients.

💧 Use from frozen, or defrost at room temperature or in a microwave.

## Salad Dressings
○ No salad dressings (vinaigrette, mayonnaise, etc.) with a high oil content should be frozen as they will separate on defrosting. Take care not to freeze dishes with a high dressing content.

## Salad Vegetables
Salad vegetables (tomato, cucumber, etc.) do not freeze for use as salad vegetables, although several of them freeze satisfactorily for other uses. *See* individual entries.

## Sauces
○ Most sauces freeze well and are useful to have in small quantities in the freezer for emergencies of for adding to existing dishes or sauces. However, heavily thickened sauces may separate on defrosting. It is better to reduce the amount of thickening, although whisking will normally reconstitute them. Do not try to freeze egg-based sauces or any sauce with too high a milk content; these will probably separate on defrosting. Milk-based sauces can be thickened with cornflour rather than flour, which will lessen the chance of separation but the sauce will need to be thinned on defrosting.
Underseason sauces before freezing as the flavours will develop in the freezer.
The following sauces are among those that freeze well: tomato, barbecue, bread, fruit-based, chocolate, curry.

☀ Make the sauce as usual, cool completely, stirring to prevent it forming a skin. Freeze in relatively small quantities; ice cubes of sauce can be useful for adding to soups, casseroles, etc.

**Storage time:** 1–6 months, depending on ingredients

💧 Add sauce cubes to soups or casseroles from frozen, or defrost in a double boiler or microwave and reheat. Adjust seasoning and check consistency before serving.

## Scallops
○ Scallops freeze well provided they are absolutely fresh; they should be frozen within 12 hours of being caught. Unless you have access to freshly caught fish it is better to buy them ready frozen or freeze them cooked. *See also* Shellfish.

☀ Scrub the shells well, open them and remove the black fringe from around the scallop. Wash the scallop well in salted water, then remove the fish and roe from the shell. Open freeze and pack in well-sealed bags or containers. Or prepare and freeze according to recipe.

**Storage time:** 1 month

💧 Defrost as slowly as possible in their containers, then cook as usual, using any defrosted juices in the cooking.

## Shellfish
○ Commercially frozen shellfish is preferable to home frozen, unless the latter is absolutely fresh; ideally it should be frozen within 12 hours of being caught in order to preserve its delicate flavour. It also pays to buy good quality frozen shellfish (especially prawns or shrimps) for maximum flavour. After about 1 month the delicate flavour of any shellfish will start to deteriorate. Where possible freeze shellfish in their shells and use the shell when cooking the fish as much of the flavour remains in the shell. Always defrost shellfish in their containers to preserve any juices and use these in the cooking process. *See also* individual shellfish.

## Shrimps – see Prawns/Shellfish

## Smoked Fish
○ Freshly smoked fish freezes well, but if you buy from a fishmonger, ensure that it has not be frozen before; it should not be refrozen unless used in a cooked dish. The smoked flavour will start to develop unpleasantly after 3–4 months and unless it is very well packed may affect other foods in the freezer.

☀ Wrap individual fish or fillets in foil or plastic cling film and freeze in very well-sealed bags or containers.

**Storage time:** 3 months.

💧 Defrost in containers at room temperature or in a microwave.

## Sorbets – see Ice Creams

## Soufflés (Cold) – see Mousses

## Soufflés (Hot)
○ Hot soufflés freeze well before (*not* after) baking, but will need an extra 20–35 minutes (depending on size) in the oven.

☀ Make the soufflé as usual and pour into a dish that will withstand freezing. Open freeze, then pack in a well-sealed bag or container.

**Storage time:** 2 months.

◖ Defrost 20–30 minutes at room temperature, then cook as usual, or cook from frozen allowing 20–35 minutes extra cooking time. If you are cooking from frozen, allow the soufflé to stand at room temperature for 5–10 minutes to lessen the shock to the container.

## Soups
○ Most soups freeze extremely well and are useful both to have in the freezer and as a way of using up leftovers. Underseason and add less spice and herbs to soups before they are frozen, as the flavours will develop in the freezer. Add cream and eggs when the soup is defrosted. Avoid soups with a high milk content as these may separate on defrosting, although they can usually be reconstituted by reheating, whisking or processing.
**Recipes:** see pages 9–15.

❋ Make soup as usual, but take care to underseason and spice. Purée soup while still warm, but cool completely before freezing. Skim any excess fat from soup before freezing. Freeze in cartons, containers or bags in preformer, leaving room for expansion, or freeze small quantities in ice cube trays.
**Storage time:** 2–6 months, depending on ingredients.

◖ Reheat from frozen in a heavy pan or microwave, or defrost at room temperature or in a microwave and reheat as usual. Adjust seasoning and add cream, eggs, etc. on defrosting.

## Spices
○ There is little point in freezing fresh spices as they keep well in airtight, opaque containers. Spices can also develop 'off' flavours in the freezer, so they should be used with caution in cooked dishes, especially cakes and biscuits.

## Spinach
○ Spinach does not retain its crispness in the freezer but is excellent for cooking. Since it is slow to blanch individual leaves, it is more practical to cook the spinach, then freeze it in leaf or puréed form.
**Recipes:** Celeriac and Spinach Bake (page 98); Spinach, Cream Cheese and Artichoke Bake (page 113).

❋ Wash spinach leaves, discarding any tough stalk, then cook as usual; the water left clinging to the leaves should be sufficient to cook it in. Drain the spinach thoroughly, then freeze in well-sealed bags or containers.
**Storage time:** 12 months.

◖ Reheat from frozen in a heavy saucepan or microwave.

## Stock
○ Stock can be made out of any fish or meat or vegetables and frozen as it is or in concentrated form. It has a better flavour than commercially concentrated stocks, which tend to be oversalted. It can also be frozen in small quantities (ice cubes) for adding to other dishes. Do not overseason before freezing.

❋ Make stock as usual. If you are short of freezer space, reduce the stock by boiling it down to a more concentrated form. Cool completely, skim off any excess fat and freeze in containers or ice cube trays. Seal well for storage.
**Storage time:** 3 months.

◖ Use from frozen, or defrost at room temperature or in a microwave and use as usual.

## Stuffing or Forcemeat
○ Stuffings can be frozen successfully, but should be frozen separately from the meat or fish to be frozen as they normally have a shorter freezer life. Heavily-herbed stuffings should be made fresh, as the herb flavours can 'overdevelop' in the freezer. 'Dry' stuffings will remain free-flowing in the freezer, which can be more convenient for use.

❋ Make up stuffing as usual and freeze in well-sealed, small bags or cartons. Do not overseason or overdo the herbs.
**Storage time:** 2–4 months depending on ingredients.

◖ Use dry stuffings from the freezer. Defrost other stuffings at room temperature or in a microwave and use as usual.

## Swedes
○ Swedes tend to be too watery to freeze well in pieces but are useful puréed or made into soup.
**Recipe:** Swede and Apple Purée (page 100).

❋ Peel or scrub and dice. Blanch for 2 minutes, then cool rapidly. Drain, dry and freeze in well-sealed bags or containers. Or cook and purée, cool completely, then freeze in well-sealed containers, leaving room for expansion.
**Storage time:** 12 months.

◖ Cook or reheat from frozen in a heavy pan or microwave.

## Sweetbreads
○ Sweetbreads freeze well, cooked or uncooked, but must be absolutely fresh. Commercially frozen sweetbreads should be transferred immediately to the freezer.

❋ Clean the sweetbreads thoroughly and soak in acidulated water for a couple of hours. Drain and dry, then open freeze or pack into well-sealed bags or containers, interleaved with foil or plastic cling film to freeze.

**Storage time:** 3 months.

❧ Defrost as slowly as possible in their containers and cook as usual.

## Sweetcorn

○ Home-frozen corn on the cob should be blanched and frozen *immediately* it is picked to be at its best. If you do not grow your own, you will get better quality by buying ready-frozen rather than freezing shop-bought sweetcorn.

❋ Remove leaves and silk and trim the cobs. Blanch for 4–8 minutes, depending on the size of the cob, cool rapidly and dry thoroughly.
The cobs can be open frozen and then packed in well-sealed bags, or the kernels can be scraped off the cobs with a sharp knife , open frozen on trays, then stored in well-sealed bags or containers.

**Storage time:** 12 months.

❧ Cook kernels from frozen. Cook cobs from frozen or defrost at room temperature and cook as usual.

## Tomatoes

○ Tomatoes have too high a water content to freeze without going mushy, so they cannot be used raw, but are excellent to freeze for cooking when they are cheap and plentiful. They can be frozen whole, puréed or stewed, or as juice. Freeze some in small quantities for adding to stews, soups, sauces, etc.

❋ Wipe whole tomatoes and freeze them whole or halved in well-sealed bags or containers.
JUICE Simmer halved or quartered tomatoes in their own juice for 10 minutes, then strain into containers, cool and freeze, leaving room for expansion.
STEWED/PURÉED Cook the halved or quartered tomatoes long and slowly until they are thoroughly reduced. You can add onions, a few herbs, etc. to make them into a sauce or purée them for later use. Cool and freeze in well-sealed carton or containers, leaving room for expansion.

**Storage time:** 12 months.

❧ Defrost at room temperature or in a microwave and use as usual, or use from frozen.

## Turkey – see Chicken/Poultry

## Veal

○ Veal freezes well both cooked and uncooked, but since it has very little natural fat, it is particularly important to prevent it drying out by keeping it totally airtight in the freezer. As it is so expensive, few people would be tempted to buy a whole carcase or side; it is better to keep just a few cuts for emergency use. *See also* Meat.

**Recipes:** see pages 68–72.

❋ Wrap joints thoroughly in plastic cling film, padding any protruding bones, and freeze in very well-sealed, heavy-gauge bags with as much air extracted as possible. Interleave chops, escalopes, etc. with foil or plastic cling film and freeze as joints. Or prepare, cook and freeze according to recipe.

**Storage time:** *joints or chops,* 6 months; *escalopes, stewing veal or cooked veal dishes*, 3 months.

❧ Cook from frozen (taking care not to burn steaks, etc. on the outside before the inside is defrosted and ensuring that the meat is thoroughly cooked through), or defrost at room temperature and cook as normal.

## Venison

○ Venison freezes well both cooked and uncooked. Fresh venison should be hung for 10–14 days and wiped over with milk every second day to keep it fresh before being butchered. Young animals should be used for roasting; older animals and tougher cuts for casseroles, pâtés, soups, etc. Because venison is rather a dry meat, it is particularly important that it is very well sealed in the freezer to exclude all air and it is better to marinate roasting joints before they are cooked. *See also* Game.

**Recipes:** A Dark Venison Stew (page 57); Venison Braised with Port and Redcurrants (page 56).

❋ Wrap prepared joints of venison, padding any bones with foil or plastic cling film, in foil or plastic cling film, then freeze in very well-sealed, heavy-gauge bags with as much air extracted as possible. Interleave steaks, etc. with foil or plastic cling film and pack as above. Prepare and freeze cooked dishes according to recipe.

**Storage time:** 6–8 months.

❧ Defrost thoroughly in the container at room temperature, then cook as normal.

## Yeast

○ Fresh yeast can be successfully frozen for relatively short periods; since it is not always easy to get, this can be worth doing.

❋ Freeze small packs of yeast (25 g/1 oz cubes) wrapped well in plastic cling film and stored in well-sealed bags.

**Storage time:** 1 month.

❧ Defrost at room temperature and use as normal (do not microwave), or crumble directly into warm water.

# INDEX